SUMMER
IS MY FAVORITE
SEASON

A MEMOIR OF CHILDHOOD
AND WAR IN KOSOVO

ILIR BERISHA

ISBN-10: 1490442243
ISBN-13: 9781490442242

Library of Congress Control Number: 2013911447
CreateSpace Independent Publishing Platform
North Charleston, South Carolina

To my parents,
President Bill Clinton and his administration,
the American people,
and Prime Minister Tony Blair and the British people

ACKNOWLEDGMENTS

Thanks to my mother who spent countless hours interviewing with me. Without her patience and sharp memory, I would not be able to remember the tiny details that are narrated in this book.

Without careful editing of my dear friend Kestal Phillips this book would not read the way it does, to say the least. I also thank Alice Rosengard for all of her help in this matter. Special thanks to Renee from CreateSpace for her editing.

I am grateful for my literary agent, Peter Riva and his staff, for believing in this story.

I acknowledge the help of all my Elon University and The University of North Carolina at Chapel Hill professors; especially Russell Gill, Sandy Smith-Nonini, Kevin Boyle, Rosemary Haskell, Cassie Kircher, Drew Perry and Marianne Gingher.

Thanks to all my friends and classmates who read it and offered me feedback and encouragement. I am forever thankful for the help of Bob and Ruthie Garner, Donald and Diane Mundy, Leon and Betty Saul, and Arlind Kastrati.

Thanks to Zana Milak for proofreading the manuscript and helping me take time off from work while publishing it.

AUTHOR'S NOTE

While I was growing up, my mother used to say to me, "You'd better not lie. Lies have short legs—they get caught." I still live by this principle, and thus the story that I tell here is true.

Map of Kosovo

CONTENTS

PROLOGUE

A WAR NIGHT

It is April 29, 1999. The earth is shaking from NATO's bombing. One of the bombs creates such a big vibration that it breaks the window of our living room, where we are gathered. We quickly lie on the floor. The Serbians follow the bombing with antiaircraft shells. It feels as if the action is happening right outside our broken window.

My family and I lie here in silence close to each other in the dark. We are waiting for someone to come to our house, break in, and murder all of us. On my father's radio, we have heard that such horrors happen every night to many innocent Kosovars.

It is midnight and we are still sitting here waiting. My father is trying to reassure my brother, Shpetim, my sister, Fjolla, and me. However, the fear is so deep inside of us that it will take much more to dispel it. After all, my father is scared the most. Looking into his eyes I can tell that he is withholding tears—tears of horror.

I turn to my mother and start to imagine what is going through her mind. Every plan and goal she had for us is buried. Her hopes that one day she would see us become professionals have been dashed.

I hear a loud knock on the door. Everyone jumps up with fear. My father goes to the door and asks, "Who is it?"

Someone with a deep voice says, "It's the police. Open the door quickly!"

My father looks at us and shakes his head. There is no choice now but to open the door. With his shaky hand, he opens it while we stand right behind him.

There they are: three masked men with pistols in their hands, one pointing at my father's ribs. Fjolla starts crying and screaming. We are about to die. I am surprised I don't scream and cry myself. These men are not even the Serbian police. They are part of the Serbian paramilitary group or mafia.

My father's horrified expression is revealed in the lamplight. They are going to kill him. We should have jumped out a window and made a run for it. Now our massacred bodies will be tomorrow's news. We will be among the victims, not the viewers. I hate anticipating the shot that will kill my father. I want to tell these men not to kill him, but I am too scared to even stay by our open front door.

The man who holds my father is taller than the other two. He shifts his gun to my father's head and says, "Give me your car keys, all your money, and your documentation."

"OK, OK, no problem at all, mister," says my father in a weak voice. His body is shaking. I have never heard him speak like this. My heart is beating wildly and my stomach is in knots.

We step back as my father and the thugs enter our apartment and go to the kitchen to satisfy the captors' demands. My father has his hands up and stays quiet. There is none of his customary display of temper this time. They are going to steal our car. That car means everything to my father, but I know that he is willing to give up anything he owns—including his own life—in a split second, just for us to survive this moment.

My father is in the kitchen with one masked man; we are standing in front of our apartment door with the other two. I am afraid to look at the guns in their hands. After a while, the other returns and huddles with the two. My father has given them all of the money and his car keys.

Now that they have what they want, they will surely kill us. I should be doing something instead of just waiting for them to pull the trigger, but I am frozen with fear. I can't run or hide. It is too late.

Fjolla is still crying. Shpetim and I are better able to control ourselves. My sister is two years younger, and I can't blame her for not realizing that her tears are not going to help us in this situation.

One of the Serbian men points to my father and asks his part-ners, "Should we take him with us?" Now they are going to take my father. This will be the last time I see him.

How did we get to this terrifying night? The trouble began long before I was born, but it would be years before I would even begin to understand it.

PART ONE

"For the survivor who chooses to testify, it is clear: His duty is to bear witness for the dead and for the living. He has no right to deprive future generations of a past that belongs to our collective memory. To forget would be not only dangerous but offensive; to forget the dead would be akin to killing them a second time."

—Elie Wiesel

CHAPTER 1

FREEDOM

I n the 1970s, around the time when my parents met, the republics and autonomies of Yugoslavia were peaceful, and people united for the common good. With Josip Tito as the president, the economy was booming and living standards were excellent. A popular leader, Tito managed to maintain peace among the different ethnic groups within the country. His chief objective was "Unity and Brotherhood" among the Serbians, Slovenians, Croats, Kosovars, Macedonians, Montenegrins, and Bosnians, who were all citizens of greater Yugoslavia.

My father, Hysen (whom we called Babi), had earned a degree in mechanical engineering and was a supervisor at an energy corporation. He had bought a cozy little apartment in Pristina. My mother, Xheva (whom we called Mami), was studying biology at the university. When they were dating, they would stroll along the tree-lined walkways in Korze, the center of the city, where people moved freely. During certain evening hours when traffic was detoured, people could safely walk amid the shops, cafés, and restaurants. My parents would occasionally stop at one of the cafés and enjoy a macchiato or go to the movie theater and watch a foreign film. Mami liked Babi because he was sincere and honest.

Mami foresaw a good future with Babi. In 1976, after a five-month courtship, they married, and Mami moved into Babi's apartment. Once she had graduated from college, she got a job teaching biology at a high school. Although they wanted to have children right away, Mami could not get pregnant. Despite their disappointment, they decided to enjoy themselves—traveling, visiting relatives and friends, and vacationing. They went to beaches in Greece, Croatia, Montenegro, and Bulgaria. Babi even went to Poland and visited Auschwitz. There, he saw skeletons and hundreds of empty shoes and hoped that genocide was something that belonged to the past. Mami and Babi even went to a natural spring in Serbia, where people swore that the water helped infertile women get pregnant.

Babi and Mami were financially well-off, and most importantly, they were free to do anything they wanted. During this time, Kosovo, although situated within Yugoslavia, was politically autonomous—meaning it was essentially an independent entity from Yugoslavia. Kosovo's citizens had virtually the same rights as citizens of the republics of Yugoslavia—Slovenia, Croatia, Bosnia, Macedonia, Serbia, and Montenegro. Mami and Babi could travel anywhere without getting stopped by Serbian police. Kosovars were free to go to the center city and watch their teams play *futboll* in their big, modern he always seems happy. But tonight he immediately sits on the living room sofa. What is wrong with him today? This is not like our dad. Babi turns on the TV and starts listening to the news closely. He also puts a blank tape into the VCR to record the broadcast.

I don't realize that the men I saw outside are Kosovar miners and other citizens who have protested because of the unjust actions of the new Serbian regime. I don't realize that Babi is worried about Kosovo.

After a while, my siblings and I join in: "Kaqusha Jashari, Azem Vllasi." Mami's reassurance that those guys are good people dissipates our fear. We enjoy chanting these names. We jump onto the living room table to mimic the men, raising our arms high and marching in place. For weeks after the protest, Shpetim, Fjolla and I continue shouting the two names. We still don't know what the words mean, even though Mami has tried to explain that they are men who work for our government, and that they have been wrongly put in prison. We know their names mean something good because Mami allows us to say them.

When we go to our uncle's house in another neighborhood, my parents, my uncle, and his wife don't mind us screaming, "Kaqusha Jashari, Azem Vllasi." They do not even mind us jumping up and down on their own living room table. They seem impressed that we have grasped these names, but they don't talk to one another while we shout.

I don't realize that we have saddened them because they know that not even a children's protest will free the public servants whom they love.

Several months later, Babi rushes home to watch the news again. Something important must have happened, because Babi puts another tape into the VCR to record the program. On the TV screen, I see the same men wearing the same helmets that have lights on them, except this time the lights are switched on. The protesters stand in a deep pit and stay there.

When he is at home, Babi watches TV constantly. He always looks distressed while watching the news. One day he enters the apartment with a stack of newspapers in his hand. He lays the newspapers on the living room table before turning on the TV and clicking the volume up to the maximum.

"You are spending all of our money on newspapers," Mami complains.

Babi doesn't say anything. Mami continues to scold him for spending too much money for the papers, money that he could be spending to buy us better clothes and shoes.

"Be quiet!" Babi yells.

He warns the three of us too. "Be quiet!" All the residents in the building must be able to hear him. Babi's voice is so loud that it sounds as though he has a bullhorn embedded in his throat. Fjolla, Shpetim, and I aren't silenced. As little children, what we do is make noise and talk. I miss the times when he played with us, when we would pretend to be the bad guys and he would chase us. Why doesn't our dad play with us anymore? The news must make him mad.

"Get out of here," yells Babi again. "Move to the kitchen." We all go to the kitchen and close the door behind us so Babi can be alone.

Mami sits on one of the chairs at our dining table. The three of us sit on her lap. We ask what is wrong with Babi, and she replies using words that are foreign to us—"autonomy" and "our rights"—but we don't know what these words mean. She must think that she is speaking to her high school students, and we are not even in first grade. When we give her puzzled looks, she holds us close and assures us that everything is going to be all right. I understand "all right," but not "our rights." I wonder what the difference is.

I'm not sure whether Babi is going to ever be normal again. Will he ever let us out of the kitchen?

I become restless sitting on Mami's lap, and Fjolla is crying now. She is more annoying than the blaring TV. Mami tries to comfort us by stroking our hair, kissing our cheeks, and tapping her feet to make our bodies vibrate. But we don't feel content. Mami is not as fun as Babi. Mami doesn't want to chase us. She hates for us to hide in the armoire. She doesn't toss us in the air. When Babi does it, she tells him to stop for fear that we'll hit our heads on the ceiling.

After a long while, Babi becomes his old self again and invites us back into the living room. He beckons me with his open arms so he can grab my cheeks with his fat fingers and kiss me.

Fjolla and Shpetim come too, and we start playing with Babi. He lifts us above his head and entertains us. He then sits us on the sofa, right beside one another, and tells us to raise the index and middle finger to form the letter V and say, "*Fitore* (Victory)." All three of us do what Babi says. When he sees us with our two fingers up, he looks happy. He grins so broadly that his cheeks rise to form pleasant wrinkles beside his eyes. I feel happy that Babi is no longer angry. He is all right again. It feels good to know that he is not crazy.

Babi takes us to the village, where we visit Uncle Skender, Babi's younger brother. We love going to his house because his son, Musa, is like a brother to Shpetim and me. Babi hands Uncle Skender a camera and asks him to take a picture. Musa, our aunt, Shpetim, and I gather around Babi, who tells us to make the victory gesture with our two fingers. I place an arm across my father's shoulders, and he does likewise to me. Shpetim lies on Babi's stomach and Musa sits by his feet. As soon as Uncle Skender counts to three, we know to say "*Fitore*." And we know that this will bring a smile to my father's lips.

CHAPTER 3
THE NEWSPAPER

Pristina is a big city full of tall buildings. Perhaps the tallest one is the building where Babi's newspaper is published. It is like a skyscraper, with gigantic blue letters on top of it that identify the name of the publishing house and newspaper, *Rilindja*.

At night, Pristina is a city of lights. Business marquees contribute to the brightness. In addition to traffic lights, headlights, and shining windows, each street and parking lot is illuminated by street lamps. But lately those lamps are not very well maintained. When one burns out, chances are that nobody will fix it. Our city is becoming darker and darker every day.

I am five and sitting on Fjolla's bed in the sunroom. A loud noise outside startles me. I approach the window and see giant metal machines rumbling down the main highway. They leave black marks on the street. They stop atop a distant hill where there are camouflage barracks surrounded by a barbed wire fence.

Babi is lying on the sofa in the living room while reading a newspaper. The loud noises get his attention. He puts down the paper, comes over to me, and grabs me by the waist. He picks me up and then slides the curtain shut with one hand. He seems to be as shocked as I am by the sight of the giant metal machines.

"Don't look out the window anymore," he says. He puts me down and resumes reading the paper. From time to time, he glances at the curtained window.

In the weeks to come, the giant metal machines move in and out of the base on the hilltop. When Babi isn't home, I love to watch them. I am fascinated by their huge size and strange appearance. Wheels spin within a big chain on each side of the machine whenever it moves. It is amazing how many little wheels there are.

I never wonder why these things are in Pristina. I just find them interesting.

During weekends, my father likes to read the paper as if he hasn't read it throughout the weekdays. Since he doesn't work on weekends, Shpetim or I buy his newspaper at a kiosk nearby. We love buying Babi's paper because sometimes there is extra change for a piece of delicious bubble gum.

Today is my turn. Babi gives me the coins to buy his newspaper. I descend the lobby stairs, exit the building, and arrive at the kiosk. Among the numerous newspapers, I recognize Babi's favorite immediately. The same blue letters atop the tall building where Babi's paper is published are printed on the front page. I give the vendor Babi's coins, and he gives me *Rilindja*. He knows not to forget the bubble gum.

I stop and smell the roses planted in the front yard of our six-story apartment building. It is the best-looking yard in the neighborhood—about the size of a volleyball field, with a border of bushes. There are roses of all colors: pink, dark red, light red, orange, and white. Their fragrance makes the air so sweet that passersby stop and thank God for the beautiful and aromatic flowers.

Our neighbor, Mr. Sejda, takes care of the property; he is an expert gardener and a real estate agent. He always wears a nice suit and a tie when he goes to work. Our other neighbors are also white-collar workers. Mr. Vokshi, from the fifth floor, works with Babi, but he has a very prestigious job. A chauffeur in a nice black car always drives him to and from work. Mr. Krasniqi, from the fourth floor, is also a big boss at the energy corporation. He too always wears a nice suit and tie to work, but he doesn't have a chauffeur and a nice company car for transportation.

I enter our apartment. Babi is still lying on the sofa, waiting for his newspaper. (Shpetim and I sleep on one of the two sofas. Mami and Babi sleep on the other.) I hand Babi the paper, and he immediately starts reading it.

The next day, Sunday, we go through the same routine in the morning, except that Shpetim gets his turn to buy Babi's paper.

We do this every weekend, until one day Babi doesn't bring a newspaper home. Shpetim and I wonder why. Maybe Mami isn't letting him spend money for it. But Mami has fussed at him about that only once, and it was a while ago. There must be some other reason.

On Saturday, when it is my turn to buy the newspaper, I ask Babi for the coins. He says, "There is no more newspaper. The Serbians have shut down *Rilindja.*" I feel bad because Babi loves to read the paper. The next time I see the *Rilindja* building, half the letters on top of the building are missing, and there are Serbian letters instead of Albanian ones. I don't know why the Serbians have taken down our letters and closed the building. Don't they realize that my father loves to read the newspaper?

Babi's face is red. He sits on the sofa and has a stethoscope in his ears, a cuff on his arm, and a machine in his lap. His blood pressure must be sky-high. When we sit at the dining room table, he yells at me for no reason. He scolds me the next day when we eat dinner too. He criticizes me because I start my meal by drinking water instead of eating food. Why did the Serbians have to make my father angry and shut down his favorite newspaper?

CHAPTER 4

THE TELEVISION

When I awaken the next morning, Mami has dressed for work. She wears a flared silk dress and a matching jacket. She takes a black leather shoulder bag before she goes out. Usually she walks to work, but today Babi takes her in his car. Shpetim, Fjolla, and I are happy because we get to ride with them too.

Babi doesn't talk much on the way. Instead of looking at Babi and expecting him to say something funny like he used to, I look out my window. There are many shops. Displayed in their front windows is an array of items such as gold jewelry and mannequins dressed in the latest fashions.

The roads of Pristina are paved but in disrepair. Workers don't tend to the roads anymore. Now there are many potholes filled with muddy water. The city's air is foul. The coal factory buildings where Babi works pollute all day and night. Sometimes the smoke is white, sometimes black. Babi's factory is in another town, but its towering smokestack is visible from Pristina.

We drop Mami off near her school, a beautiful yellow building, three stories high. During the drive back to our apartment, Babi still doesn't say a word. When we get home and finish vacuuming, watering Mami's flowers, making the beds, and dusting, we sit and enjoy watching a children's program in Albanian on Radio-Televizioni i Prishtines (RTP).

Eventually Babi gets over the fact that he no longer has an Albanian newspaper to read, and he doesn't yell at me anymore. Today I watch the cartoons while he is taking a nap. I know that he'll wake up and start watching the news at 7:30 p.m. At that time Fjolla, Shpetim, Mami, and I always go to the kitchen, because we know Babi wants to be alone when the news starts. Usually we close the kitchen door and wait thirty minutes until we no longer hear the news anchor's voice, but this time the newscast stops after only a few minutes. I slide off Mami's lap, wondering about the sudden silence. What happened to Babi's news? We wait and then hear loud sounds erupt from the living room.

Mami rushes there. We follow her and see Babi throw the remote control toward the TV. He strides around the room like a madman. He then takes books out of the armoire and throws them on the floor. He swears and stomps and fumes. Something bad must have occurred. The room is in shambles. Books and old newspapers litter the floor, and one of Mami's potted plants has fallen onto the carpet. Babi must have knocked it over. Mami shrieks at him for making a mess.

I later learn that while we were in the kitchen during the telecast, Serbian policemen attacked the anchor, grabbed him by his neck, pulled him out of his chair, and dragged him out of the studio. That incident marked the end of Albanian news programs.

Babi takes his blood pressure and glares at the needle on the machine, which moves like one on the speedometer of a furious driver. He looks at Mami and me but doesn't speak. This silence scares me more than his rant did. I fear what he might do next. At any moment, he could resume his rage.

He tosses the blood pressure monitor aside and stands defiantly. He is going to harm us as a punishment for our coming into the living room. We should have stayed in the kitchen.

He walks to the armoire and gets a vial of medicine out of a drawer. I slowly walk backward toward the kitchen. He pops some pills into his mouth and swallows them without water. I have never felt so afraid of my father.

Babi doesn't hit us. He sits on the sofa and rechecks his blood pressure every two minutes. After he checks it three times, he throws the entire apparatus at the wall. Babi starts pacing again, kicking aside everything he has thrown on the floor. He keeps his head down, staring at the carpet. Is he going to slap us or order us out of the apartment?

Mami approaches him and tries to gently place a hand on his back.

"What is wrong?" she asks him.

He immediately swats her hand away.

"Enough!" he yells.

Then I get an idea. If I raise my two fingers and proudly exclaim "*Fitore*," then he will not be so angry. He will remember the day he taught me that.

I feel a close connection between Babi and me. I had always bought his newspaper when it was available, and he always appreciated that. I even look like Babi; everyone says so. Uncle Skender calls me Little Hysen. "You're just like him," he tells me. "Same brown eyes and broad forehead." I can imagine that Babi's mood will shift immediately as soon as I remind him of our motto. That will give him hope. That will make him happy. My dad will love me again.

He is still walking around the living room but less frantically. I step in front of him. His head remains bowed, his mood sullen.

"Babi—"

He slaps the back of my neck hard and shoves me toward the kitchen before I can raise my two fingers.

I should have known better than to interrupt his rage. I should have known that he wants to be alone.

There are no more cartoons in Albanian. The singers sing in Serbian, the children speak Serbian, the men on the news speak Serbian, and even Bugs Bunny has become Serbian! I can't watch *Pippi Longstocking*. The children's program in Albanian is replaced by a version in Serbian. No Kosovar kids are shown singing songs and reciting poems. I now realize why Babi is so angry about the television. I feel like reacting the way he did when Albanian newscasts were banned. I feel like yelling and throwing things.

I rarely watch the Serbian children's program for longer than five minutes. The show is hosted by a man my dad's age. He has long, dark hair, and the children call him "Drugar." In the studio are a lot of Serbian kids who seem to be having a really good time. Drugar must be funny, because they always laugh. I sit in front of the TV and wish I understood the jokes so I could laugh and enjoy myself too. I guess Kosovar Albanian children aren't meant to laugh anymore.

CHAPTER 5

LEAVING KOSOVO

I'm happy when summer begins because Mami has finished teaching school until the fall, and we can go to our house in the village of Drenovc and play in our yard. We don't need TV to entertain us. During summer, I don't have to watch Drugar and his group of Serbian kids. My friends here—my closest cousin, Musa, and some neighborhood kids—speak Albanian. We have our own jokes and games.

In the village, I can go outside whenever I want and feel safe because most of the neighbors are my relatives. There are four family houses in a row; three belong to my uncles—Sefer, Skender, and Ismet—and the other one is ours. Uncle Ismet's house, like ours, has three stories and was built during the same time when my parents built theirs, when they earned a lot of money. Uncle Skender's and Uncle Sefer's houses are two stories, but the top floors are unfinished. Each house has a fence made of red bricks, and all have big front yards. In our yard there are different fruit trees: pears, plums, peaches, apples, and quinces. Mami and Babi also grow strawberries, tomatoes, hot banana peppers, and beans. My youngest uncle, Fatmir, owns the empty lot beside Uncle Sefer's property. He lives in Switzerland so he can earn enough to build a house in our village too. I always look forward to his visits because he brings us Swiss chocolates and new clothes. I love all my uncles and cousins, though. In Kosovo, close familial bonds are traditional and important.

Several families live across the road. They too have multi-story houses that are unfinished but inhabitable. The exteriors are unpainted because money has become scarce for Kosovar Albanians.

Drenovc is surrounded by mountains. To the right of our house, cows and sheep graze on green slopes in the distance. A dirt road meanders toward another village. The clean air is a welcome relief from the pollution in Pristina.

If you turn left onto the narrow dirt road in front of our house and walk for about four minutes, you will see a pond. Sometimes fish leap above the surface, which is an amazing sight. Tread the same road for another three minutes, and you will see the Llapi River. Its rushing water is cold throughout the year.

Among my favorite activities is going fishing with Cousin Armend. We also like to pick and eat apples that are green and sour.

Throughout the summer I attend Musa's *futboll* matches. He plays for the village's *futboll* club, Traktori, on the junior varsity team. Musa is four years older than I am, yet we are the same height. He has the best reflexes on the team, and he can kick the ball into the net like a bullet. His muscular legs are bowed, like the letter "O." This is a good sign, Musa tells me—a sign of talent. Several professional *futboll* players, he points out, have legs like that.

Once we return from one of his games, he tries to teach me how to play *futboll* and explains some rules. We are in his front yard with an inflated ball that we borrowed from a neighbor. We make the red fence of his yard our goal and use white chalk to mark the boundaries.

My scrawny little legs can't kick the ball anywhere near the goal. Musa demonstrates how to kick the ball with the inside and outside of my foot, but I can't do it. He then tells me to use my toes. Success! I score; I feel great.

But my favorite season passes quickly. One day my parents announce that we are returning to Pristina, because Mami has to resume teaching and Shpetim has to begin the first grade.

At the apartment, I am isolated. All I have is the boring children's TV show in Serbian. Mami and Babi rarely allow me outside because they are scared somebody might kidnap me. I've heard stories of children like me being abducted and murdered. Their remains are then ground and used in consumer products such as soap and shampoo.

On New Year's Eve, we return to the village. Babi's side of the family has gathered at Uncle Skender's house, and Uncle Fatmir has arrived from Switzerland, bringing us different varieties of Swiss chocolates—some with almonds, some plain, and some white, which look strange but taste delicious. At the party, everyone has a good time. Even Babi looks happy and acts calm for once. Babi and my uncles, who call me Lili, drink from a glass bottle. The beverage makes them jolly and relaxed.

After midnight, Uncle Sefer motions for me to come to him. He hands me a bottle and says, "Hey, Lili, drink some of this."

I gladly grab it with both hands. I want to get as happy as he is. I take a couple of sips. The taste is so bitter it makes my lips pucker. Uncle Sefer and Uncle Fatmir laugh. Uncle Sefer grabs me and holds me high in the air like Babi used to do. He kisses my cheek and rubs his face against mine. His beard tickles.

Uncle Sefer coaxes me to take more sips from his bottle. I start to feel giddy. Uncle Fatmir and Uncle Sefer are laughing like crazy with me.

It is a week after New Year's Eve, and Uncle Fatmir is going back to Switzerland. He has come to our apartment in Pristina to say good-bye. Uncle Sefer is with him. They are both dressed in nice suits and wear shiny shoes. They look neat, and their cologne smells wonderful. Why has Uncle Sefer dressed up just to say good-bye to Uncle Fatmir?

Uncle Sefer announces that he is going to Switzerland with Uncle Fatmir with 500 deutschmarks (the equivalent of $250) he has borrowed from Uncle Azem, Mami's brother, who used to be a chauffeur for the former president. Now, because the Serbians govern Kosovo, Uncle Azem works as a driver for a private bus company. I am shocked that Uncle Sefer is leaving the country. He has two babies—a son, Duart, and a daughter, Donjeta.

"What about Duart and Donjeta? Are they going with you too?" I ask.

"I will return to Kosovo as soon as I make enough money, Lili," he says. "I can't take them with me."

How will Aunt Shpresa, Uncle Sefer's wife, take care of Duart and Donjeta by herself? She is now going to be left just like Aunt Fatmire, who has been living meagerly in a ghetto since her husband emigrated to Czechoslovakia. Aunt Shpresa's house is just as bad as Aunt Fatmire's.

"Our bus is leaving. We have to go," Uncle Fatmir says. My uncles kiss me on the cheek and say, "Good-bye, Lili." My father embraces his brothers and then turns away to wipe tears from his eyes.

I want my uncles to stay with us forever. They are entertaining, and we love each other. Now they will never give me strange drinks, and Uncle Sefer will never tickle my face by rubbing his beard against my cheek. Will we ever celebrate another New Year's Eve together? I hate the new president that Babi complains about for making matters worse in Kosovo. It must be his fault that Uncle Sefer can't find work here anymore and must go to Switzerland, away from us.

After they leave our apartment, I go to the sunroom window, sit on Fjolla's bed, and watch Uncle Sefer and Uncle Fatmir walk toward the bus station. Once they disappear from view, I feel pain in my stomach and heart. The cologne that they wore lingers in our apartment. I stare out the window a long time and wish they had taken me with them. For the rest of the day, I often gaze out the window and hope to see my uncles return.

During the same day, the giant metal machines are interspersed among the usual highway traffic. Atop each one is a man positioned behind a short metal pipe mounted on a circular base. Many of the machines display Serbian flags. I wonder what the machine is actually for. What does it do? Do the men who ride on top of the machines steer them by using the rotating base that the metal pipes are mounted on?

CHAPTER 6

STOP

When the weekend arrives, I beg Babi to take us to the village. There I can spend time with Musa and learn to become a better *futboll* player so the other kids can't steal the ball from me when we play.

He usually replies, "I don't have any gas in my car." I realize that this is true, but our village house is only twenty minutes away. Surely he can afford to buy that much gas.

On this weekend, though, he expresses fear about getting a traffic ticket from the Serbian police.

"Why would they give you a ticket, Babi?" I ask.

"Just because they want to, son," he responds.

"Come on, Babi, they are not going to stop us. *Të lutna, të lutna.*" Shpetim and Fjolla start to beg him too, and pretty soon even Mami joins our side.

"Hysen, you don't have a paper to read and you don't have news to watch," says Mami. "You don't have anything to do. Let's all go for a little bit, and maybe we could work in the house a little and straighten up some things."

"All right, all right, we'll go. But I know they are going to stop me."

We quickly get ready. The sooner we leave, the sooner we will get to the village. It's February and cold, so I dress in layers. Since it's snowing in Pristina, it must be snowing twice as hard in the village. There are more mountains there. I take my toboggan and gloves with me too.

We get in the cold car. As cold as it is, I figure there won't be any police on the roads. Babi buys some gas, and we get on the highway. Shortly afterward, I see a police car and realize that I was wrong. As we get closer, a policeman gets out of his car and stands in the middle of the road. He holds a sign that has these letters: S T O P. Babi pulls over and stops. He rolls the window down and starts to speak in Serbian. Even though 90 percent of the people here are Kosovars, all of the policemen are Serbs now, so we have to speak their language to communicate with them. All Kosovar security forces, including police and military troops, have been fired.

Babi hands some documents to the cop, who glances at them and then returns them to him. The policeman checks the back of our car and then speaks to Babi again. I don't understand what they are talking about, but Babi's shaky voice becomes loud and angry. It sounds as if he is trying to defend himself. The policeman yells at Babi. My father says nothing but removes the wallet from his pocket and pulls some bills from it. The Serbian policeman must have demanded money. With bribe in hand, the policeman leaves. We then resume our drive to the village.

"I told you that I would get stopped and fined," Babi fumes. "I don't know why I listen to you all!"

"Why did he take your money, Babi?" I ask.

He doesn't answer. "He told him that Babi's brake lights didn't work," Mami answers.

"I know the things work. He just wanted some money. Fuck his mother," curses Babi.

"Don't curse in front of the children," cautions Mami.

Babi stops cursing but vents his anger with loud sighs through clenched teeth.

Once we reach our driveway, Babi has Shpetim tap the brake pedal. When he does so, the lights flash bright red. When Shpetim lifts his foot off the brake, they go out.

I am angry that the Serbian policeman fined us. Now Babi will never bring us to the village again. He'll say, "No, you remember what happened last time." I'll tell him, "It won't happen again," and he'll growl, "Yes, it will."

I play *futboll* with Musa in the snow, but I don't have as much fun as I would have if Babi hadn't had to pay that hefty fine.

On the ride back to our apartment, Babi stays quiet.

The only time Babi cheers up is when we have guests. Then, in the Albanian tradition, he becomes a genial and relaxed host.

This evening, Uncle Azem visits us with his wife, Hava. Uncle Azem has short, dark hair. He is tall and slim. Babi's mood brightens and he immediately starts talking and smiling. Babi and Uncle Azem discuss politics and Kosovo; their conversation is animated and impassioned. We are happy that Uncle Azem is here. For one thing, he has brought us treats from Switzerland: chocolate bars and a big bottle of Coca-Cola.

After a while, Uncle Azem asks me to massage his left leg, which was broken years ago in a bus accident. A surgeon stabilized the fracture by implanting a metal rod, held in place by screws. The skin that healed over the surgical scar frequently itches. Whenever he visits us, Uncle Azem asks me to massage that leg. He lies on the sofa and places his leg on top of my thighs, and I begin the physical therapy.

"*Bravo, bravo, djali i Dajes* (Uncle's boy). You are the best," he says and falls asleep shortly thereafter.

I'm sad when Uncle Azem wakes up and leaves. We will miss him, but he promises that he'll be back and bring us more chocolates and Coca-Cola.

After Uncle departs, Shpetim, Fjolla, and I argue over who is going to get the biggest portion of chocolate. We finally agree to divide the chocolate equally, but one piece looks bigger and has more almonds than the other pieces.

Shpetim claims it immediately. "I'll take this one," he says.

Fjolla doesn't say anything. She is content with whatever piece we give her.

I wish that Mami and Babi still had money; they could buy plenty of chocolates for everyone. Instead of having to bribe a policeman, Babi could have bought us treats with that money.

CHAPTER 7

JOBS

Since Babi is often angry and sick from hypertension, he takes some time off from work. He immediately feels better and plays with Fjolla and me all day. We often go for walks and shop for loaves of bread. Babi lifts one of us onto his wide shoulders, making us feel taller than everyone else in the world. He buys Fjolla and me candy canes and takes us to the park, where we play on the slides, ladders, and seesaws. I feel as if he has changed. I hope he never returns to work. Mami can teach, and my father can stay with us.

In the evenings, Babi likes for Shpetim and me to wrestle, and he always roots for me, the underdog. He teaches me a tactic to defeat Shpetim. Babi tells me to wrap my arms around my brother's waist and place one foot behind his ankle and then push him. I am afraid, but with Babi's coaching, I am confident I can win.

I push Shpetim with all my strength as I position my foot behind his ankle and take him down. I am so excited that I can't stay still. Babi is just as happy as I am. He grins and teases Shpetim for not beating his smaller, ten-kilos-lighter younger brother. My happiness lasts all night.

It is Monday morning, and this is the last day of Babi's medical leave. Babi, Fjolla, and I walk with Shpetim to school, the same one where I am going to start first grade next year. During the past three months, we took daily walks with Babi. I worry about how things will be now.

"Babi. Promise me that we'll take walks even after you start work!"

"OK, *djali i babit*. I promise," he says.

The next day, I wait by the door at the time when Babi usually returns home from work. Maybe Babi will bring Fjolla and me some candy canes or chocolates.

Suddenly I hear the door open. Babi rushes by me. Maybe he has to use the bathroom immediately. I greet him, but he ignores me. He throws his shoes to the side and slams the door shut.

Babi doesn't go to the bathroom but to the living room. Something is wrong; something serious must have happened. I start to worry that Babi will never again take Fjolla and me for walks and to the park. Babi has a Serbian newspaper in his hand; he angrily throws it on the living room table. It is unwise to say anything to him now. I had better stay quiet and wait for him to calm down. Perhaps he might relax enough to wrestle with me.

He turns on the TV and starts listening to the Serbian news, something that he hasn't done during the past three months while on medical leave.

Later that evening it's clear that Babi is in no mood to play games. Mami talks to him and then comes to us.

"What happened, Mami?" asks Shpetim.

Mami tries to explain what is bothering our father, but we don't understand. She uses words that are strange to us—words like "directors," "terminated," "medical leave," and "supervised." Later, I learn what happened. When Babi arrived at work, he noticed that something was wrong. He didn't see any of the thirteen Kosovar workers whom he supervised. The only other Kosovar there was Destan, who had also returned from medical leave. Destan explained to Babi that the other Kosovars had been terminated by the new Serbian directors. Many workers were fired for participating in public protests against Milosevic's punitive policies toward Kosovo. Some were given vague explanations for their dismissals.

The only thing I understand is when Mami says, "His workers who were also his friends don't work with him anymore." I can imagine how Babi must have felt when he didn't see his friends at work. He may have expressed his objection initially but then decided to keep quiet for fear of losing his job too.

Babi sits on his sofa and watches more Serbian news. The Serbian media reports that the Kosovar workers left voluntarily. Such lies anger my father even further.

He doesn't say a word to anyone. When he walks past us he keeps his head down, and we know not to get in his way.

I wish Babi had been fired too. He was much happier when he was home with Fjolla and me. Now he drags himself to work, knowing that his Kosovar friends aren't going to be there, and comes home looking as if he wants to kill somebody.

I notice that Mr. Vokshi from the fifth floor no longer has a driver to pick him up in the fancy black car. I never see Mr. Krasniqi from the fourth floor wearing his nice suit and tie.

I go to Mami and ask, "Mami, why doesn't Mr. Vokshi have a driver anymore?"

"He has gotten fired, like Babi's friends," she says.

"You mean his driver will never come pick him up with the black car again?"

"Yes."

"What about Mr. Krasniqi?"

"He lost his job too."

"Really?"

"Yes, son. Most of the Kosovar workers have gotten fired. Kosovar doctors have gotten kicked out of hospitals, Kosovar clerks out of post offices, Kosovar lawyers out of their practices, Kosovar police out of their posts, Kosovar workers out of factories."

From Fjolla's window, I see men, women, and children crowding into buses. There aren't enough seats for everyone. Passengers carry suitcases. People say good-bye and blow kisses to those who get on board. There is a lot of crying and waving of hands as the buses depart for Switzerland or Germany.

No one wants to stay in Kosovo anymore. Milosevic and the politics that make Babi angry are making things worse for everyone. People are leaving Kosovo, never to return. It saddens me to watch them go. They will probably never see their family or friends again. I remember when Uncle Sefer left Kosovo. He never came back.

The buses leave, and the giant metal machines follow. I think it would be cool to sit on top of one of those machines. I would be high above the ground and could see everything; it would be like sitting on Babi's shoulders the whole time. I would have a nice pair of goggles, like the ones the camouflaged men wear.

CHAPTER 8

SCHOOL

I am almost six-and-a-half, and eager to start first grade, since Babi doesn't play with me anymore and all I do is look outside the window and feel bored. School will be fun. Today I am so restless that I go to the bathroom and try to shave like Babi. I cut my face. Maybe in school I'll learn how to shave like my dad. And maybe I will learn something about those strange machines and why they are in Kosovo.

On the first day, Mami accompanies me to school, even though it is only a five-minute walk. I am excited to enter the orange school building and see what it looks like inside.

The school has a big front yard made of concrete. I see hundreds of Kosovar first-graders standing in rows. At the front of every other row stands a teacher. One of those teachers is mine. Mami knows her name, finds her, and introduces us. Her name is Ajshe Sherifi, and she seems to be my mother's age. Her hair is dark red, and her perfume smells like the roses in Mr. Sejda's garden. I fall in love with her immediately.

The students are well groomed. The boys' hair is neatly combed and slicked down with water. The girls have long ponytails. Two of the girls in my class are beautiful; I glance at them and then shyly look away. After telling Mrs. Sherifi that she is a teacher too, at a high school, Mami takes me to the end of one row to stand and wait. She kisses me good-bye and leaves.

It's my class's turn to enter the building. An elderly, strict school clerk makes sure that the rows are straight. All the students march in perfect formation. Once inside, I am amazed how high the ceilings are. The floors are covered in green tiles. Our classroom, located on the second floor, is huge.

We are assigned seats. I sit next to a boy who has rosy cheeks and the same last name as mine. After everyone gets settled, the teacher asks us if we know the famous Albanian poem "*Qesh i vogël, dhe u rrita*." I have heard Mami teach it to Shpetim, but I don't know all the lines. Some students raise their hands. Our teacher says, "We are going to do some practice here," and she starts reciting the poem slowly.

> *Qesh i vogël, dhe u rrita.*
> *Në prehen të nënes u merzita.*
> *Sdi me shkru as me lexu.*
> *Mirpo drejt në shkoll du me shku.*

> (I was little, and now I am grown.
> On my mother's lap I am bored.
> I don't know how to write or read.
> But straight to school I will proceed.)

At the end of class she says, "Let's make sure we all learn it by tomorrow."

At home, I practice my poem. The next morning I feel I am ready to recite it to Mrs. Sherifi. I wash my hands, brush my teeth, and comb my hair with water like some of the boys in my class. As I'm getting dressed, Mami appears and says I can't go to school.

"What do you mean I can't go to school? Why? I am supposed to learn the *Qesh i vogël, dhe u rrita* poem, and I did. Mrs. Sherifi is going to love it when I recite it. She'll love that I have learned every line of it." Mami tries to say something and I keep insisting, "I am pretty sure she wanted me to learn it by today. She told everybody to learn it."

31

"I know, I know, son," says Mami, crying, "but they have closed the school."

"Who closed the school? Those school clerks that stand by the door? They are mean," I say.

"No, not the mean school clerks, but the Serbian police. The Serbian police are the ones that closed it."

"Why?" I ask.

"They don't want you to go to school. They want you to be illiterate."

I am in disbelief. I thought they mostly stayed on the sides of the highways and stole money from Kosovars. I didn't realize they would shut down our school. I can't believe I can't go to school. I wanted to go back and see those pretty girls with ponytails, learn something about the metal machines and maybe learn to shave like Babi. I can't believe it. I won't get to make any new friends. My classmate with rosy cheeks and I were becoming friends. We were meant to be friends; we have the same last name.

Mami follows me to the living room. I notice that she isn't wearing her leather shoulder bag or her silk dress. "Did they close your school too, Mami?" I ask. "The yellow building?"

"Yes," she says.

The next day, I am confused when I see Mami dressed up as if she is going to school.

"Where are you going, Mami?"

"I am going to protest the closings of our schools."

What does "protest" mean? She must be going to march like the miners did.

Since we can't go to school this semester, the fall of 1991, Mami begins teaching me the alphabet. The Albanian alphabet has thirty-six letters, so I have a lot to learn. Shpetim is supposed to be in second grade this year; Mami starts to teach him math and how to write better.

When she teaches us something and we don't understand it immediately, she reminds us of Babi. She breathes slowly and calmly when I recognize the different letters, but if I mispronounce a letter or mistake it for a different one, she becomes agitated and slaps me.

Every day and night she sits between Shpetim and me on the sofa. I'm to her left side and Shpetim is to her right. Shpetim and I each have a book on our laps. Mami shows my brother how to multiply two times three. While he muddles through that, she resumes teaching me the alphabet. She instructs me how to pronounce and write the letter *R*. Then she turns her attention back to Shpetim.

"What is two times three?" she asks him.

Shpetim looks down at his book. His face turns red. He doesn't know the answer. "Eight?" he says.

Mami smacks the back of his head and yells, "Not eight, but six." I feel nervous and forget my lesson about the letter *R*.

She turns toward me. She points her index finger to the letter *R* in my book. "How do you say this letter?" she asks.

I look down and think hard, but I can't remember it at all. Mami expects so much of us. We are only seven and eight years old—first- and second-graders.

"Uh…*Q*," I say.

She smacks the back of my head and shouts, "Not *Q*. *R*. How many times do I have to tell you that?" She told me only once, but I don't dare correct her.

She raises her hand, and I cover my head. She smacks me anyway, and then she pulls her hair in frustration. "How could you forget? I taught you it's the letter *R*, not *Q*. Just two seconds ago. Can't you remember anything?" I am sure that our neighbors hear her scream.

Finally, Babi comes home. He still doesn't talk to us, but I am happy because I know he is going to watch Serbian news. Shpetim and I feel relieved that our lesson is over, but Mami continues and punishes us whenever we give wrong answers. Babi turns on the TV and gets mad at what the Serbian reporters say. He orders us to move to the kitchen and do our work there.

"This is more important than your stupid news," Mami screams at him. I don't think Babi has realized how frustrated and angry Mami has been since we haven't been able to go to school. "*You* don't bother us. And you're listening to the Serbian news, the same people that say, 'The Kosovars don't want to go to school… They suddenly have decided not to go to school because they are stupid anyway.' The same people that say, 'They don't want to go to work, they don't want to read, they don't want to have a channel in their own language.'"

Babi doesn't respond to Mami or do anything else except turn down the volume so I can continue learning my ABCs and Shpetim his multiplication tables.

Shpetim and I dutifully study as Mami demands. Every day, I think how I would much rather learn the alphabet in Mrs. Sherifi's class.

One day I ask, "Why are you angry with us all the time, Mami?"

"I am sorry you feel that way," she says. "I really shouldn't be angry at you. I am just afraid that you are going to be illiterate, and I don't want you to get behind."

I am surprised at her response. I thought that Mami believed we were stupid, and that's why she was angry. Now I realize she is mad at those mean policemen and Milosevic, who don't let us go to school. Mami is probably afraid that she won't be allowed to teach at her school again too.

Mami lets us take a break from studying. I gaze out the living room window. I observe more people boarding buses to leave Kosovo. Since we can't go to school and study in our own language, I wish that we had gone to Germany or Switzerland with my uncles. I am sure there are no Serbian policemen in those countries.

I tire of looking out the window and feeling sad. Shpetim and I take advantage of Mami's calm mood and beg her to let us go out and play for a while. Mami says the kind of "no" that really means "yes," so Shpetim and I go out to play basketball.

We go to the basketball court near our apartment and see that there are Serbian kids playing on it. This means we have to wait until they leave. The Serbian kids never let us play with them, because they think they are better than us. We just sit around the court and watch them. Other Kosovar kids have come to the court too. The Serbian kids dribble the ball in between their legs and think they are good. They don't know that we can do that too; it is not that hard.

I am angry that we have to wait. This playground is supposed to belong to everyone. Also, both the basketball and the *futboll* stadiums are being used only by Serbian teams. So I am not surprised that we are treated like this here on our local court. My next door neighbor—the son of Mr. Sejda, the gardener—is over seven-feet tall, the second tallest man in Kosovo and a professional basketball player, and the Serbians won't let his team play in the city's big stadium either.

The Serbian kids finish playing. Before they leave, three of them go behind the back board. Two of them grab the third one by his thighs and knees and hoist him up. With a wrench, he unscrews the bolts, and then removes the whole rim. The Serbian kids laugh as they depart with the rim in their hands. Now we have only the board, and all we can do is aim the ball at its center.

Once the Serbian kids are out of earshot, one of the Kosovar boys shouts, "They think we are going to eat the rim."

"They don't want us to have fun, that's all," someone else shouts.

"We should have fought them and taken the rim that belongs to everyone and not just to them," an older kid says. "Fuck their mother."

Eight of us take to the court anyway. Divided into two teams of four, we start playing. We wish we had the rim so we wouldn't have to fight about whether or not someone has really scored a point in the little square. It is hard to tell because the ball always touches one of the lines of the square and never quite hits the very middle.

I wonder why Serbians hate Kosovars. Why do I have to be afraid of them? I'm certain that it's not because of the way we look. We look alike. Most Serbians and Kosovars have dark hair and black or brown eyes.

I know that religion doesn't play a role in their hatred toward us. My family is Muslim, but we aren't devout. Neither Mami nor Babi prays five times a day. They don't fast prior to Ramadan. In regards to Mami, not only does she not pray and fast, but she also immediately stops Babi from teaching us Koran verses on the rare occasions when he is tempted to do that. After studying advanced biology and evolution, Mami is convinced there is no God. She believes that "Nature" is the only deity. Often I ask her what she means by that, because I picture God as a person with a big bald head and long arms who lives in the sky; I imagine that his eyes are so big that he can see everybody.

Mami answers, "Nature is the air we breathe, the water we drink, the earth we live on, the wind, the trees—everything." Her description of God confuses me.

"Besides, we are converted Muslims," she continues. "We were converted from Catholicism to Islamism during the Ottoman Empire." I heard this at school. And Babi once said, "Six generations earlier we were Catholics."

The only occasion when I go to the mosque is during Ramadan, but I don't go inside, because it is crowded, and once you take off your shoes, somebody can steal them. Instead, Musa, Shpetim, and I wait in the mosque's yard and eat snacks. Once we went inside, but we pinched and tickled each other's feet and made funny faces while the adults stood and sat or knelt and bowed.

Some Kosovar teenagers celebrate Christmas even though they are Muslims. On Christmas Eve, they gather in the city center with Kosovar Catholics to party and have a good time. In my school, the teacher reads a letter from the principal wishing all staff and students a merry Christmas. Although my classmates are Muslims, no one feels offended. Instead, we are happy to have a vacation for that holiday. Most Serbians are Orthodox, but we never disrespect them. They never disrespect us in that regard either.

Only years later, after reading history books by American and British historians, do I understand the hatred between the two groups. It began on June 15, 1389, when the Serbians were defeated by the Ottomans in the Battle of Kosovo. The Serbian historians assert that their people were exiled from Kosovo as a result, allowing the Albanian population to gradually increase. Serbians believe that Kosovo is their ancestral land and thus belongs to them. American and British scholars agree that Kosovar Albanians are the descendants of Illyrians, who were native to the Balkans and settled in Kosovo centuries earlier than the Serbians. Kosovars believe the same. That is why Mami and Babi named me Ilir.

The belief that Kosovar Albanians took over Kosovo after the battle is also fueled by Serbian nationalist myths, which have been the subject of many books written by Western scholars. For example, the Serbians were taught that until World War II, the majority of the population in Kosovo was Serbian; yet the population census of 1948 shows that Kosovars constituted 68.5 percent of the Kosovo population and the Serbians 23.6 percent, with other ethnic groups making up the remainder.

The next day at home, while I am learning the letter *U*, I hear the phone ring; Mami answers it. Whoever she is speaking to is making her happy. She hangs up the phone, smiling.

"Who was that, Mami?"

"It was the school principal, *pllumb*. He told me that the department of education has converted a private house into a school," she says with great excitement. "I must call my students because we are having a meeting to restart school in this private house."

Mami starts phoning her students and telling them to secretly meet in Germi, a mountainous region; the park that Babi took us to is located there. She warns her students to be careful when they come and to watch out for the Serbian police. If the Serbian police discover that Kosovars have reopened school secretly, Mami fears they'll teargas the students and arrest her.

Mami meets her students on Saturday. After she comes back, I ask her, "Mami, did the Serbian police see you and your students?"

"No, *pllumb*. Fortunately, they did not. Now we are going to start school on Monday in the new schoolhouse."

Hearing Mami talk about her school makes me think about mine. When am I going to restart first grade?

Mami, Shpetim, and I walk to our school and see a white sheet hung on a window in front of the orange building. Mami stares at it for a few seconds and her face brightens. She smiles at us and says, "You are going back to school." Shpetim and I are as happy as Mami. We are relieved that we won't get slapped anymore, and Mami is happy that she won't have to slap us anymore either. Most importantly, she is ecstatic that we won't be illiterate.

CHAPTER 9

TWO UNEQUAL HALVES

It is Monday morning. Shpetim and I are on our way to school. A minute passes, and Shpetim and I encounter two Serbian policemen. Both of them have big guns strapped across their chests. They have billy clubs hanging from their belts. They are wearing dark blue helmets. I realize these are the same people who didn't let us go to school. The two Serbian policemen see the book bags on our shoulders. I'm frightened; Shpetim and I are alone. I wonder if the policemen are going to kill us for going to school. I know Mami had to meet her students in secret because the Serbians don't want us Kosovars to have our own schools.

The policemen are slowly walking on the right side of the road toward us, looking in our direction. Shpetim and I move closer to one another, trembling. I look around to call out for help, but I don't see other Kosovars. I want to run home, but I know that we will be quickly caught. I try to inch closer to Shpetim. I want to get inside his body and hide, but he draws his body closer toward mine; he must be thinking the same thing. What are they going to do to us? We are so scared that we freeze.

The policemen are only a few steps from us; I stare at them. Their uniforms are scary. Their bodies are huge. They wear calf-high black boots. Shpetim pushes me toward the left side of the road, away from them. My heart is pounding faster and faster as they near us. I wish Mami or Babi were by our side. This is why they usually don't let us outdoors on our own. This is why Mami walked to school with me the first time. These hulking officers tighten their lips and give us the meanest looks I have ever seen.

All of a sudden, they walk past us. My brother and I start running away from them and hope they don't decide to turn around. I feel relieved to have escaped. After a little distance, we see several other kids walking to school too. We are no longer alone, but when we reach the school, I see more Serbian police. They are in front of the rows of students. The same scary feelings chill my body. I think they are not going to let us into the school. I remember what Mami said.

I don't know what else to do but part from Shpetim and try to get into the school with my classmates. I get in the row where they and our lovely teacher, Ajshe Sherifi, are standing. Seeing our frightened faces, Mrs. Sherifi assures us, "Don't worry, they are not going to touch you." In front of the building, where the police are standing, I notice the sign displaying the school's name has changed. Our school's name was Dardania, which is the Albanian name for our neighborhood, but now the sign says "Владімір Лэніх Лэнін (Vladimir Ilyich Lenin)" in Serbian Cyrillics. I wonder who changed our school's name. It must have been the Serbian policemen.

Mrs. Sherifi was right. We walk inside, and the officers don't touch us. I am so happy to leave them behind and get inside.

The interior of the school has changed as well. The Kosovar classrooms have been divided with thick walls. Our school is now divided between the Serbians and us in two unequal parts. Even though there are three times as many Kosovar students as Serbians, we have the smaller space.

Mrs. Sherifi directs us to the same classroom as last time, but now it is half its original size. There are half as many desks and chairs. Some of us must share chairs. I share one with a classmate who wears thick glasses and whose name is Labinot. Our school desks are each supposed to accommodate two students, but at ours there are four. I feel as if I can't breathe. Learning the alphabet with Mami on our big sofa was not so bad after all.

Soon every chair has two students and every desk four or more. There are still some classmates standing. Mrs. Sherifi asks one of them, a blond-haired boy, to use his book bag as a seat. The blond boy quickly says no; he tells her that he has rulers and triangles that he will break if he sits on his book bag.

It takes us almost the whole day just to get started. I am sweating because I am wearing heavy clothes. I can barely move my hands, but I don't say anything. I hate to complain because Mrs. Sherifi has just started to explain something. I don't know what she is teaching. I can't concentrate. Maybe it is one of the letters of the alphabet. Good thing Mami has taught me the letters. I wait for my classmates who are standing to start whining or crying. It won't take much to disturb Mrs. Sherifi, because she herself doesn't have room to move. Beads of perspiration trickle down the sides of her face, and she sighs often. I pretend to pay attention, but I'm really thinking about her sweaty, dark red hair.

Mrs. Sherifi notices that we are not paying attention and yells at us. "We are behind, dear students. Focus! Focus! We have a lot of letters and numbers to learn. I repeat. We are behind."

"But it is so hot in here, teacher," someone finally whines.

"I know, I know, but we have to try to focus. That's just the way it is."

We stay for only three-and-a-half hours instead of the usual five and then go home. Now that our classroom space has been reduced by half, we go to school in shifts. The next shift of Kosovar students will arrive shortly to take our place.

We continue to go to school. Each day we deal with the same problems in our classroom while trying to pay attention and learn. The classroom floors start getting dusty from our dirty shoes. During the break, some of us boys run or fight with one another, which stirs up clouds of dust in the air that we breathe. When our teacher returns from the break and opens the classroom door, she waves her hand in front of her face to keep from inhaling the dust. Then she yells at us for running and fighting. Sometimes she has to waste the entire three-and-a-half hours determining who exactly was misbe-having so she can notify those students' parents.

Once I get home, I start to complain to Mami about the dust, the crowdedness, and the shortage of chairs and desks.

"Oh son, oh son," she says. "My students don't even have any chairs or desks. They sit on the floor. I have thirty-two students, and I teach all of them in a small bedroom in the house."

"Really?" I start to feel better. I'm one of thirty-six students, but our classroom is bigger than a bedroom, and we don't have to sit on the floor.

"Yeah, I'm not kidding. My students all sit on the floor of the bedroom that isn't any bigger than twelve-by-fifteen feet. They sit in rows. Some of them place their notebooks on the back of the person in front, and some of them curve their legs and place their notebooks on their thighs to take notes." Hearing this, I feel even better about my classroom. Even though I share a chair with Labinot, at least we have a desk to set our notebooks on.

"There are twelve-hundred students who study in the house," Mami continues. "All of them are divided in three shifts and among twelve rooms. None of the rooms have blackboards, of course. My students just listen to me talk. At least there is a blackboard in your classroom." I can barely understand the lesson if my teacher doesn't write on the blackboard. I don't know how Mami's students learn without one.

"Yes, son. You shouldn't complain. Your school is near our apartment. My school is far away; I have to walk an hour and a half each way."

"That is true," I say. It takes me only five minutes to reach my school, and I don't have to stride uphill to the Lagjja e Trimave neigh-borhood like Mami. She is right: I shouldn't complain anymore.

"I'm sorry that you have to walk so far away, Mami. I wish Milosevic was dead so you wouldn't have to walk so much," I say.

"I wish so too," she says.

CHAPTER 10

DARK AND CRUEL PERSONALITIES

I t is 1992, the start of the fall semester of my second grade. I am almost eight, and I still go to the same crowded classroom—and I still complain. To make matters even worse, Mami and Babi have run out of money. Mami doesn't get paid for teaching at the schoolhouse. Babi says the 1,000,000 dinars a month he gets are not worth anything.

"With the inflation of Kosovo's economy and its rapid fluctuation, my wages are equivalent to a pack of cigarettes by noon and not even a piece of gum by afternoon," I hear Babi tell Uncle Fatmir in Switzerland on the phone. "Milosevic has ruined our lives, the economy, and everything else."

To save energy, the three of us take a bath at the same time and only once a week. We don't buy any new clothes as we ordinarily would at the beginning of a school year. I wear clothes from last year and Shpetim's old, smelly shoes, which have holes in them. My feet get cold, and because the shoes' soles are loose, the rain and snow get inside them and make my socks wet. Babi doesn't have money to buy us even the cheap, counterfeit Nike shoes.

At least my classmates don't make fun of me. Most of them have torn shoes too. Most of them are in a similar economic situation. Three of them don't even have their dads around to buy them anything. Their fathers fled Kosovo because of Milosevic; two were politicians and one was a policeman. When they talk about how much they miss their dads, they get very sad, so everyone in class knows not to mention them.

At home, Mami bakes bread before going to school. That is about the only thing that we have to eat. Mami says baking bread is cheaper than buying loaves of it at the store. So she wakes up at five o'clock every morning, prepares the dough, and puts it in the oven. We eat the bread sprinkled with plain sugar. I quickly learn to hate bread and sugar to the point that I am disgusted by the thought of it. I ate little even when Mami cooked a variety of delicious foods all the time, much less a diet of bread and sugar three times a day.

With the current inflation, Babi's monthly wages are sixteen deutschmarks, but we cannot purchase anything except more flour and sugar. Even buying these two items becomes a problem because of the rising prices.

Babi starts to plant wheat on the little piece of land we have in our village. During the weekend when Babi sows the seeds, Shpetim and I ride with him. Babi teaches us how to spread the seeds on the ground at intervals. I am hungry and worry we may starve to death. I don't understand that it will take eight months for these seeds to turn into wheat, and that only then can we harvest the crop and take it to the mill to grind into flour. I hate to think that when we return home, there isn't going to be bread on the table because Mami did not have flour to make it with.

There is also a critical shortage of gasoline, so we can't go to the village as often as we should to tend the field and harvest the grain. Nevertheless, Babi turns this crisis to his advantage by driving to the neighboring country, Macedonia, and buying some of its cheap gas to sell in our city for a higher price.

On his first trip, my brother and I beg Babi to take us with him. He takes us and five empty twenty-liter gasoline canisters. We see ourselves as his junior business partners and are very excited to take this trip. We want Babi to make lots of money, but most of all, we want to travel in his car, see new places, and get out of our boring apartment.

Babi fears we are going to be fined again by the Serbian police. He leans close to the steering wheel and keeps his attention focused on the road. From the back seat, I can see his wide eyes in the rear-view mirror.

Shpetim and I enjoy the one-hour ride. We see lots of mountains, houses, and livestock. I like the roads that are downhill at first and then turn uphill. When coasting downhill, Babi cuts off the engine to save gas and doesn't restart it until we get to the top of the hill and the car doesn't move anymore.

At the Macedonian border, there is a line of cars about two miles long. They too are waiting to buy gas. We will have to wait hours; now Shpetim and I regret that we came. The cars move so slowly. We become cold, bored, and sleepy. It gets dark before we reach the gas station, and the attendant tells Babi that he can fill only two of our five canisters.

Babi doesn't like this. He pulls the car to the side, takes a rubber hose out of his trunk, and sticks it into the gas tank to transfer the fuel to the three empty canisters. Babi can then refill his gas tank at the pump. Babi puts the other end of the hose in his mouth. He inhales through the hose like a straw, but he stops and takes a fresh breath of air; he must be nauseated by the smell. He tries again but inhales harder this time—too hard. Gasoline is suctioned out of the tank through the rubber hose and into Babi's mouth. Babi spits it out and quickly puts the hose in the canister. His mouth burns from the taste of gasoline, so he spits and spits, wiping his lips with the cuffs of his shirt sleeves. His face is withered, as if he just drank a glass full of vodka. He suctions the hose twice more and then almost faints as he continues to cough and spit; he gasps for air.

Babi manages to fill two canisters from the tank and doesn't fill the last one. He says, "Fuck its mother," and gets into the car. The smell of gasoline infiltrates our car, and I quickly come to hate the overpowering odor. I used to like it, but never again.

"I am sorry that you had to suck that gasoline out of there, Babi," I say.

"Well, son," he says, taking another big breath, "you have to stay alive somehow."

The next day is Sunday, and we accompany Babi to sell the gasoline at a busy intersection. Shpetim and I approach people's cars and ask, "Do you need any gas? My dad is selling it if you need some.

He is right there." We point toward Babi's car. Some of them want one liter, some of them five, and occasionally someone can afford to buy twenty liters. There are other older men like Babi selling gas, and sometimes customers trust grown men instead of boys like us. Others don't care, so we direct them to Babi, who transfers the gas from the canisters into their gas tanks.

At the end of the day, a Serbian police car with two officers stops at the intersection, and Babi shouts, "Ilir, Shpetim, come here." We run to Babi, and he tells us, "Get in the car quickly!"

From their car, the Serbian policemen spot another man selling gasoline. One shouts from his open window, and the man gets into his own car and follows the police.

"Babi, where are they going?" I ask.

"To the police station," Babi responds.

"What are they going to do to him?"

"Confiscate his gasoline and arrest him."

I feel sorry for the man even though he was our competitor. He had to wait in that long line in Macedonia for hours just so he could get some gasoline to sell in order to feed his family. They could have arrested us too. It must be illegal to resell gasoline on the street. I am probably a criminal for helping Babi sell gas, but we are hungry.

We sell all of our gas without the Serbian police harassing us. The trip turns out to be a success. With our profit, Babi buys milk, eggs, and more flour. Mami cooks us thin pancakes and scrambled eggs. I start to eat more.

We continue to help Babi with his business for a year until one day someone hits the back of his car at a stoplight and damages its trunk. "The car could have exploded," Babi says. "I had three canisters full of gas in the trunk."

No gas profit means no eggs or milk. We go back to bread and sugar until Babi fixes his car and a friend of his who owns a mini-market says, "Hey, Hysen. I know that you resold some gasoline you bought in Macedonia. Well, I don't need gas, but what I do need are one-hundred-gram cans of chicken paste called Argeta. They are made in Macedonia, and if you go there and buy them for me, it will be worth it for you."

"Really?" says Babi.

"Yeah, really," says the owner of the mini-market. "They sell well here, and I need them fast. I need fifty cans."

Before we know it, Babi, Shpetim, and I are on the way to Macedonia again, but this time to buy Argeta. We go to the capital of Macedonia, Skopje. It is nighttime, and the city looks similar to Pristina, with lots of tall apartment buildings and lights. We find an open shop and buy a hundred cans of Argeta. We plan to sell fifty of them to the mini-market owner and the rest in the street market in Pristina.

It is Tuesday, after school. Shpetim, Babi, and I take our fifty Argeta cans to the street market. Tuesday is a busy day when a lot of people attend this market, which is called *tregu i grave* (women's market) because a lot of the shoppers are women. People sell various products, from food to clothes to working tools. There are vendors and customers from all neighborhoods of Pristina and the surrounding villages. When we arrive, I see that inside the market are people selling their wares on top of beach cots. One person has used shoes spread all over the cot. It would be hard to find two shoes that match. The vendor beside him has jeans for sale, and the next one has sweaters and new counterfeit shoes. I wish I could buy a pair. There are rows of these beach cots and a lot of customers browsing. Some vendors have beach umbrellas to shield their products. Even though there are a lot of beach cots and umbrellas, you don't get the feeling that you are at the beach; people are wearing heavy clothes on this cold late October day, and the sea is nowhere to be seen.

Beside *tregu i grave*, there is *tregu i pemëve dhe perimëve* (the fruit and vegetable market), where big trucks are parked in rows and their trailers display fruits and vegetables. Few people can afford fresh produce, so they look but don't buy. It has been a long time since Babi has bought any bananas. I could eat three of them right now; I love bananas. Maybe if we sell enough Argeta, Babi will buy me some.

Near these two markets, there is a road where a lot of cars have parked on the sidewalk, and their owners display products for sale on the top of the hoods. These are men like Mr. Vokshi, our neighbor. They used to have real jobs, and now they have to sell stuff on the street. Mr. Vokshi, the big boss with a chauffeur, is now a blacksmith. Instead of working in a nice, spacious office, he works in a cramped storage room in the cold basement of our apartment building.

Babi gets the crate of Argeta from the trunk, and I grab an empty box and follow him. We find a space between *tregu i grave* and *tregu i pemëve dhe perimëve* where lots of people walk by. We place our Argeta cans on top of the empty box, and the people start to direct their attention toward us.

I see other children doing business too. I am glad Shpetim and I are not the only ones. Some of them sell cups of sunflower seeds or pumpkin seeds from a white bucket. Others sell eggs, sodas, and cigarettes. In *tregu i pemëve dhe perimëve*, some children offer to carry shoppers' goods for a small fee. They look around to see who is buying boxes of fruit and vegetables and roll their wheelbarrows up to them and say, "Do you need assistance? I won't ask for a lot of money. You know you don't want to carry those heavy boxes all by yourself."

I don't want to be seen by my classmates here. There is an embarrassing image associated with child vendors. To be a child vendor means that you are poor. My classmates and I are all poor, but we hate to openly admit it on the streets. I am afraid that if my classmates see me, they might think I am delinquent and don't care about my education. Often, child vendors are forced to drop out of school. If they do go to school, they are rarely able to attend, so they can't keep pace with other students. They must make money to help their families, like my friend Labinot, who sells cigarettes.

In less than two minutes, we sell our first can of Argeta to an elderly lady. If we continue to sell like this, we will have money to buy more food. Babi might buy me bananas. We sell several more cans, but then we see armed Serbian policemen walking up and down the rows of vendors. Everyone is smiling at the officers, trying to be nice and hoping they won't be fined, but the two Serbian cops stare at them coldly. What if they come closer to us? I am scared they are going to take our cans of chicken paste.

Babi smiles when he looks toward them. I'd better smile too. I remember the police taking that man's gasoline, and I suspect they are going to take something from someone. I watch them nervously as they move from vendor to vendor, picking up little things from the cots to see whether the items are appealing. The vendors greet them and talk to them politely in Serbian. "Hello, *gospodin* (mister in Serbian)," they say. "How are you doing today?" The Serbian police don't reply.

Finally, a girl almost my age with lightly curled hair, selling sunflower and pumpkin seeds, passes them as she carries her white bucket. She doesn't seem to realize who they are.

"Stop!" I hear the Serbian police yell. One of them takes a cup from the bucket, fills it with white sunflower seeds, and pours them into the palm of his hand. Instead of paying for the seeds, the policemen give her a cold look. The girl runs away. The two policemen finish walking through *tregu i grave* and disappear.

After we sell twenty-five cans of Argeta, Babi agrees to buy us six bananas in *tregu i pemëve dhe perimëve*. Then we spot the same policemen in their patrol car, driving in between the parked fruit and vegetable trucks. One of the officers gets out of the car and points to a box of cucumbers and a box of tomatoes, and the next thing we see is the salesman putting both in the back seat of their car. Those thieves, jerks, devils. They shouldn't be able to do that.

Once they leave our immediate area, the salesman swears, "Fuck their mother." He is angry, and I am too. I don't understand why we allow them to take our merchandise. I hate that we smile even though we don't like them.

Their next stop is a truck that sells fruit. This time they don't even get out of their car, and a box of apples is loaded onto the back seat. The policemen finally drive away and the vendors start to vent their anger by complaining and cursing.

We go to the vendor whose apples were taken. Babi buys the bananas from him and says, "They are jerks."

"What can we do?" the vendor sighs.

We put our bananas in our car and start home. I eat one banana on the way and think about the two Serbian bullies in the market. With them on my mind, I can't enjoy my banana.

As time goes by and I continue helping Babi sell Argeta cans, I learn more about the Serbian police. Young Kosovar children and teenagers, especially the vendors, refer to them as the t'zi (the brute or the dark) because of their dark, cruel personalities. They have more power than I first thought. I see a girl drop her bucket of seeds just to flee the cops. Serbian officers seize bottled drinks from children who are trying to sell them. They steal cigarettes from a boy—several packs of them. Worst of all, I see a cop slap a vendor my age to the ground. Witnessing these things makes me angry. I picture myself as a superhero who will rescue my fellow vendors. Together my imaginary friend Zllumzllak and I scare off the police. They run away and never return.

Each time I see another one of these incidents, I know that it is just a matter of time until my brother, father, and I are going to be victims. Despite my vigilance, it's impossible to avoid the vicious tactics of the police.

CHAPTER 11

BOSNIAN BOYS

We have now made some money from selling gasoline and Argeta, and no longer eat the same foods over and over again. Mami cooks a variety of dishes.

One day Babi decides that it is time to quit watching the insanely biased Serbian news and buy a satellite dish. I am thrilled when we install it outside our balcony. Now we are able to watch an Albanian channel that is broadcast for an hour and a half between 6:30 and 8:00 p.m. Within this time slot, there is a twenty-minute children's show I love. The show is similar to Drugar's program, except the kids and the host speak Albanian. I always make sure to watch the show at 7:00 p.m., right after the thirty-minute news segment Babi watches. When the children in the show laugh, I do too, because I understand the jokes. The satellite also brings us channels from all over the world, including America, Italy, Great Britain, France, Germany, Turkey, Saudi Arabia, and Croatia.

Now I am so busy with school, watching TV, and helping Babi that I hardly remember that last time I looked out Fjolla's window and saw the metal machines move.

After the daily Albanian TV shows end, Mami and Babi watch the Croatian channel. I watch it with them. This channel shows people with their heads, arms, and legs cut off. I see dark faces with eyes missing from their sockets. Among these people are boys and girls like me aligned in rows on the floor of a house. I quickly turn away from the television. Still, those images keep replaying in my head. Is that a horror movie Mami and Babi are watching? I decide it's not, because all they watch is news, so those images must be real. Those mutilated bodies couldn't have been faked. Once an arm or leg is severed from its socket, it can never be reattached. When I face Mami and Babi, they look just as terrified and disgusted as I am.

"What is that, Mami?" I ask.

"It's the war in Bosnia, son," she answers.

I turn my head to watch TV again. I see metal machines. They have Serbian flags hoisted on them like the ones on the highway near our apartment. They are driving on dirt roads and directing their long pipes toward houses and shelling them. The roofs catch fire. The houses ignite. If the houses don't burn to the ground, they are left with big holes in their white facades. There must be people in there. The machines' gunners are chanting, smoking cigarettes, and waving their Serbian flags. These are the same metal machines as the ones I watch on our highways.

I have been a fool for not knowing what the giant metal machines were for. During all the time I watched them go to their base, I never realized that the purpose of the rotating gun was to kill people and destroy houses. I am in disbelief. How can the men on the machines be capable of killing people and burning houses? Until now, I felt they were so fascinating. I should have known that nothing good could come out of the dark, loud machines that damaged our highway with their chains as they moved to the base. The ominous signs were there all along, but I missed them all.

The men atop the machines are not drivers but Serbian killers. I am stunned by this harsh reality. I was stupid enough to want to drive the machines when I grew up. Now I never want to see one again.

Had they anticipated those images, Mami and Babi might not have watched them, much less allowed me to see them. Like me, they sit on the sofa, fascinated and alarmed by what they see. Those massacred Bosnian children my age were real. They once played just like me, but they will never play again.

My new understanding of the machines—they are called tanks, Babi tells me—makes me fear them being so close to our apartment. I am afraid they are going to blast our building and kill us. The base where they are stationed is less than half a mile away from where we live. They could probably shoot their grenades through their long pipes from the base to our apartment. The men atop the tanks could fire their rotating guns and wipe us out.

I am inside the room as the massacred Bosnian children are lined up. I try to escape and I succeed. I awaken, gasping for air. My heart is pounding. I realize that we are all alive in our living room; I tell myself we are all right. Babi is snoring on the next sofa, and Shpetim is breathing quietly while asleep beside me. I lie in the dark and keep my eyes open. I fear I might fall asleep again and see the bodies of Bosnians. I hide my face under the blanket and curl up like a snail, with my hands between my legs. I pass the night with little sleep. I wonder why the Bosnian parents didn't save their children, but then I realize that the Serbian soldiers probably killed the parents too.

CHAPTER 12

THE SERBIAN GOVERNMENT

More than a year has passed. I am ten, and I still think about the tanks and the murdered Bosnian children, especially during the night.

Babi has expanded his business. He now goes to Bulgaria, buys merchandise, brings it back to Kosovo, and sells it for a profit. Tonight Babi is in Bulgaria, and I feel insecure without him. What if the Serbians decide to crank their tanks and shell our apartment? What will we do without Babi? What if my nightmare of being killed like those Bosnian children comes true? I cannot stop thinking about their corpses. I am really frightened of becoming a victim of my former idols, the tank gunners. Lying next to Shpetim, I cover my whole body with a blanket and try to make myself invisible.

The next evening Babi arrives home with a huge duffel bag full of stuff in one hand and a suitcase in the other. I wonder what kind of products he will have to resell. Did he bring the shoes I asked him to buy for me? Fjolla, Shpetim, and I run and hug him. We open the bag and the suitcase to see if Babi has brought us gifts.

"Did you buy my shoes, Babi?" I ask.

"Sorry, Lili. I invested all my money in the merchandise. I will buy them next time, after we sell this stuff," he says.

I'm not upset because I know Babi does not have much money. After selling these goods we are going to double our income. Then

Babi will buy me new shoes. Inside the bags we see the items that Babi bought. There are hygiene products like toothpaste, toothbrushes, shaving cream, and sponges. There are car tools and parts including wrenches, fog lights, tire chains, and car brakes. There are toys; I especially like the remote control cars. The cosmetic lotions and perfumes smell good. We unpack Turkish coffee, chewing gum, blank VHS tapes, decks of cards, water pumps, and pens. I am eager for Tuesday to come so we can sell these things and make more money. Finally, I see a chocolate. Fjolla, Shpetim, and I rush to grab it.

On Tuesday and on Sunday at the *tregu i kerreve* (auto market), where goods other than cars are sold, we sell a lot of merchandise. We lay a thin plastic cloth on top of our car's hood and windshield and then place the goods on top of it. As many as fifteen customers gather around to browse or buy. On both sides of the street, vendors like us park their cars next to each other. Those without cars display their wares on beach cots and crates, as is done on Tuesdays in *tregu i grave*. The vendors sell anything you can think of. There is even an old man who sells puppies. Shpetim's and my job is to tell the customers the prices of the goods and watch for greedy hands that might try to snatch something without paying for it.

Soon after we sell most of our goods, Babi goes to Bulgaria again with his empty duffel bag and suitcase.

"Babi, don't forget to buy my shoes," I tell him. I am not particular about color, brand, or even size. I just want some new shoes. I'm tired of walking in old, leaky shoes. It's fall, and there are lots of rainy days.

"I won't forget, son. I will buy them."

"You promise?"

"I promise."

"Thank you." We kiss him good-bye and he leaves. He will park his car near the Grand Hotel in Pristina and then take the bus to Bulgaria.

While Babi is away, I get a terrible toothache. My suffering is so intense I believe there is no greater pain in the world. This tooth has hurt before, but not like today.

My mother hears my fussing. She tells me to open my mouth and point to the tooth that is hurting. After she takes a look, she announces that we are going to the dentist.

Mami and I walk to the nearby clinic. She holds my hand and I still complain about the pain. We come to a white building I recognize from the times when I was younger and sick; I came here and got sharp needles in my behind. As we walk through the clinic doors, the odor of medicine reminds me further of how much those shots hurt. Right now, I fear the dentist more than the Serbian policemen.

We climb the stairs to the second floor and enter the dental office. Mami gives my health card to the receptionist, who tells us to sit in the hallway to wait our turn. Other people are waiting to see the dentist too. Some of them speak Serbian and some Albanian.

There are two dentists' rooms in this clinic. An older dentist wearing a white coat exits one of the rooms and speaks to the Serbian patients. I don't understand them. The few Serbian words that I know are the ones spoken by Serbian policemen to Albanians, which include *jebem ti majku* (fuck your mother), *bezi odavde* (get out of here), and *Šiptar* (an offensive word for Kosovar).

The older dentist ushers the next Serbian patient inside.

"Mami, do all the dentists speak Serbian?"

"Yes, *pllumb*, those are the only ones here now. The ones who speak Albanian have been fired."

From a different room comes a young man in a white coat who doesn't look like a dentist. He is scrawny, has black hair, and resembles my cousin Bekim, Uncle Azem's son, who is a guitarist. He calls out a Kosovar name and then shouts a few words in Serbian. A young Kosovar fellow gets up and goes into that dentist's room.

Both Serbian dentists continue to call other patients. The older man always calls the names of the patients who speak Serbian, and the young one calls the ones who speak Albanian. A boy slightly older than me runs from the young dentist's office crying and screaming. A teenager leaves the older dentist's office looking calm and relaxed.

The young dentist finally calls my name. Mami gets up and takes my hand, and we enter his office.

"Mami, is he the dentist?"

"He is an intern." I don't know what that means, but I hope he knows what he is doing.

I sit on the dentist's chair and the intern asks me something. Mami translates. I point to the tooth that hurts. The pain is so bad I don't think it could be worse if it were pulled. The intern's assistant, a young woman, hands him a pair of shiny white metal pliers. *Oh Zoti im* (Oh my God!). I never realized they were going to take out my tooth with a pair of pliers. I thought they were going to somehow pull it with their hands instead.

The intern instructs his assistant to hold my head still while I open my mouth. I tell myself to be strong, that it will be worth having relief from the pain. The dentist sticks the shiny metal pliers into my mouth. I glance at Mami. She watches nervously. Suddenly I decide that this is not what I want, but it is too late now. The pliers grab hold of my tooth. The assistant holds my forehead with one hand and my chin with the other. The intern pulls my tooth several times, but it doesn't budge, even though he is pulling it with both hands and with all his strength. I hear a cracking sound in my mouth. Did the tooth break? He pulls harder. His face turns red. I am convinced that this guy doesn't know what he is doing. I want to leap from this chair and bang the wall with my head.

I cry and scream. The intern releases his grip on the pliers. The pain is now even more extreme—the maximum pain that I can tolerate—and the tooth remains in my mouth.

Mami screams at the intern in Serbian, but before she can finish what she is saying, the redheaded assistant grips and opens my jaw, and suddenly the pliers are back in my mouth. I squirm because the pain is so great. Mami tries to calm me, but I resist even more. I thrash wildly and my heels stomp the footrest of the chair. The scrawny Serbian intern is pulling as hard as he can with both his hands again. The young woman tells me something in Serbian. Mami says, "Son, don't move." I want to flee, but I feel helpless. I want to die. I can't breathe. The intern finally tugs again, and this time I see my big tooth has been removed. I spit a large amount of blood into the sink.

My pain is indescribable. I feel dizzy, and I nearly faint. We shouldn't have come here. The pain would have eventually gone away, as it did before. I am never going to come to this place again.

At home I spit out almost one liter of blood. I can't sit for longer than five seconds. The pain makes me pace throughout the apartment, covering my mouth with my hand. I question the purpose of life. Why is there so much pain? Are we born only to suffer? Will my pain disappear the way the tooth did?

That intern was sadistic for not numbing my mouth before the extraction. It makes me sick to my stomach that the Serbian government has fired all Albanian dentists and doctors. I wish I could destroy all Serbian government buildings with a tank.

When Fjolla's baby teeth loosen, Mami refuses to take her to the dentist. Instead, Babi ties a string around each one and pulls it out. When our big teeth hurt and Babi can't yank them out with string, Mami agrees that we shouldn't go back to the clinic. Instead, we cope with the pain. Mami tries to comfort us as best she can. She tells us to put cold water in our mouths and gives us aspirin. Babi tells us to drink some of his vodka to numb our teeth, but Mami doesn't let him give us any.

My teeth look bad too. The front ones look OK, but the back teeth are black and hollow. At least my classmates don't make fun of me, because their teeth are just as bad—or worse.

CHAPTER 13

THE SHOES

The next morning, Sunday, the bleeding stops and my pain eases. When I think of the shoes that Babi has promised me, I cheer up—so I think about them constantly. I picture a pair of counterfeit black Adidas similar to my classmate Pruthi's original Adidas shoes. I imagine myself walking in them on my way to school and all the kids staring at my shoes with envy and admiration. My classmates will love them. They'll want to be me. They'll want to be in my shoes. My feet will be warm and dry instead of cold and wet as they were for over a year from wearing Shpetim's raggedy, smelly shoes.

I wait for Babi until late at night. The bus from Bulgaria usually arrives in Pristina at one thirty in the morning. I feel tired, but I'm too excited to sleep. How will my shoes look? I imagine the smell of the new fabric. Just thinking about them gives me a thrill.

Shpetim and Fjolla try to stay awake to see what Babi brings. Fjolla falls asleep, but Shpetim is still waiting with me.

"Go to sleep," Mami tells us. "When Babi comes back, I'll wake you up."

"You will never wake me up, Mami. I know you won't," I tell her. "You've said this in the past and you never woke me up."

Mami and Babi bought a new sofa and placed it in the kitchen behind the dining room table for them to sleep on. The good thing is that now Shpetim sleeps on a sofa formerly used by Mami and Babi instead of sharing one with me. The bad thing is that I rarely hear

Babi when he comes back from Bulgaria, because he goes straight to the kitchen.

"This time I will," Mami says.

I let exhaustion overtake me. "All right, I am going to sleep, but *të lutna, të lutna,* Mami, make sure that you wake me up as soon as Babi gets here."

I go to sleep, but the excitement wakes me up after fifteen minutes. I go to the kitchen to see if he has arrived. I see only Mami there.

"He hasn't come back yet," she says. "Go back to sleep, and really sleep this time. I promise I will wake you up." Babi is already supposed to be home. It is almost 2:30 a.m. I worry that something bad has happened to him.

Another five minutes pass. Babi comes through the door without his duffel bag and suitcase. He looks livid; he has that grim, red face. I look at his hands again, and they are empty. Babi isn't even holding my new shoes. He also looks as tired and weak as a beaten dog. Where are Babi's bags? Maybe he is weary from the long trip and has left them downstairs for us to fetch.

"What's wrong?" asks Mami. Babi does not say a word; he just throws his shoes to the side and goes to the kitchen.

Mami demands that he tell us what happened. "What is wrong?"

"They took them from me," he says.

"Who took them from you?" asks Mami.

"The Serbian police," he says. "I did everything I was supposed to do. I even paid a large customs fee. Yet when I arrived at the Grand Hotel, a police officer stopped me and took them away. He even slapped me."

"What about my shoes?" I ask. I hope that they weren't taken somehow.

"I bought your shoes, but the policeman took the bag they were in."

Why did he take my shoes? I looked forward to receiving them all weekend. They were so important to me, but then all of a sudden a Serbian policeman decided that those should not belong to me. I want to kill him for that. I was so close to finally having a new pair of Adidas or Nikes. If the bus had arrived in Pristina only a few minutes earlier, the *t'zi* wouldn't have seen Babi.

This incident is a major loss, and Babi is never going back to Bulgaria to buy me shoes. The *t'zi* have stolen everything that Babi hoped to sell for profit. Instead of being in a position to make money, Babi is broke. Just like that.

In four hours it will be time to go to school. I go to the bathroom and shut the door so no one will hear me crying.

When the dawn finally comes, Mami sees my face and says "*Pllumb*, I assure you that when Babi returns to Bulgaria, he is going to buy you another pair of shoes."

"Yeah, right, Mami. How do you know that he's going back to Bulgaria?"

"I am sure he is, *pllumb*."

"He is never going back. He has spent almost all his money. How is he going to go back to Bulgaria?" I know Babi's finances better than Mami does; I used to work with him. Babi had invested almost all his money on that last trip. Now that money is gone, thanks to a tyrannical policeman.

When Mami opens the door for me to leave for school, I carry my old shoes in my hands. I look at them and feel ashamed. I cannot believe what has happened.

On the walk to school, I often look down at my old shoes and wonder if I am going to be wearing them for the rest of my life. By the time I reach school, my socks are wet and my feet cold, and when I return home, my socks are soaked and my feet frozen.

CHAPTER 14

ROCKS

For several months we haven't bought much food. Babi realizes that something needs to be done so we can have milk, eggs and plenty of flour.

We are in the living room waiting for the news program to start. Mami, Shpetim, and I urge Babi to go back to Bulgaria and try his luck again. Though I am only eleven years old now, I have already learned that business is about taking chances.

"Come on, Babi, you have to go back to Bulgaria," I tell him. "I am sure the Serbian policemen are not going to take your goods again."

"Take a chance, Hysen," Mami tells him. "You know that soon we are going to run out of what little money we have anyway; might as well risk it."

Babi does not say much in response, but when Friday comes, he is ready to leave with two new totes. He looks determined but nervous. Shpetim, Fjolla, and I kiss him good-bye.

"Have a good trip, Babi," we tell him. I don't mention the shoes. Food is more important. Babi takes a big breath and walks out the door. I know that he dreads the thought of Serbian policemen. Perhaps he could subdue them if they didn't have their batons and guns. I like to picture Babi on the winning side, despite his being unarmed. Those cops had better not mess with him, because he might beat them up. He has strong arms and can throw harder punches than they can. They are unaware of the fierce lion hidden inside my dad. If they harass him, they will regret it.

It is Sunday. Although I am excited that Babi will be back tonight, I'm worried that he will come home empty-handed again. I am determined to defy sleep tonight. I want to be the first person to open the door for him when he gets here with his hands full. I imagine that Babi has bought a lot of merchandise that will sell well this Tuesday and Sunday—things like Turkish coffee and toothpaste.

I look at the clock. It's 1:45 a.m. I think I hear someone climbing the stairs of our apartment building right now. I hope it is Babi and wait for him to knock on our door.

Silence.

What if the *t'zi* took his bags again? We might starve to death or be forced to roam the streets and beg for money. I might have to quit school, borrow a wheelbarrow from Uncle Skender's house in the village, and use it at *tregu i pemëve dhe perimëve* to haul customers' purchases to their cars.

Sitting on the sofa in the living room, I listen for footsteps in the foyer of our building. The door creaks a little, but there is no way that this could be Babi. He would have made a louder sound when his bags hit against the lobby door, but I rush to check anyway.

I see nothing but the dark hallway. I step forward and look down at the main entrance. Surprisingly, I see Babi make his way through them with two heavy bags of merchandise.

Yes, he made it! It's such a relief to see him. I won't have to quit school to beg on the streets.

Behind Babi is an older friend of mine and Shpetim's. He is helping Babi carry items from his car. His name is Faton, and he lives in the apartment building next to ours. Neither of his parents has a job. He admires Babi as a businessman who is able to make money, and I suspect he wishes his own father could do the same.

Once they put the bags on the kitchen floor, Babi tells Faton, "I know that your father is unemployed. So I'll give you a job. Come and help us on Tuesday, and I will pay you."

"OK," says Faton gratefully. He leaves. I go to Babi and kiss him. I am proud of my father. I know other kids would love to have a dad like mine, because he is the best. Now we are going to earn money again. There will be plenty of food, and then I will have new shoes.

On Tuesday, Faton helps us, and Babi pays him ten deutsch-marks. "Thank you, Mr. Hysen, thank you," he says. "I will never forget." He looks at the money in his hand, jumps to his feet, runs out the door, and shouts, "I will never forget. I am going to show this to my parents. I will never forget, Mr. Hysen."

We sell merchandise successfully on Sunday too, and Babi goes to Bulgaria again. When he comes back, he opens a big striped bag and says, "I've got something for you."

He reaches into the bag and pulls out a pair of black counterfeit LA Lakers. They are very good-looking—almost too good-looking to wear. They are ankle-high and ideal for protection against wet and cold weather.

"Let me lace the shoes for you," says Babi. No way. I can't wait for that. I put them on without the laces. I picture myself walking around the classroom with my classmates eyeing my new shoes. They are going to love them, and they are going to wish they had a dad like mine who would buy them a pair. No more smelly old shoes for me. I let Babi thread the shoelaces. I want to sleep in them tonight. I will take good care of them.

At school a lot of my classmates compliment me on my shoes, and the others just stare at them enviously, just as I had imagined. You can barely tell that the shoes are counterfeit. Only the letters L and A are a little misaligned. When Labinot sees them, he tells some other classmates that the reason I have nice shoes is that I'm rich. Some classmates stare at me in awe. It's a good feeling when other people think you're rich. Of course, they don't know that I worked hard at the markets twice a week for more than two years to earn these.

Initially, I take good care of my shoes: I avoid muddy places and jump over puddles. After about two months, though, they look as if they have been worn for a year.

Today, with my friend Artan, I play *futboll* in my new shoes on a muddy field near our apartment. As Artan and I pass the ball to one another, a rock about the size of a small potato lands between us. Then another one lands. We look all around but don't see anyone. When two more rocks come flying toward us, we start running in the direction from which they are coming, which is the garden of an apartment building.

Two Serbian kids our age walk steadily toward us, full of menace. One of them has a shaved head and small eyes, and the other one has curly hair, blue eyes, and a scar on his face. They stride toward us angrily, as if we were the ones who threw the rocks at them. I guess they are surprised that we inferior little *Šiptar* will challenge them. They are getting closer to us, walking with the same deliberate pace, ready for combat. Surely our anger will enable us to slam them down to the ground and punch them hard. We can probably beat the devil out of them. I am the son of a boxer, and I know how to wrestle.

But then I imagine the two Serbian boys directing the *t'zi* to our front doors, after which they take Babi to the police station and beat him for my troublemaking. I don't want my dad to be assaulted by Serbian officers; I know this happens to many Kosovar parents. From the window in Fjolla's room, I have seen the *t'zi* beat fathers and young men with billy clubs and then load them into blue and white vans to take them to the police station for more beating. There is a Serbian gang—the skinheads—who could corner me somewhere on my way to school and leave me for dead. I'd better calm down. But do these thugs expect for us to say, "*Izvini* (sorry), we will not be in the same place where your rocks land next time?"

"Fuck your mother, *Šiptari*," says the one with the shaved head.

We don't hesitate to respond to their insults. "Fuck your mother, *majmuni* (monkeys)," I shout.

"Fuck your mother, *majmuni*," repeats Artan.

"Fuck *Šiptari*," says the one with the scarred face.

"Fuck Slobodan Milosevic," I say.

"Fuck Ibrahim Rugova."

They just cursed our president. Their president, Milosevic—not ours—is the villain.

"Fuck Slobodan Milosevic," says Artan. We run away from them. They chase us, but we arrive at our apartments in time.

CHAPTER 15

THE COAT

W e are lucky. The next two times Babi returns from Bulgaria, the *t'zi* don't seize his goods, and we sell the items without a problem.

My rich classmate, Pruthi, asks me if I am interested in joining a karate club. I ask Babi whether or not he can pay the fee, and he says yes, since the business is going well. I practice with Pruthi and graduate from white belt to yellow and then to red. I like karate and do it well, but I'd much rather play *futboll*—but only if Kosovars had access to our nice stadium.

It is Sunday—another business day at the market. The November air is chilly, and I am wearing a light jacket. What I hate most about the business is the cold weather. At the *tregu i kerreve*, Babi parks our car beside that of another businessman who has already started to display his goods on top of his car's hood and windshield. There are several cars parked on both sides of the straight road, and more are arriving. A Serbian police car patrols the street. I take my hands out of my corduroy pants pockets and begin to help Shpetim and Babi. We start arranging our hygiene products, kids' toys, car tools, food items, and car parts.

Customers will be here soon, so I memorize the prices. As the morning progresses, customers come to our car. Some of them haggle with Babi.

Not far from us is the old man who sells puppies. He has placed them in an open banana box. Someone has bought one and carries it inside his brown leather coat. You can still see the puppy's cute face peeking out. Even with its thick fur, it seems as cold as I am.

Near the end of our business day, Babi is counting the money. So far, he says, we have done well. His announcement almost warms me up. I rub the palms of my hands together and jump up and down. Maybe I will soon have a new warm coat.

My enthusiasm doesn't last long, because the blue and white car stops right in front of ours. The two *t'zi* get out and start talking to Babi in Serbian. When I see their weapons, I am terrified. Babi's voice soon changes from a calm tone to a high pitch.

The police start screaming words that sound familiar: "Fuck you, *Šiptar*." Babi cautiously steps back. I want to protect him, but they have guns and billy clubs.

One *t'zi* smacks Babi's face hard and loud. The slap leaves a red mark on his cheek. I want to do something. Will the *t'zi* smack me if I try to help Babi? They probably will. I feel horrible. Watching your father being beaten is the worst feeling in the world. This is the second time he has been assaulted. I wish Babi would retaliate and pull some boxing moves, leaving them lying on the ground like Muhammad Ali's opponents. Then I could stomp their faces.

Babi doesn't defend himself. The *t'zi* start toward their car. Babi tells Shpetim and me to hide some of the expensive merchandise in a ditch behind us because the *t'zi* have ordered him to transfer all of our stuff to their car.

"Hide the water pump, quickly," Babi says. While the police have their backs to us, I grab the pump and run to the ditch behind our car. Shpetim starts to cry.

Babi, Shpetim, and I reluctantly transfer our goods to the *t'zi's* car trunk. With tears in his eyes, Shpetim looks like the sad, cold puppy that was taken away from the banana box. I probably look the same. The business that we worked so hard to establish means nothing now. No merchandise, no income. Babi's money from today's sales won't last long. We'll be left penniless, with nothing to sell.

We close the trunk with what we hid in it. The *t'zi* get in their car and drive away. Just when we were able to make good money and could afford eggs and milk, we are back to a diet of bread and sugar.

Babi is resigned to never resuming his business. There is no point anymore, he says. I agree with him. Even if three trips to Bulgaria go well, the fourth one won't, and then we will be right back to square one.

I quit the karate class because Babi can't pay my monthly fee, and there is a rumor that the arena where we practice is going to be filled with Bosnian refugees. I would rather let the poor Bosnians whose families were killed by Serbian soldiers live in that arena. They have nowhere else to live.

The only thing that gets us through the winter months with enough flour and sugar is Mami's income. For over four years, Mami wasn't paid so much as a dollar to work at the schoolhouse. Finally, she has started earning sixty deutschmarks a month. Mami gets the money from Kosovar immigrants living abroad who donate three percent of their wages to teachers in Kosovo. Some of Mami's sixty deutschmarks go toward her bus and taxi fares. Varicose veins have begun to form on Mami's legs; they bulge underneath her skin in a weird and horrible way. Her body can no longer endure the long walks to school plus the household chores.

CHAPTER 16

A PLACE FOR THEM TO ENJOY AND US TO ENVY

It is a Saturday in December, and Bekim, Uncle Azem's older son, has invited us to Brezovica, a ski resort in the Sharri Mountains. Uncle Fadil and Bekim have bought a bus and have opened a route that connects Vushtrri, the city where Mami grew up, to Pristina. Uncle Fadil drives the bus, and Bekim collects the fares from the passengers.

Uncle Fadil and Bekim have gotten a request from some high school seniors to take them to Brezovica for their graduation. Bekim said he has a few extra seats for us younger cousins from Mami's side of the family.

It is early morning. Shpetim and I wait for the bus on the main highway. Since I don't have a warm coat or skiing apparel, I am wearing a couple of sweaters underneath my jacket and two pairs of pajamas underneath my trousers.

When the bus comes, Uncle Fadil stops it right in front of us and we climb aboard.

"Hello, Uncle Fadil. Hello, Bekim."

Both of them have thick black eyebrows. Bekim takes a seat right beside Uncle Fadil's. When off duty, Bekim still loves to play his guitar, and Uncle Fadil loves to attend to his pigeons. He has fifty pigeons and a special little house for them in his yard. The pigeons are beautiful and colorful: white, black, brown, gray, purple, and

73

some with combinations of colors. Uncle's pigeons are distinguished from wild pigeons by their unusual coloring and short beaks. They gather around your feet and let you touch them. Whenever Uncle lets his birds loose, they always return to him, eager for the corn and grain that he feeds them.

With a touch of a button, Uncle Fadil closes the doors. "Hello, nephews," he says.

"Hello, nephews," says Bekim. Biologically, we are his cousins, but since he is older than we are, he likes to call us his nephews.

In the two front seats I see my wonderful cousins Fisnik and Valdet, who, like Shpetim and me, are in the fourth and fifth grades. They are also brothers and vendors like us. They sell fresh cold drinks in the market in Vushtrri on weekends and occasionally after school. They load a wheelbarrow full of ice and drinks. Fisnik, the younger one, has blue eyes and a skinny body; he pushes the wheelbarrow, and Valdet collects the money.

Another cousin of ours sits in front. His name is Besnik, and he is Uncle Fadil's only son. Even though Besnik is almost our age, he is bigger than us, his classmates, and the boys in his neighborhood. He has brown eyes, blond hair, and enough strength to overpower the four of us simultaneously—but he doesn't. He loves us, and we love him the way cousins do. I am excited to see them, and I know that the trip to Brezovica is going to be fun.

Besnik, Fisnik, and Valdet rise from their seats, shake our hands, and give us hugs. They shout, "*Ku jeni* (What's up?)," "*Qka po bëni* (What are you up to?)," and "*Qysh jeni* (How are you all doing?)." Other than my cousins, the bus is filled with high school students. Our cousins make room for Shpetim and me to sit with them, and we are on our way.

Uncle Fadil drives slowly and cautiously like Babi does because the *t'zi* stop bus drivers too. He also drives the long bus past hills and mountains. Near the Sharri Mountains the roads are wet and slippery, but he is a skillful driver, and we arrive safely at a point from which we can walk to the ski resort.

Once we get out and start walking, we are awed by the beautiful sights. The slopes and hills of Brezovica are completely covered in white. Ski lifts are transporting skiers up and down mountains. I see big bulldozers that remind me of tanks. We have never seen such things.

But when skiers and snowboarders begin to glide all around us, our amazement turns into envy. We know they are all Serbians. There isn't a single Kosovar on the course. I see Serbian kids smaller than me wearing skis longer than their bodies. Their parents are wealthy and able to rent skis, snowboards, and rooms in the nice wooden multi-story hotels here. We can only watch them. We don't even inquire about the price of renting skis; we know that we can't afford them. Instead, we imagine ourselves gliding down the slopes.

"How nice it would have been if we had a pair of skis," says Besnik.

"We would be coming down that slope fast," I say.

"It seems that these monkeys are having a lot of fun," continues Besnik.

Valdet points to a group of Serbian kids. "You know, if these little Serbian boys can ski, we could ski too."

"Yeah, it's not that hard," says Fisnik.

"Hey, you know what?" Besnik shouts. He is bigger than any of the Serbian kids skiing.

"What?" we ask.

"How about we bump into one of these Serbian kids and make him tumble down the hill?"

We laugh and think it is a great idea, but we know that Besnik is joking. No Kosovar would dare do such a thing to a Serbian kid, even if he pretended it was accidental. Instead, we curse at the skiers in Albanian every time one of them comes near us. If only one of them would trip, hit a pole, or fall off the ski lift. Nothing of the sort happens, and we get even angrier.

We cannot help feeling bad that we are unfortunate, inferior, and poor. At home we are surrounded by Kosovar kids like us, but here we stand out like patches of grass in the snow.

"What is wrong, nephews?" asks Bekim.

"Nothing," says Shpetim.

"Oh, we're fine. This is fun," another one of us lies.

"What do you mean, 'This is fun'? Why are you lying to me? You are just standing there and watching. What is wrong, nephews?"

"We're fine, really," says Shpetim. We haven't the heart to tell him how upset we are. After all, he was nice enough to bring us to this beautiful place.

Bekim doesn't say anything else. Instead, he watches us and the Serbian skiers. When he hears Besnik curse at a Serbian kid who tips on one of his skis and wobbles a little but doesn't fall, and then hears us ridicule a fat Serbian kid on skis, he understands.

Since Bekim is several years older than us, he does not envy the Serbian kids as we do. Or, I guess, since he is older and wiser, he accepts things more readily than we do. Yet he doesn't become philosophical and say, "My dear nephews, this is how things are, whether you like it or not. You must learn to accept it." Instead, he buys each of us a cold, refreshing can of Coke.

We are happy for a moment. We pop our drinks open and raise our cans in the air, following Bekim's lead. As we toast one another, Bekim says, "Here's to the freedom and independence of Kosovo, nephews."

"To the freedom of Kosovo," we all repeat. We take long sips of our drinks. A long silence follows, during which we just look at one another. My body shakes and I begin to sob. How do we know what freedom is? We just stand in silence and think about the freedom we do not have and the things we cannot do.

CHAPTER 17

SUMMER

It's my favorite season, and we are in my favorite place—the village. I feel much better now. "Let's build a basketball goal," Shpetim suggests. Musa and I like the idea. We get a plank from Uncle Fatmir's unfinished house, a board lying on top of the well at our house, and a large, bent piece of scrap metal. We assemble these materials, dig a big hole in Uncle Fatmir's front yard, and put our basketball goal in place. Now we can play whenever we want. No Serbian boys live in our village, so we are free from bullies. Our Kosovar friends play with us, and we play until it gets dark and we can't see the ball.

On days when we don't play basketball, we play *futboll* on mountainous pastures. We find the flattest one, where shepherd friends have their cows and sheep grazing. The goals are marked with upright sticks. The shepherds join us, and we start the game. This field is dry and grassy, unlike the muddy and rocky yard at our apartment. Most importantly, my village opponents don't throw rocks and try to beat me up.

Shpetim and I play daily for two months but then, on a beautiful, sunny day, Mami hands each of us a book and says, "Go in your rooms and read the first forty pages. I want a summary of those pages after you read them."

"Oh, come on, Mami, don't do this to us in the middle of summer," I complain.

"Come on, Mami," says Shpetim.

"If you two want to get out of this house, you've got to give me the summaries of those forty pages."

Reluctantly I climb the stairs to my bedroom, and Shpetim goes to Mami and Babi's bedroom. I lie on the sofa and think of what is occurring everywhere else but in the book. I don't want to read during our summers in the village. We want to have fun while we are here. Why is Mami punishing us?

Finally, I open the book and look to see if there are any pictures in it. There are none. How boring. But to play outside I must study and give Mami a summary. Once I start to read, my mind wanders from the Serbian bullies to the *t'zi*, to basketball and then to kissing and making love to an older girl. As I recall some girls I saw on a TV channel Musa, Shpetim, and I discovered, I pull my pants down and start playing with my penis.

The door opens. Mami sticks her head inside the room as she says, "How are you doing with your readi—" I roll my shorts back on and grab my book quickly. She pretends she doesn't see me and tells me I'd better start getting interested in this book if I want to go outside today. She leaves.

Embarrassed, I read forty pages and summarize them to Mami, and she lets me go out. Shpetim is freed too, and we go to Musa's house. When we hear that the village boys have arranged a date to collect blackberries, we each grab a white bucket and head toward the mountain. The air is so fresh that I never want to breathe the filthy, dusty air in the city again. We fill our stomachs and buckets and go back to play basketball.

After the game, we go home and have a nice meal, starting with a mouth-watering salad prepared with our garden's tomatoes and cucumbers and topped with Aunt Hanumsha's homemade cheese. We have fresh eggs thanks to Grandmother's chickens, and hearty steaks thanks to Uncle Ismet's cattle. Our stomachs full, we run to go fishing in the Llapi River. I put a cherry on my hook and catch a big fish. Musa and Shpetim don't believe it.

"You didn't," says Shpetim.

"Who caught it?" says Musa.

"I did," I say. "You can ask Kuci. He was with me."

Our friend Kuci confirms my feat. "He caught it. I had to help him pull it to the shore because it was so big."

"Good job, Ilir," says Musa. They are proud of me. I am proud of myself. We show my fish to everyone.

I want summer to never end, but we have to return to Pristina.

On the ride back to the city, I dread the thought of my tiny, dusty classroom. I dread being chased from the basketball court. I dread playing on the concrete and muddy *futboll* fields. I dread living where I am unwanted. I dread Serbian policemen. I fear becoming seriously ill. If I were a shepherd, I wouldn't have to live in the city. I would have plenty of milk and would never eat bread and sugar again. There would be plenty of meat, eggs, cheese, tomatoes, and cucumbers.

Babi does not take the usual route, but we still get pulled over. According to the *t'zi*, Babi was speeding and driving recklessly.

CHAPTER 18
FUTBOLL STADIUM

During the fall in Pristina, the only thing that helps me overcome the feeling of hopelessness is watching *futboll* on TV. Usually after nine o'clock at night, Babi finishes watching the news. Then I can enjoy watching my favorite player, the Brazilian Romario, and my favorite teams, Inter Milan and Borussia Dortmund. When national teams play one another to qualify for the World and Euro Cup, I never miss a game. Because it is not independent from Serbia, Kosovo can't participate; Kosovo is represented by the Former Republic of Yugoslavia (FRY) team, even though Kosovars object. I am not a fan of FRY, because all the players are Serbians or Montenegrins.

Whenever I see German, Italian, or French kids wearing replicas of their national teams' jerseys, I wish I had a Kosovo team to support. I envision our team's jersey as red and black—the colors of the Albanian flag—and picture wearing it all the time.

Kosovars are very good at *futboll*. My cousin Besim, for example—Uncle Azem's middle child—is one of the top scorers in the Kosovar premier *futboll* league and plays for one of the best professional teams, 2 Korriku. Besim could play for FRY in a beautiful big stadium, but instead he and his teammates play in a small, dilapidated stadium.

Since I think so much about *futboll* and Besim, I decide to attend a game. I walk to the "*Šiptar*" stadium. It is located on the city's highest point, so I have to trudge 150 steps uphill. I finally reach the summit, gasping.

The stadium is situated beside the city's cemetery and a grove of trees. It looks more like a swamp than a stadium. The field is uneven, muddy, and rocky. There are no seats for spectators. People have gathered around the field; I join them and watch the game while standing. The tall men in front of me block my view. I can only peer through the spaces between their bodies. I can't even see my cousin's feet. The tall men are too close to the outer lines and seem as though they are trying to get in and play. The sideline referee often stops the game, waves his flag, and orders them to step back. They cooperate for a minute and then move forward again, cursing at the visiting players and threatening violence if they score.

I stop watching the game. I turn around and see the main stadium down the hill, where the Serbian players are practicing. That field is trimmed, verdant, and leveled perfectly. The facility is modern and similar to the ones Inter Milan and Borussia Dortmund play in. There are over 30,000 seats and big, metal overhangs that shelter them and cast shade on the lush, green field. I close my eyes and imagine sitting comfortably in one of those seats while watching my cousin. He dribbles and kicks the ball superbly. I see his every touch, pass, and shot. I stand and applaud loudly.

I quit daydreaming and refocus my attention on Besim's team. I join some kids watching the game from a hill far from the field. The players look small from here, but at least I can see them. Despite the rude fans and horrible conditions, they are playing wonderfully. Both teams move the ball smoothly, making long passes and great crosses. They kick the ball hard at the goal, and the keepers are making spectacular saves.

It's unfair that we can't show our talent to the world. I will never forgive the Serbians for banishing our players and seizing our stadiums. Nevertheless, I love *futboll*. The game is exciting and beautiful. The Serbians can never take that passion from me. Never.

In school, I share a seat and desk with my classmate, Betim. We have become best friends because both of us love *futboll* and enjoy talking about it.

Betim says to me today, "Hey, Ilir. Have you ever heard of the Albanian *futboll* players Altin Rraklli and Igli Tare?"

"No," I am sorry to say.

"They play for Albania's national team. They also play for professional teams in Germany's league."

"You must be kidding me. How come I didn't know this?"

"You have been missing out, Ilir. They play matches on the German TV sports channel, DSL, every Tuesday, right after we get out of school."

Wow. Albanians from mainland Albania are the same as Kosovars. We speak the same language and share the same culture. I can cheer and be proud of them; they represent us too. As Betim said, I have really been missing out.

On Tuesday I run home from school. Once inside the apartment, I throw my book bag on the floor and turn on DSL. The TV screen is fuzzy and green. A German commentator is announcing the names of players and teams, showing the scores and highlights of each team in Germany's second league of *futboll*. I'm afraid I'm going to miss their highlights. *Oh Zoti im.* I reposition our satellite dish. That makes it worse. I move the dish back to where it was, and I hear the commentator say "Igli Tare" and then some German words. The player who has the ball is Igli Tare. This is so exciting. He either has blond hair or he is albino; I can't tell, but I love him anyway. He sees that the goalkeeper is away from the goal; he has been helping the offense. Igli kicks the ball from midfield. He almost scores. Oh so close. The ball goes only slightly up over the post. Excellent shot.

DSL shows two other teams, and then the sportscaster says, "Altin Rraklli, *Albanischer spieler* (Albanian player in German)." I get excited. Altin is short and has black hair. His legs are muscular and bowed. I watch him even when he doesn't have the ball. Then he receives a pass just near the eighteen-meter mark and he kicks toward the goal. Wide right. Next time, he scores from a pass close to the goal. I jump up and down. Altin Rraklli is proof that Albanians, and thus Kosovars, can play. The commentator is excited too when he calls Altin's name and says, "*Albanischer spieler.*" That's right, Albanian player. They can score.

Every Tuesday after school, I watch the two. They both play well and score a lot of goals. Whenever they don't play well, I worry that the whole world will think that Albanians and Kosovar Albanians aren't competitive.

One day after Betim and I have been talking about them, he says, "Let's join a *futboll* club."

"Good idea. I have been meaning to ask you the same thing. You know my cousin plays for 2 Korriku. He might find us some spots on the team," I say.

"2 Korriku is far away; there are too many steps to climb there. And you have to pay a monthly fee. Let's join Ramiz Sadiku. It's much closer and it's free."

I want to be a professional *futboll* player like Altin Rraklli and Igli Tare. I dream of playing for Inter Milan or Borussia Dortmund. Everyone in Kosovo will follow me. I imagine them saying to one another, "Who said Kosovars can't play *futboll*? Who said Kosovars are not talented? Look at our boy, Ilir Berisha. He will prove you otherwise."

"All right then, let's join Ramiz Sadiku," I tell Betim.

Betim and I are on our way to *futboll* practice, on our way to make everyone proud of us. After walking uphill for thirty minutes, we reach a concrete field where a lot of kids have gathered around a short man who must be the coach. The field is near the University of Pristina, and it looks like a parking lot. At each end of it are two big rocks that mark the boundaries of each goal. The coach takes our names.

After a little while, over fifty kids arrive. The coach slowly divides us into two teams. By the time he is finished, everyone forgets who's on which team. The coach places a flat ball on the field, and we scramble after it like five-year-olds. When one has the ball, he is confused because he doesn't know who to pass it to. We all want to dribble it. While running, one kid trips over the foot of another, and they both fall hard on the concrete. They leave the field with bloodied elbows and scraped knees. I quickly learn not to run after the ball as fast as those kids did.

A ball comes near me, but it is high. The practice ends with my never touching the ball. Betim didn't touch the ball more than two times.

We decide not to come back.

Mami lets me ride with Uncle Fadil and Bekim to Vushtrri, where there is a concrete *futboll* field. My cousins Besnik, Valdet, Fisnik, and I join other Kosovar kids, and we start a game. Within two seconds I get the ball. I pass it successfully to Besnik so it won't get stolen from me. I feel my confidence increase. I am getting better already. Soon the ball comes to me, and I make another good pass. This is great.

When the ball reaches Valdet, he freezes and stops the game.

"Come on," we tell him. "Throw the ball." He hesitates. We wonder why. Then we turn around and see seven Serbian kids watching us, holding empty glass jars and glass beer and Coke bottles. They are looking at us coldly.

"Put the ball in play, Valdet," someone says. "Don't be scared."

Valdet throws the ball, but we are distracted by the Serbians' presence. I attempt to focus on the ball.

"Watch out, watch out," shouts Besnik. "Get off the field." A beer bottle shatters beside me, with a piece of glass hitting my shin. I run off the field. The Serbian kids hurl more jars and bottles toward us. They are laughing at us. Before long, broken glass litters the concrete.

I look at my cousins and the other Kosovar kids. We outnumber them two or threefold. We could pursue them and beat them up, but no one moves. Even my big, powerful cousin Besnik is motionless like the rest of us. The Serbian kids slowly walk away, laughing and giving us the finger. My heart pounds wildly with rage, but I and the other Kosovars remain silent and still.

I return home, devastated. The next day at school, I tell Betim what happened.

"Ilir," he says, "let's restart practicing with Ramiz Sadiku. At least we won't have bottles and jars thrown at us there."

We practice with Ramiz Sadiku. Because fifty kids are playing, I never get a chance to touch the ball again. Afterward, I decide I can earn enough money to pay the fee to practice with 2 Korriku, where there won't be as many kids playing, and we'll get the chance to touch the ball more.

On the way back from Ramiz Sadiku, we stop by the city's main *futboll* stadium. I am stunned by the size of the building. On the outside of it, there are hundreds of vendor stalls, beach cots, and umbrellas. We want to get inside, but all the doors are locked and chained. Betim and I climb over a door and land hard on the ground. I am more stunned by the interior than I was by the exterior. The field is clean. Like other European stadiums, it is striped with two shades of green grass. There are gigantic lights overhead for night games. The rows of seats ascend so high that they appear to touch the clouds.

More importantly, the field is empty. Betim and I could play on it right now if it weren't for the Serbians who might see us and call the *t'zi*. Despite the fact that this stadium was built by Kosovars, Milosevic says we can't use it. When Kosovars controlled it, we allowed the Serbians to play on it. Why won't they let us use it part of the time? It is not fair for ten percent of the population to hog what belongs to us all.

"Let's get out of here before someone comes," says Betim.

We climb back over the door and leave. I don't want to stay in the stadium anymore. It makes me want to kill Milosevic and hate life in general. At home, I envision my imaginary friend, Zllumzllak, and me playing in the main stadium. Zllumzllak beats up all the Serbian kids and assures me that no *t'zi* will arrest us. We practice until it is dark.

CHAPTER 19

CIGARETTES

Babi comes home from work angry again. His Serbian supervisors have transferred him to a location that is farther away, but for no stated reason. He has worked in the same place for over twenty-six years. For a long time he stares, alternating between the wall and the carpet. His face is flushed.

Babi's anger and disappointment last for days. He resumes smoking. While we were babies, he stopped smoking, as he realized how harmful it was for us. I guess he feels that cigarettes will help him cope during this latest crisis.

He takes a medical leave from work and goes to Bulgaria to buy twenty cartons of cigarettes. He decides to sell some of them. However, the competition is fierce; there are many whole-carton vendors. There are nineteen cartons of cigarettes of different brands stacked on the kitchen floor, waiting to be sold. How can we sell them?

I remember that kids at the markets sell cigarettes by the pack. Since most men in Kosovo smoke, those kids make more than the sunflower seed or drink vendors. I decide to go out on the streets and sell Babi's cigarettes pack by pack. I need money to pay the monthly fee for practicing with 2 Korriku and to buy *futboll* shoes. Most importantly, my family needs money in order to afford a healthier diet. Mami and Babi are doing everything they can to get us these things. I need to help them out, just as other kids help their parents.

I figure that the key to selling cigarettes must be finding a group of men gathered at a café or restaurant. There are a number of these close to our apartment in a strip mall. Men congregate there and chain-smoke all day and night.

Leaving my book bag at home, I take three individual packs of Pall Mall. As I walk to the cafés, I think about the dangers of selling cigarettes. One cigarette vendor was found dead in a storage room of an apartment building. He wasn't much older than I am. No one knows who killed him. Nothing should happen to me, though. I will be all right.

When I reach the strip mall, I see other boys selling cigarettes, all competing for customers.

My first sale occurs quickly. Soon two other men buy my remaining packs. Once home, I put the money in a glass jar like the ones that were thrown onto our field that Saturday. I will sell enough packs to fill the jar with money so I can give some to my parents and save the rest for my monthly *futboll* fee.

There are seven packs of Pall Malls remaining. After school the next day, I take them all. I hold four in my hands and place the rest in my pockets. I clip the four packs with my fingers. Whenever I see a group of men in cafés or one walking in my direction, I holler, "*Cigare?*"

I sell only one pack before one of the boys yells, "The *t'zi*, the *t'zi*." We run away. The only time my fellow vendors cooperate with one another is when they see the *t'zi* coming. Whoever sees them first sounds the alarm for other vendors. Then everyone scatters and hides.

We glance at the two policemen. They are on foot. With their heavy uniforms, round helmets, billy clubs, handguns, hand grenades, and AK-47 rifles, they can't run fast enough to catch us. Still, the sight of them frightens me. What if they shoot at us? What if I encounter them some other time? I feel faint. This business is not as easy as I first thought. The hardest part of the job is not competing with other boys, but avoiding the *t'zi*.

After a little while, someone announces that the coast is clear. We return to the streets and cafés. I often look around for the *t'zi*. The rest of my cigarettes sell fast—probably because I look nervous and people feel sorry for me.

Back home, I put the money in the jar. Its bottom is covered with coins and bills. I forget about the *t'zi* and think of 2 Korriku, Altin Rraklli, and Igli Tare instead.

The next time I sell cigarettes, Babi follows me. We soon start walking together. I try to impress him by demonstrating how I accomplish a sale.

We approach a café full of men and I say to him, "Babi. Watch. I am going to sell at least one pack of cigarettes in there. Just stay out here and watch."

He agrees and observes me through the café window. I hold the cigarettes in my hand and walk to every table. I shout, "*Cigare*, Pall Mall." At each table the men refuse to buy; this makes me feel terrible. I was certain I would sell at least a pack and that Babi would be impressed and proud of me. As I walk out, some of the men inside the café notice Babi. They seem to be telling him, "Hey, you lazy bum. Why are you making your son sell cigarettes while you are standing there?"

When I approach Babi, he starts moving away as if he doesn't want others to know I am his son. I understand how he feels, though. People do not understand that Babi did not make me sell cigarettes. He is not lazy. Babi tried to sell cigarettes but didn't succeed. My family and I needed money, so I took his unsold cigarettes and sold them by the pack.

I catch up with him. We walk home with our heads down. We do not say a word to one another, but I know that this is my last day selling cigarettes.

CHAPTER 20

A FISH OUT OF WATER

The only thing that saves us from starving this time is a visit from Uncle Fatmir, who is accompanied by one of his nephews, my twenty-year-old cousin Armend.

Uncle Fatmir brings us Swiss chocolates, a bag of clothes, and 500 deutschmarks. Shpetim, Fjolla, and I open the bag of clothes and find a sweater and a tee shirt for each of us. We hug and kiss Uncle Fatmir many times over. Babi can now let me have some money. The spring *futboll* season has already begun, so it is too late to join 2 Korriku, but at least now we can buy milk and eggs.

My uncle and cousin sit on our living room sofas. Everyone starts talking and laughing. While Mami serves hot tea in small cups, Uncle Fatmir tells the story of when Uncle Skender moved to Switzerland to work without taking Musa and his wife, Aunt Hamide. Uncle Skender cried every morning for his son and wife. It wasn't long before he returned to Kosovo because he could not take living in a foreign country anymore—he decided that he would rather move back to Kosovo and live with his family in poverty than live in Switzerland by himself in prosperity.

While Uncle Fatmir is telling the story, I remember Uncle Skender saying that he missed even the muddy roads, the dust, the old cars—everything. "You must adapt to so many changes," he told me.

The story is sad, but the way Uncle Fatmir tells it is funny. He makes fun of how Uncle Skender would wake up every morning, and cry, "Musa, my son, my son. Hamide, my wife, my wife. I should never have left you." He would bawl like a baby for more than fifteen minutes, and then he would go to work with Musa and Hamide still on his mind. We all laugh; Armend claps his hands and then falls to the floor, laughing hysterically.

Later the same evening, Armend takes Shpetim and me for a ride in his dad's Golf Rabbit. He drives the car fast, and we are amused by it. He doesn't fear the *t'zi* patrolling the streets. Babi never drives this fast. When we get close to an intersection where the *t'zi* sometimes lurk, we tell Armend to slow down. He makes a 180-degree turn, and my body is thrown from one side of the back seat to the other. I like the feeling.

During our summers in the village, Armend's dad, Uncle Ismet, always yells at him for driving his car recklessly. When we get back to the apartment, I stand in the middle of our living room and imitate Uncle Ismet, pointing my finger at Armend and yelling, "Are you out of your mind? Why do you race my car like it's a horse?" Armend claps his hands and falls to the floor again, laughing.

Then I learn that Armend is going to Switzerland with Uncle Fatmir.

I should be happy because now we have some money, but I am sad because Armend is going away. I am grieved that he has to work abroad. Will he be like Uncle Skender and miss his family? Without the presence of people who love him, there is no way that Armend can be happy in a foreign land.

The next summer I fish at the pond and the Llapi River near our village. Musa, Shpetim, and I reminisce about Armend. In the past, Armend took Shpetim, Musa, and me fishing at the river. Armend had a talent for knowing where the biggest fish were, and he would mock their bulging eyes. He pointed at one and said, "Look at that fish; he has glasses on—prescription glasses." Then he would point out a different fish and exclaim, "Uhh, look at that one. He has sunglasses." Armend was funny and made us laugh like crazy.

Musa says, "Hey, look at that fish's glasses," but we don't laugh. He doesn't say it like Armend. He doesn't even point to a particular fish the way Armend always did.

"All right, Ilir and Musa, guess what Armend is doing at this moment?" Shpetim says.

Musa and I think about it for several minutes, but we don't know. I am curious. How would Shpetim know? Perhaps Armend has come back. The thought makes me scream with happiness.

"What? Is he back?" I ask Shpetim.

"No, he is not back. Musa, do you know?"

"No," says Musa.

"He is breathing," Shpetim says.

I hate him for tricking us.

Even though he is breathing the fresh Swiss air, Armend must feel as stifled as a fish out of water.

CHAPTER 21

CHECKPOINT

When it is time to go back to the apartment from our summer house, I ask Babi if Musa can come to the city with us for a couple of days. Musa can make my summer last longer. He can help me cope with the awful reality of Pristina being ruled by tyrants. Babi says we don't have enough room in our apartment. I try to persuade him otherwise, but he quickly gets angry and threatens to slap me.

When we reach our apartment, I feel isolated. The gloom descends as soon as I go through the front door. I hate the smell of our apartment. It's not bad, but it reminds me that summer is over and mocks me, as if to say, "You are back to me now. Your fun times are over." I don't hate the apartment itself, but rather its location in a city where you can't even sell a pack of cigarettes without being chased by policemen.

When we return to the village two weeks later, I cheer up. Shpetim and I realize our parents rarely buy potatoes and never cook us French fries. "Let's explore the fields of the farmers who have planted potatoes," Musa suggests. "We can collect the ones that they missed or didn't want."

Pushing a wheelbarrow, we make our way to the potato fields. Potatoes are scattered everywhere. The farmers have dug them up but have not yet collected the crop.

"Let's take some," Musa says.

I know Mami and Babi will kill us if they find out. Should some-one in the village see us, everyone will hear about it, and we'll have a bad reputation for the rest of our lives. Everyone will gossip about us, likening the potato fields to a bank. They'll say, "Those three Berisha boys robbed a bank. Can you believe that, as young as they are?" Or they'll compare the fields to a house. "Those Berisha boys—they burglarized a house. I don't know whose house it was, but they sure enough did. Those Berisha boys, as young as they are? They ought to be ashamed of themselves—with the kind of parents they have." Whenever someone steals something in the village, they'll say, "It's the Berisha boys. Those boys. Aha."

We risk it. These potatoes will make delicious fries—my favor-ite food. I love potatoes in general. Mami cooks the best potato soup, and she sometimes bakes them. I don't care what the villagers say. We'll just take some. It's not our fault that Milosevic came to power and has forced us to steal in order to survive.

We load the wheelbarrow with muddy potatoes and push it as fast as we can. Sometimes the wheelbarrow gets stuck in the mud, and one of us must lift the front of it. Instead of taking the usual road to our house, we go through our friend Kuci's yard and directly to Uncle Sefer's door. We wash the potatoes and tell our parents the farmers forgot to dig them up.

Mami cooks fries. The aroma and sizzle increase our anticipa-tion; we scarf them down as if we hadn't had anything in weeks.

The following weekend, I go to Vushtrri and play *futboll* with my cousins. With the new season approaching, I must prepare for 2 Korriku. I hop aboard Uncle Fadil's bus and wait for it to leave. As usual, I sit in front and talk to him and Bekim.

"Are you getting a lot of passengers, Uncle?"

"It's kind of slow, nephew, and these *qena* are killing us." Uncle Fadil refers to the Serbian policemen as *qena* or dogs.

We wait a bit longer and twenty passengers get in—a pretty good group. Bekim begins to collect their fares. He has a coin dis-penser clipped to his belt and a wallet. Uncle Fadil starts the journey.

By the time Bekim collects all the passengers' money and sits down beside Uncle, two *t'zi* ahead raise a stop sign and motion for Uncle to park there.

"Oh, these *qena*," sighs Uncle Fadil. Bekim doesn't say anything. His face usually reddens with anger and frustration before he'll speak to the *t'zi*.

"I haven't seen these two before," says Uncle Fadil. He smiles politely while rolling his side window down. Uncle shows his documents to the *t'zi*. He often offers them packs of cigarettes or money to avoid getting fined. Today I don't think he has any packs of cigarettes, and I know Bekim doesn't want to bribe them with money.

The *t'zi* inspect Uncle Fadil's papers and hand them back. The policeman talks to Uncle in a rough tone.

"They want money," Uncle Fadil whispers to Bekim.

"For what?" Bekim asks.

"Just because we are alive," Uncle replies.

"Just because we are alive?"

"Yes."

Bekim looks on in disbelief as Uncle Fadil hands the money to the *t'zi*, who snatch the bribe out of Uncle's hand. He sneers and says, "*Fala* (Thank you in Serbian)."

As Uncle Fadil drives off slowly, I hear the passengers in the back cursing the *t'zi*: "Monkeys...Jerks...*Qena*...Fuck their mother..." While we were stopped, no one dared say a word. Given my size, I can't fight back, but most grown-ups are as big as the *t'zi*. Will I ever see someone challenge them? My classmate Betim told me a story about a young Kosovar karate fighter who had struck a *t'zi* with one kick. I would have paid money to see that—except the part where the Kosovar was arrested.

During the rest of the drive, Uncle Fadil and Bekim smoke cigarettes one after another and stare straight ahead at the road. Occasionally Uncle Fadil curses the two *t'zi*, muttering, as if he is afraid they will hear him. Bekim has propped his right elbow on the dashboard and rests his forehead in the palm of his hand. I stay quietly in my seat. I don't speak to him because I know that he wants to be in his own world.

After letting passengers off at the final bus stop, Uncle Fadil drives the bus to his house, parks it, and immediately goes to his pigeon roost. I follow him. I am fascinated by the birds; they are beautiful, colorful, and as loyal as dogs. Uncle opens the door of the pigeon coop and lets them out.

Meanwhile, Bekim walks to Uncle's house with his head down and his arms stiffly by his side, with both hands clenched.

The pigeons greet Uncle Fadil with a knowing look and then fly out the door. As they soar skyward, Uncle just watches them and relaxes. He seems to have forgotten about the *t'zi*. After a few minutes of dancing in the air and brightening up the sky, the pigeons return and gather around his feet. With his head tilted toward the sky, Uncle Fadil grins.

Once they return, Uncle starts feeding them grain and corn. He has attached bands to the feet of his favorite birds. He talks to them and they appear to understand. I sit on a bench, fascinated. Uncle coos, "*ngu, ngu, ngu*," as he spreads their food on the ground. A white pigeon has distanced itself from the rest of the flock as if angry at Uncle, but he coaxes the bird back to him by gently calling its name, "Bardhosh." He has a name for each one.

I realize why Uncle's pigeons are dear to him. I understand why he had fought with his parents when they wanted to get rid of his pigeons. They tried to destroy the coop because they thought it was childish for a grown man to play with pigeons. At one point, they broke the pigeons' eggs and roost, but they still couldn't keep Uncle Fadil from raising his beloved birds.

When I go back to the house to invite my other cousin, Besnik, to play *futboll* with me, I see Bekim smoking a cigarette, sulking. Unlike Uncle Fadil, he does not have pigeons to soothe his anger.

I find Besnik in a better mood than Bekim. Together with our two cousins Valdet and Fisnik, Besnik and I head toward the concrete field where we had played last time. The pieces of glass from the bottles and jars the Serbian kids had thrown are gone, apparently removed by Kosovar boys. Luckily no one bothers us this time.

When it is time for me to return to Pristina, my grandmother gives me a two-liter Coke bottle filled with milk. I am almost as happy as I would have been if the bottle had been filled with Coke, because now Mami can make us pancakes.

When I enter our apartment, I see Babi quietly sitting on a sofa, reading the paper. It must be *Koha Ditore*, the Albanian newspaper that recently began publication. Babi has on two pairs of reading glasses, one over another; one pair rests on the bridge of his nose and the other directly underneath. He bought a bunch of cheap eyeglasses in Bulgaria, but none of them match his prescription. So he combines two pairs of glasses to improve his vision. Mami also wears two pairs of glasses when she grades students' papers. She cannot afford a visit to the optometrist to get the right prescription.

CHAPTER 22

THE TEN-DEGREE MUDDY SLOPE

I am on the way to my first practice for 2 Korriku. I am excited to start playing for a new team. This should help me become a star *futboller*. I now have the money to pay the monthly fee (Babi gave me some of it, and I took the rest from my savings). My cousin Besim accompanies me to register for the team. We take a long walk and climb the 150 steps to get to the field.

The coach announces the roster of players and asks for our monthly fee. More than a third of the kids do not have the money, but we start playing anyway. There are fewer kids playing for 2 Korriku than for Ramiz Sadiku, but the field is worse here. It is a ten-degree muddy slope, and rocks mark the goals. I touch the ball only twice.

When I return home, Mami and Babi insist that I not play *futboll* anymore because they can't afford the monthly fee. I tell them that I will walk to practice every day and that Besim will take care of my fee. They relent; maybe there is hope that I'll become a *futboll* star.

Mami and Babi hope that one day they will be able to send either Shpetim or me to study in America. To augment the three-and-a-half hours of school, I am enrolled in a private English class. It's best to know how to speak English before going to America, so I had better learn it. Babi has a friend who sent his son to study in America, and the boy was required to take a test in English.

There is a monthly fee for my English lessons. For two months I attend English class and *futboll* practice, but then Babi explains that he has spent the money Uncle Fatmir gave him. I consider continuing the class without paying the fee, but I know the teacher will only send me home, as she did a friend of mine who couldn't afford lessons.

I still go to *futboll* practice because the coach doesn't mind if we are late paying our monthly fee. He sympathizes with our situation more than the English teacher does.

The next day before practice, I observe from our balcony several Serbian police cars lined on a street in a distant neighborhood. We soon hear that two *t'zi* were killed by a Kosovar in one of those houses. Serbian soldiers and policemen are searching for the killer.

Even though the situation outside looks unsafe, I slip on my shoes and head for practice. A pair of *futboll* shoes with cleats would be more suitable for running up and down the muddy slope, but I am lucky enough to have a pair of tennis shoes. Some people play barefooted. As I leave the apartment building, Albert, the twenty-year-old neighbor from the fourth floor, asks me where I'm going.

"To practice," I respond.

"Did you see what's going on outside?"

"Yes, but I'll be all right," I tell him. If Mami and Babi knew what was happening outside, they would not have allowed me to leave the apartment.

After a bad practice under horrible conditions, I'm discouraged. I might as well have stayed home. How can I improve my game when there is no good field for practice? How can I get better without the proper *futboll* equipment? Mine is an impossible dream. I decide to forget about *futboll* and consider something else.

Soon afterward, I decide that my career ambition is to be an actor, a comedian. I love to make people laugh. I mimic Sali Berisha, president of Albania, who always begins his speeches with, "*Ju përshëndes, ju përshëndes, motra the vllëzer* (I greet you, I greet you, sisters and brothers)." He uses a lot of hand gestures, talks slowly in a loud voice, and repeats himself. I imitate perfectly everything that he does, and my audience loves me. At school, I make the students laugh by making funny comments during lessons and mimicking Kosovar comedians.

I have it all planned out. First I can perform in Kosovo; then I can go to America and make Americans laugh and tell them I am from Kosovo, a country they don't know. Then I can tell them about how talented my people are and how horribly we are oppressed by the Serbians.

Instead of trying to be a star *futboll* player, I can be a passionate fan. One day, Kosovo will be independent from Serbia and have a team that competes internationally and plays in Pristina's big stadium. I will wear a red and black jersey to games and cheer for Kosovo until I lose my voice.

PART TWO

"The atrocities that [Kosovar] Albanians faced deserve another book."

—Noel Malcolm, in *Kosovo: A Short History*

CHAPTER 23

USHTRIA ÇLIRIMTARE E KOSOVËS (KOSOVO LIBERATION ARMY)

These past two days, rumors have spread about the identity of the man who killed the two *t'zi* in the neighborhood near our apartment. According to news reports, other *t'zi* were slain elsewhere in Kosovo. Our president claims that the Serbians are killing their own *t'zi* and then blaming Kosovar Albanians for those deaths. Others speculate that Kosovars are killing the *t'zi* to protest their brutal targeting of civilians.

I discuss these theories with my classmates. We want to believe that some Kosovars are resisting the Serbians. We are happy and say that it is about time to retaliate. Enough is enough. We won't take it anymore and must fight the oppression and tyranny of the Serbs.

However, my father believes that our president is right. Since the Serbians have always dominated us in politics, he thinks that they will go as far as killing some of their own people to lay blame on Kosovars and to further Milosevic's political agenda.

During this time, I show what a good actor and comedian I am. Three classmates and I decide to prepare a skit for *dita e flamurit* (Flag Day), on November 28. We adapt material from an Albanian comedy that almost every Kosovar knows. It's about a girl who has a blind date with three boys. One of them is a gypsy; I choose that part because I like putting on a gypsy accent and because he is the funniest character. Betim portrays a Kosovar hillbilly, and Valon plays the part of a city boy. Erleta, the loyal fan of the Backstreet Boys, plays the part of the girl who will select one of us as her date.

Our teacher of Albanian literature, Mr. Gashi, likes our idea of the skit and lets us rehearse in front of the class. Betim, Valon, and I take three seats up front, facing our classmates, and Erleta takes a seat to the side. She asks each of us the same questions.

"If I chose you as my boyfriend, where would you take me on a romantic date?" asks Erleta. Betim and Valon give their answers and then comes my turn.

"If you chose me," I say in my exaggerated gypsy accent, "I would take you to the beach. We would lie on the sand, you in a bikini and I in my Speedo, and we would start to make love." My classmates laugh at my accent. "I would serenade you," I tell Erleta. I get up from my chair and start singing a rap song for her.

> *"Oj, Erlet', oj, Erlet'.*
> *Unë e ti shkojm për lezet.*
> *Nëse u shkru ti mem marr mu,*
> *Drejt ne Gjermani kena me shku."*

(Yo, Erlet', yo, Erlet',
Me and you match like perfect.
If it's meant for you to choose me,
We'll go straight to Germany.)

Everyone starts to laugh, including Mr. Gashi. That makes me feel great about myself.

"Tell me a joke," says Erleta.

"One day, there was a woman whose husband was at work," I start. "She invited her next door neighbor over, and they started making love. Suddenly her husband returned. The neighbor and the woman heard his car pull into the driveway. What were they to do? Before the husband entered the house, the neighbor hid behind the TV set. When the husband walked in, he immediately sat in his favorite chair and started watching a *futboll* game. After a few minutes, the referee blew his whistle. Startled, the neighbor popped his head up from behind the TV set. The husband saw him and was taken aback. 'Neighbor, what are you doing?' he asked. 'The referee just kicked me out,' the neighbor responded."

My classmates start to laugh again. I know that I will be a much better actor than *futboll* player. At the end, Erleta doesn't pick me as her lover because I am a gypsy and nobody likes gypsies, but I don't care. My classmates and Mr. Gashi laughed, and that is all that matters to me.

At home, I watch the news with Babi. We are more eager than ever to know who killed the two *t'zi* in the nearby neighborhood. The news anchor says that at the funeral ceremony of a Kosovar teacher killed by the *t'zi*, three armed Kosovar men appeared and claimed to be a part of a militia called *Ushtria Çlirimtare e Kosoves*, or UÇK (Kosovo Liberation Army, or KLA). Taped footage of the incident shows the men wearing military uniforms; they speak Albanian. One of the UÇK men says that the killings and persecutions of innocent Kosovars such as the teacher won't go unpunished. Another one says, "Serbia is massacring Albanians. The UÇK is fighting for the liberation [of Kosovo]." Babi seems surprised by this development, since he believed that the president of Kosovo was right in supporting a peace movement.

The news continues; mourners begin to cheer in response to the statements of the UÇK soldiers. They chant, "UÇK, UÇK, UÇK." I shout, "UÇK, UÇK," too. Finally, Kosovar Albanians are retaliating against vicious Serbian policemen.

The next day at school, my classmates and I proclaim these UÇK troops to be our heroes. Some of us start writing "UÇK" on desks and walls. One student carves the three letters on the back of a wooden chair with the needle of a compass. Outside the classroom everyone is talking excitedly. We are relieved and elated that an army is fighting for our rights.

At home, Babi watches the news with Ymer, a neighbor. They discuss the UÇK troops with enthusiasm. "Ymer," Babi says, "this seems too good to be true."

Is it possible to defeat the *t'zi*, who kicked us out of schools, shut down our Albanian television channel, took away our autonomy, and prohibited *Rilindja* from publication? Can the UÇK really stop the Serbian police who took my new shoes, gave Babi a false fine for a traffic violation, and demanded a bribe from him? Is it true that someone is raising a hand against the same Milosevic who robbed us of every freedom? Is it true that someone is stopping the same brute and vicious hands that kicked us out of our stadiums, our playgrounds, our hospitals, our clinics? Is it true that we Kosovar Albanians are no longer intimidated and have decided to fight for what is rightfully ours?

UÇK men continue to appear on TV. Classmates spray-paint "UÇK" on the outside walls of the school, taking care not to be seen by any *t'zi*. On my way to school, I see "UÇK" written with paint or chalk on the walls of most apartment buildings.

After a month, *Ushtria Çlirimtare e Kosoves* becomes a part of our daily vocabulary, like the phrase *How are you?* UÇK is in the heart of every Kosovar. However, we must remain cautious. If we mention our militia in front of the *t'zi* or any other Serbian, we could be killed. I heard that after an elderly man inadvertently said "UÇK" in front of two *t'zi* on a crowded public bus, he was beaten unconscious.

From Fjolla's window, I notice that the tanks and other military vehicles move in and out of the Serbian base more frequently than usual. Are the Serbian forces mobilizing to kill us? No. Bosnia is the place where that happens, not Kosovo.

CHAPTER 24

DRENICE

I am at Uncle Azem's New Year's Eve party. The last thing I think about is getting killed by the Serbians. Many of my dear cousins, including Besnik, Valdet, and Fisnik, are here too, and the atmosphere is joyful. Uncle Azem has laid bottles of Coca-Cola and bars of Swiss almond chocolates on the table. When you have plenty of Coca-Cola to drink and plenty of Swiss chocolates to eat, there is no way you can have a bad time even if you are alone.

Uncle Azem, Babi, and Uncle Fadil are drinking beer. While Uncle Azem isn't looking, I grab his bottle and drink about half of it. He does not say anything because I massage his leg, and we love each other no matter what. After I drink the beer, the night gets even better; I start to feel giddy. During the massage, Uncle Azem begins to doze, and I get up to join my cousins.

We borrow Bekim's guitar and drumsticks and pretend to make music. I swing the drumsticks in the air and sing Albanian rock songs along with Valdet. I also pretend to drink liquor out of a closed bottle. The year to come, we say, will be better than the ones before—the UÇK will liberate us. This is our New Year's resolution.

Three months after the New Year's Eve party and a week after my birthday, we learn that 1998 is not going to be better than recent years. Hell has already broken loose; the Serbian forces have started killing innocent Kosovars. After a fight between the UÇK troops and Serbian forces, the Serbians ravaged the villages of Likoshan and Qirez and killed twenty-four Kosovar civilians, including women, children, and the elderly. This can't be. I didn't think that Kosovo was going to be another Bosnia. It doesn't seem real. I must be having a nightmare. When I awake, the genocidal campaign against us will turn out to be a gruesome fiction.

Thanks to our dad, for the next two days we see the images of these massacred Kosovars on TV and in the newspaper, and we hear about them on the radio. The image that haunts me is the one of Rukie Nebihu, a twenty-seven-year-old pregnant woman. Her big stomach is covered with a baby blue sweater. Her face is slashed diagonally, and it's covered with so much blood that you can't see her eyes, mouth, or nose. All that is recognizable is her black hair, her chin, and a naked forearm. The news anchor says she was already a mother of two when she was killed. I feel disturbed and helpless. Who would have thought that it would come to this in our country?

After watching the news on the Albanian channel, Babi turns to Euronews. The same images are displayed across the screen except that at the bottom appear the words "No Comment."

Tonight I watch the 7:30 Albanian news with Babi and Ymer. Another massacre has been committed by the Serbians, this time in the early morning in the village of Prekaz. Fifty-eight Kosovars were killed, including eighteen women and ten children under the age of sixteen. Among the victims are Adem Jashari, the UÇK commander, and all of his family.

"Babi," I ask, "how far is Prekaz from here?"

"Forty minutes," he shouts.

I knew Prekaz was close, but not this close. Still, I try to convince myself that the Serbian forces will attack only villages and not major cities like Pristina. They can't come to our city, I tell myself. I don't have to worry. We will be safe here. There are Serbians who live in Pristina, and the Serbian forces will be too afraid that they will kill their own people.

Suddenly my thoughts shift to Musa. He lives in the village. He could be killed. This thought hits me like a hammer. Musa must come live with us immediately. We must make some room in our apartment for him. Not just for Musa, but for Grandmother, Uncle Skender, and Aunt Hamide too. We must save as many people as we can.

"Babi, will there be war in our village?" I ask.

Babi doesn't answer.

"Ilir, don't worry," Ymer says. "The war will go on only in Drenice."

Drenice? Actually this makes sense because the villages of Likoshan, Qirez, and Prekaz, where the slaughter has taken place, are all in the region of Drenice, the center and heart of Kosovo. In our Kosovar history class, we learned that our bravest heroes were all born in Drenice. Its citizens are courageous and have always fought for Kosovo's independence from the Serbian minority rule. The UÇK was born there.

Still, I want Musa to come live with us.

"Babi, can Musa come live with us here?"

"Why?" His voice changes. "Have you finished your home-work?"

I nod.

"Go read or something," he says. I asked him too many questions. I go to the kitchen. How am I supposed to concentrate when the Serbians are killing people forty minutes away? Of course I don't read anything. I just sit on one of the chairs at the dining table and worry that the Serbians will invade our summer village.

At around 11:00 p.m., Ymer goes home, but Babi still keeps watching the news on TV. He turns on the radio at the same time. Over the next few days, I begin to suspect that Babi is really scared that something bad will happen to us. Every time someone knocks on our door, or Babi hears an unfamiliar noise, he immediately jumps up and asks, "Who is it?" with a troubled look on his face.

When I wake up the next morning, I am surprised to find that despite the news of the previous night, everything is the same. Babi has gone to work, and on my way to school I see that stores are open as usual. Other students exit their apartment buildings and walk alongside me. In class, everyone has heard about the death of Adem Jashari and about his legacy as the bravest UÇK commander. He died for Kosovo along with his parents, wife, children, brother, nieces, and nephews. In every picture of him shown on TV, he is dressed in military uniform and carries a big gun. His hazel eyes, like those of a wolf, scan the horizon for Serbians approaching his village. He becomes our hero. We carve his name on desks, chairs, and walls.

In the days to come, the pictures of the dead are displayed on TV over and over. I identify the most with Adem Jashari's youngest son, Kushtrim. He was my age. In a picture taken before he was killed, he looks like his father. His hair is pulled back; his facial expression is somber, as if to say, "I have nothing to smile about." When I see a picture of his lifeless body, I get as emotional as I did when I saw the body of the pregnant Rukie Nebihu.

Kushtrim and his family died for the freedom of Kosovar Albanians like me.

CHAPTER 25

WORLD CUP

The war has moved closer. It is now in Pristina.

My new friend Burim is a refugee in our apartment building. After fleeing their homes in Llaushe, a village in Drenice, he and his immediate family and other relatives have moved to Ymer's apartment. The number of people living there has grown to thirty. With their presence, the apartment building is noisier. The babies are always crying, and Ymer's front door opens and closes at least a hundred times a day. My family and the neighbors try to help them as much as possible by buying them food and inviting them to our apartment.

Burim is a year younger than I am and has curly hair and a squeaky voice. We have become very good friends and always play *futboll* in the yard of our building. I talk to him about war a lot.

"Me and my family had to sleep in the forest," Burim tells me, "on the ground. In the distance we could see houses burning. We could hear grenades explode and tanks rumble."

"Was it scary?" I ask.

"Yes, it was scary," he says. "There were guns being fired everywhere. They never stopped."

"Did you see any dead people?"

"Yes, one of our neighbors got shot. Then we left. I didn't see anybody else."

"Burim, don't worry about the war anymore. We are safe here in Pristina," I say.

"I am happy here," Burim replies. "I am lucky."

My classmates and I continue to praise our UÇK soldiers and Adem Jashari. Luckily nothing bad happens, and we forget about the atrocities. On TV, we see pictures of UÇK battalions, soldiers marching in perfect formation, dressed in matching military uniforms and carrying a variety of guns. They are our army, and that makes us proud and happy. There are so many of them; they look as if they popped up from the forest ground, but in reality they are random brave young men and women who are tired of Milosevic's reign of terror.

The TV commentator refers to the different UÇK units with specific names. My favorite one shown on the Albanian channel is *Njesia e Forcave Speciale* (the Unit of Special Forces). They wear black uniforms, do impressive training exercises, and look bigger and tougher than the men in other units. But I love all our soldiers equally. They are all fighting for the freedom of our country.

All soldiers have official UÇK emblems sewn on their berets and on the upper right sleeves of their uniforms. These emblems have the double-headed eagle—the same insignia as on our flag—encircled by the words *"Ushtria Çlirimtare e Kosovoes-UÇK."*

It is summer, and we are in the village, where everything and everyone is the same as the last time we were here. The fruit trees in our yard have started to bloom, and Musa, thank God, is still alive. Uncle Fatmir has returned from Switzerland with a German car—an Opel Ascona—and Swiss chocolates. He continues working on the house he is building beside Uncle Sefer's.

The only thing that seems different is the presence of refugees who have moved to our village from their own houses in Drenice.

Among them are some boys our age whom we invite to play *futboll* with us. Outside the mini-market across from our house, a group of men often gather around two tables, playing chess and cards, and after *futboll* games they buy the refugee boys cold Coca-Colas and ask them to talk about the villages they had to leave.

Babi usually sits at the chess table. He taught me the game, so I watch him intently and wish for him to win. I would rather watch *futboll*, though. The World Cup is being played in France, and Musa, Shpetim, and I watch it all the time. We all want Croatia to win, because there is a Kosovar, Ardian Kozniku, on that team. Like every UÇK soldier, he is our hero. But the coach never allows Ardian playing time.

After watching these games, Musa, Shpetim, and I always join the men playing chess and cards outside the mini-market. One day while discussing the World Cup, we learn that someone has seen a vehicle in the forest—a red Golf Rabbit—with three UÇK soldiers in it. In the shop, everyone is speculating aloud about their presence near our village.

"Perhaps they are here to recruit new members," someone says.

Whatever they do, I hope they don't attract the attention of the Serbian forces.

The red vehicle disappears. After a tense silence, there is a collective sigh of relief, and conversation about the World Cup resumes.

Once the World Cup ends, most of what is broadcast on TV is news about Kosovo's massacres. There are new images of Kosovars hiding in forests, mountains, and other remote locations. They aren't all from Drenice. Some are from its surrounding villages. The chill of fall and the bitter cold of winter will sicken and kill many of these people.

To escape the news on TV, I go outside to the mini-market to find the men playing chess and cards.

One afternoon the *t'zi* come to the village, arrest several young men, and take them to the police station, where they are beaten severely for no stated reason. One of the victims is Agron, Musa's cousin. After he is released from the police station, he comes to Musa's house to ask Uncle Fatmir to transport him out of the village to avoid getting brutalized by the *t'zi* again.

Fjolla and I ride along with Uncle Fatmir as he takes Agron out of the village. Agron's face is bruised and swollen, especially around the eyes. His fingernails are black. He tells me that the *t'zi* hit them with a baton and then they clubbed his head.

"My hands are numb, and I have a severe headache," he says. "I was beaten repeatedly from ten o'clock in the morning until five in the afternoon. Three policemen beat my shoulders until I couldn't hold them up anymore. Then they battered the sides of my body, my legs, shins, ankles, and my feet."

Agron looks extremely weak. He must be in great pain. He slumps in the passenger seat, places his hands on his swollen face, and moans. Throughout the summer, while he was helping to build Uncle Fatmir's house, he was always happy and funny. He made fun of Uncle Fatmir's music. I laughed hard when Agron would say, "That French music is making me cry. We are not in Switzerland. We are in Kosovo. Play some Albanian music." The only French song he liked and sang aloud was, "*Voulez-vous coucher avec moi?*"

But now Agron doesn't say anything funny. He looks anguished. "I never want to go back to the village," he says. "I want to disappear."

I daydream about being a soldier in the UÇK's *Njesia e Forcave Speciale*. I have Agron direct me to the *t'zi*. He points his finger at the one who beat him the most, and I kick and punch the *t'zi* to avenge the vicious assault on Agron. "Hit him one more time, one more time," Agron shouts. I beat the *t'zi* to the ground and then I let Agron punch and kick his assailant too. Agron weeps with gratitude and embraces me for bringing him justice.

CHAPTER 26

DR. ROBAJ

The beautiful season ends much too quickly. Reluctantly we return to our apartment. Another summer will come, I tell myself, and I can go back to the village.

We can now hear occasional distant gunfire at night. Still, I deny that the war is coming our way. The UÇK won't let that happen; I'm sure of that.

My classmates and I start eighth grade with the same patriotic spirit we had when the semester ended. We hurl pens, pencils, markers, and compasses across the room, pretending that they are grenades being thrown at Serbian forces.

After school, I resume my *futboll* practices. Despite what I said about being an actor, I still have hopes that one day, somehow, I will become a professional *futboller*. Burim, the refugee kid, and I sometimes play *futboll* in the parking lot or the muddy backyard of our apartment building. Burim has expertise about different kinds of guns that he shares with me. A Kalashnikov, he explains, is the same as an AK-47. He also knows more about tanks than I do. He has witnessed them in action.

The following day, I learn that Pruthi, my rich friend and karate practice partner, has gone to America. I miss him and at the same time I envy him. If my parents were as rich as his, we could go to America too. It would be safer to get out of Kosovo until the conflict has ended—to escape being tortured, murdered, and mutilated. In America, I would be closer to Hollywood, closer to my dream of becoming an actor.

When Babi turns to the Serbian channel, we hear Serbians claim that the massacre of a family in a village called Abri i Eperm is a plot by the Western media and the UÇK.

"Why is the world not doing anything to stop these massacres?" Babi asks rhetorically. "This is genocide—and no one is doing anything about it."

In school today, I learn that my classmate Erleta's father, a doctor for the Red Cross, has been killed. I am in shock. While traveling to Abri i Eperm to help the refugees who escaped the massacre, he and his colleagues were killed by a Serbian land mine.

Erleta's desk is empty this morning. All that is left is a heart pierced by an arrow. Erleta wrote her name above it and "Nick" below. She loves Nick and the Backstreet Boys.

During the funeral procession, my classmates and I walk in unison. We talk about Erleta and her dad; knowing Erleta, we believe she will never stop crying. She used to cry when she got a less than perfect grade, never mind now that her father is dead and she will never hear him comfort and praise her again.

Erleta was close to her father. Several times he had tried to call Nick of the Backstreet Boys in California, just to make Erleta happy, but he could never get in touch with him. He was going to tell Nick how much his daughter loved him. Since he couldn't make direct contact by phone, he had helped her write and send letters to Nick. I would go crazy if my father had been killed by Serbians—even if he had never helped me call or send letters to my favorite *futboll* players.

We walk to Erleta's grandparents' house, where Dr. Robaj's coffin rests. The line of mourners is long—about two or three miles. It seems as if the city's entire population is here. I figure that most of these people don't know Erleta's father personally, but they do know that he was an honorable man who risked his life to help others.

We are now on our way to the cemetery. Some classmates and I want to get to the front of the line; perhaps we can see Erleta. Others scold us as we run past them. We are almost near the beginning of the line, but we do not see Erleta or her younger brother. Instead, we see Mrs. Robaj and other family members, who weep during the entire graveside service. One of them holds a framed picture of Dr. Robaj wearing a white shirt, thick glasses, and a big smile. Now he is a picture and no longer a person living among us. Many people will suffer and die as a consequence of his murder.

When Erleta returns to school one month later, she tells us that she couldn't bear to witness her father's burial. Apart from being a dad to her, she says, he was also a friend who always made her and her little brother laugh.

November 1998 passes with the Serbian forces still committing massacres against Kosovar civilians and offering nonsensical excuses for their actions. In addition to killing thousands, they have burned the homes of thousands more. Babi continues to watch the news and buy the Albanian newspaper. He becomes so exhausted with worry that after work, he lies down on the sofa and falls asleep while the news is still on.

One night, as Babi starts to snore, I switch the channel to a *futboll* match. Suddenly he opens his eyes and says, "Go back to the news." I obey immediately. I am surprised that Babi watches the news even when he is asleep.

The anchor on Babi's news program states that diplomats from Western countries are flying to Serbia to warn Milosevic to cease the genocide and ethnic cleansing of Kosovars, threatening military intervention if he doesn't stop. Milosevic appears cocky and unconcerned. When Babi hears that NATO air strikes are being discussed to combat Milosevic's evil mission, his eyes open wide. "Milosevic will never concede," Babi says. "Just bomb him."

In school, my classmates and I tell one another that NATO is coming with Nike Air shoes. The West will come to our rescue.

In the meantime, here in Pristina, everything seems normal. If it weren't for Babi's news and the frequent movements of tanks, I wouldn't know we were engaged in a war.

CHAPTER 27

UNCLE AZEM

On New Year's Eve, Uncle Azem is called by the coach company to pick up a group of passengers in Northern Serbia. Their bus has been disabled by a mechanical failure, and they need transportation to Hungary.

We spend this New Year's Eve at Uncle Azem's apartment while he is en route to Serbia. On the living room table are Coca-Cola bottles and Swiss chocolates. Uncle Azem's daughter, Gëzime, the architecture student, serves the guests these goodies. His two sons, Besim and Bekim, are present along with my family.

It seems unfair that Uncle Azem has to work on New Year's Eve. Without him, things are not the same. Tonight, Mami and Aunt Hava are worried that Uncle Azem is traveling on roads near villages where Kosovar civilians have been attacked and killed by Serbians. Babi attempts to reassure them that Uncle Azem will be safe.

Uncle Azem was supposed to come back on January second. It is now January ninth, and he still hasn't returned. We have not heard a word from him.

The threat of war in Pristina is growing. Tank tracks on the highway and their noisy rumblings are more frequent. Kosovar emigrants from rural areas roam the streets, gather, and then disperse when tanks or *t'zi* approach. I watch them from the window in Fjolla's room. When I see them later on TV, close-ups of their faces reveal their fear. Little children cry and beg to be held by their mothers or grandmothers. People look lost, their eyes vacant. The news reports confirm that the refugees come from different villages and that they have no shelter, food, or protection in Pristina.

I see a man who resembles Uncle Skender on TV. Could that be him? I point to the screen and ask Mami and Babi.

"Hush," cautions Mami. Perhaps I am the only one who noticed the resemblance. I am afraid to ask more questions.

It is mid-January, and Uncle Azem is still missing. Strangers call Aunt Hava on the phone, telling her that if she wants to see her husband alive she will have to pay a huge ransom. The owners of the coach company that employ Uncle Azem have paid those people, but Uncle has not appeared. Maybe his bus broke down on the way to Serbia or he got arrested by the *t'zi*.

When Uncle Azem's son Bekim comes to our house, he smokes cigarettes, one after another, while staring at the carpet. Every few minutes, Mami phones Aunt Hava and Gëzime to see whether they have heard anything about Uncle.

I try to be optimistic. He is going to come home alive, I tell myself. There is no need to panic. No one can hurt Uncle Azem. He is tall, strong, and clever. If someone tried to hurt him, he could run over them with his bus. I know my uncle well. He can take care of himself.

Feeling reassured, my mind shifts from Uncle Azem. While changing channels to find a *futboll* match on TV, I see news of another massacre in Reçak, about fifteen miles away from where we live. There are forty-five victims, including a boy who looks like me. One channel shows people piled in a ravine, where they were shot dead. Their corpses were then taken into a mosque. The bodies have been placed on the floor, faceup, row after row. Little numbers scratched on bits of paper are placed on their chests. These people are reduced to numbers now.

As I am about to change the channel, Babi comes into the room.

"Leave it alone," he commands. He stares at the images. His jaw drops a little.

Some boys and men are shirtless, as if they have been killed in the morning right before getting completely dressed. Others are wearing thick sweaters and long pants suitable for cold weather. Still others are dressed in clothing and gear traditionally worn by Kosovar farmers. Some of the women's breasts are naked and bloodied. Some have been decapitated.

In the mosque, family members walk around the rows of the dead, often walking in pairs, leaning against one another for support. One pair embraces tightly and prays, as if that will somehow ease their pain and revive the dead. Their faces are buried in one another's shoulders as they weep uncontrollably. I suddenly feel as if my mind is detached from my body, as if I'm floating above a sea of blood. It is surreal. How can the world allow these heinous crimes?

One evening during the second week of Uncle Azem's disappearance, Mami asks me to buy loaves of bread at a bakery near the place where I once sold cigarettes. On the way, tobacco vendors approach me as if I want to buy cigarettes from them. Desperately, they ask everyone to buy their cigarettes, no matter one's age or gender, just as long as you are not a *t'zi*. I am sorry, I say; I am only going to buy some bread. They turn away from me and approach someone else. I should feel sorry for them, knowing how disappointing it is to get turned down by a customer, but I still feel incapable of empathy.

I enter the bakery and barely nod to the baker, an older man whose apron and shirt are covered with flour. I purchase two warm, soft loaves of bread. The man cheerfully says good-bye. I exit his shop, not knowing that I will never see him again.

Once outside, I hear a *booooooooom*. The blast echoes for several seconds. The earth vibrates. Two older men, a cigarette vendor, and I fall to our knees, crouch, and cover our heads with clasped hands. Judging from the direction of the blast, it seems to have occurred in a little market in the neighborhood of Ulpiana, not even 300 yards away from us. I release a big sigh. The explosion caught me by surprise, and I don't know what to do. I am afraid that another one will land even closer. I start to run home, a loaf of bread clenched in each hand. The men and the cigarette vendors flee too.

The blast has jolted me to my senses. The Serbians have begun to destroy our city.

"What happened?" Mami asks when I reach home. While taking deep breaths in the middle of each sentence, I tell her about the explosion. Mami wraps me in her protective embrace and holds me close. I recall that Serbian forces had thrown grenades in a Sarajevo market to inaugurate the carnage there.

Starting today, Pristina is like Sarajevo.

The next day after school, some classmates and I walk to the site where the explosion occurred. Ground zero is near the entrance to the flea market. Upon arrival, we see a crowd near two charred buildings. All doors and windows are shattered and collapsed inward. The merchandise is unrecognizable and the walls are blackened from smoke. The air smells like gunpowder. Dried blood is splattered on the ground. Two or three Kosovars were killed. I imagine a likely scenario: a *t'zi* drove by, tossed hand grenades out of an open car window, and sped away.

Another week has passed and Uncle Azem is still missing. While returning home from a friend's house, I try to imagine what happened to Uncle. Was his bus involved in an accident?

Once inside our apartment, I see my brother, Shpetim. His face is flushed and his eyes are wet with tears.

"What's wrong?" I ask.

"Uncle Azem is dead!"

"Who?"

"Uncle Azem."

"How did he die?"

"They killed him."

"Who killed him?"

"The Serbians."

Stunned, I go to the sunroom to be alone.

I can't imagine life without Uncle Azem. He will never say, "Lili, will you massage your uncle's bad leg?" His voice is stilled forever. I am denied new memories of him. Now he belongs to the past, like Dr. Robaj. My dear uncle will never stride with his long legs, nor say another loving word, nor initiate another humble act. No one can replace him.

My earliest memories of Uncle Azem have faded, but I try to conjure them anew. Once Uncle Azem had carried me on his shoulders as he walked to the bus station. I enjoyed being aloft so I could see distant cars on the highway; Uncle Azem often stopped to talk to people. Many greeted him with kind words and a handshake. Uncle introduced me to all of the well-wishers. "This is my nephew, Lili," he would tell them. He was proud of me; I felt special.

The company bus that Uncle Azem drove was beautiful. When washed, it looked brand new. I remember how Uncle Azem would get into the driver's seat and start the bus, letting it idle for a bit to warm up its big engine. He could easily handle that big vehicle and execute any maneuver flawlessly. I found it amazing that small men like Uncle Azem could control such big things as buses and trucks.

I return to Shpetim to make certain that he knew what he was talking about. He is still crying. His eyelids are swollen and his face is red.

"How did they kill him?"

"They shot him. Him and Valdet, and then they took their bus." Valdet Regjaj was his twenty-three-year-old assistant who was with Uncle on that trip. Shpetim turns away. I doubt that Uncle and Valdet did anything to provoke the Serbians. There would be no reason for the murders—except cruelty.

Before long, Mami comes home from work, crying. She has already received the news. She takes a seat in the corner of the kitchen, where she looks outside the window in the direction of the bus station. She sobs quietly and does not talk to us.

I learn that Babi and Uncle's best friend are in Serbia to claim the bodies. When Babi returns from the trip, I ask him for details about Uncle and Valdet's deaths. I must know the truth, however grisly.

It turns out that the call from the group of passengers to the coach company was a ruse on the part of the Serbian mafia. When Uncle arrived to provide transport for the allegedly stranded passengers, he and his assistant were shot at close range. This operation is believed to have been ordered by Arkan, leader of the Tigers, a paramilitary group hired by the Serbian government to torture and kill Bosnians and Kosovars.

A farmer found two big black plastic bags in his field. When he looked inside them, he discovered the dead. The cold January temperatures had preserved the corpses from substantial decay. The farmer notified local police, who arranged transfer of the remains to a morgue. The owners of Uncle's coach company, Uncle's best friend, and Babi had picked them up. Uncle Azem's body is now back in Vushtrri, near the village where he was born and will soon be buried.

It is January 21, 1999, the date of the burial. It is cold and snowy. We are traveling in the car Uncle Fatmir had left behind for us when he returned to Switzerland at the end of the summer. During the drive to Vushtrri, no one speaks. I stare out a window at the whitening landscape.

Mami is aggrieved most by Uncle's death. They played and studied together. As her elder brother, he guided and inspired her. He was an emotional and financial support for her. Still, what we will all miss most is his vitality, compassion, humor, and love.

Finally, the silence is broken. "He was always caring for others," Mami says. Uncle Azem was once the chauffeur for the president of Kosovo's assembly, and after Mami gave birth to Shpetim, he drove the two of them home from the hospital in the president's luxurious black Mercedes. Shpetim and Mami were brought home like a queen and her baby prince.

Uncle Azem was a good and generous man. He earned a little more money than his siblings and always helped them, including our family, by buying them food and clothes. In addition to Coca-Cola and chocolates, Uncle Azem also bought us thick sausages that Mami sliced, fried, and mixed with scrambled eggs. He helped his two older sisters even more because they were poorer than we were and lived in remote villages. One of them had twelve kids and the other seven. Uncle often paid their bills.

Before this tragedy, Mami seemed invincible. I had never seen her cry until today. Even during and after Babi's fits of rage, Mami never cried. She was always composed, even when we were prevented by the Serbians from going to school.

But not this time. Mami isn't assertive and stoic today. She has been hit where it hurts the most. Her habitually disciplined nature can't tame her grief. She mutters to herself, as if she belongs in a hospital's psychiatric ward.

While disturbed and even frightened by Mami's distress, I understand her agony. One time I had a dream about Fjolla getting massacred; I awoke panicked and ran to her bedside. Discovering that she was alive, I was so relieved that I softly kissed her cheek and sobbed. Ever since that dream, I love my sister more than ever.

But Uncle's death is not a dream. It's a living nightmare. His death is an aching reality.

Babi has not only our loss on his mind but also fear of being stopped by the *t'zi*. If that happens, he has rehearsed a plea that will persuade them not to fine him for no reason. He will tell them that there has been a death in our family. After looking at our faces, they will surely be able to see that our grief is genuine. Members of their families have probably died as well, so they will have empathy toward us.

Already we have passed two *t'zi* checkpoints with no incident, but the one where everyone gets stopped is ahead. There is a line of four or five cars in front of us waiting to be inspected by the *t'zi*. The authorities stop and search the cars, buses, and tractors that wind in both directions on the highway.

When our turn comes, a young *t'zi* motions for Babi to roll down the window. He peeks at my siblings and me sitting in the back seat and then says to Babi in Serbian, "License and registration." (My Serbian vocabulary is much better now. I understand almost everything.) Babi shows the documents, which are abruptly snatched from his hand. The *t'zi* examines them and says, "This is an imported German car." Babi is ordered to get out and open the trunk. There is nothing in it.

"Twenty deutschmarks to pass with this car," barks the officer. Babi has already registered our car and gotten a plate after paying all the necessary taxes and fees, but the young *t'zi* wants more.

"I have registered the car," says Babi.

"I don't care," the officer replies gruffly.

Babi points to Mami and explains, "She has a brother who died, and we are en route to the funeral. I don't get paid at work. I don't have any money."

The *t'zi* doesn't seem to care. "Pay or turn back," he demands. "Hurry up. There are other people in line that are trying to get through."

Babi opens his wallet and surrenders the money he has left. We are allowed to pass.

When we arrive to see Uncle Azem for the last time, we find the house crowded with people. We all go to the room where the casket is. Made of gleaming, polished wood and nicely carved, the casket is surrounded by my aunts, cousins, and other family members, most of whom are women. All of them are crying.

I slowly approach the casket. Uncle Azem's eyelids are slightly swollen and his skin looks jaundiced. His once-vital body is rigid. I lean forward to kiss his forehead, but Bekim says touching a corpse violates some religious rule. He orders me to get out of the way so other people can see the body. Overwhelmed with sadness, I move away but stay in the room, leaning against the far wall and staring at Uncle Azem from a distance. I never expected this. I had remained hopeful that he would be found alive.

I remember when a lot of my little cousins and I were around Uncle Azem. He always asked, "Who loves Uncle the most?"
We raised our hands and said in unison, "Me, me." We all loved him. Then we would all pile onto his big belly to kiss his soft cheeks. He

would then choose one of us to massage his bad leg. Uncle would ask me, "Lili, will you massage your uncle's bad leg?" I would sit on the couch, he would put his leg on top of my thighs, and I would rub his shin until he was pleased or fell asleep. Now Uncle Azem has gone to sleep forever. I hate Arkan and his Serbian paramilitary troops for killing my uncle. I hope someone will bring them to justice before they kill more people.

I stay in the room until the lid of the casket is closed, locked, and transferred to the van that is going to take him to the cemetery.

Uncle Fadil wants to ride with his dear brother. He sobs in a low tone. Tears stream down his cheeks and he sighs deeply. His pet pigeons can't bring peace to his heart after this. Syla, a cousin of Uncle Fadil's, stays close to him. Fisnik tells me that Syla is staying with Uncle Fadil because they are scared he may not survive his grief and kill himself.

The yard is crowded with people, and hundreds more line the road. It seems that all residents of the town are attending the funeral, like the mourners of Erleta's father. Some of them had met him; others had not but knew how great a man he was. There are Uncle Azem's family and friends, of which there are many. Besim's *futboll* team and coach have come to pay their respects. The wife of our former president has come to honor the man who chauffeured her husband for years.

The mourners will travel to the gravesite in buses, cars, vans, and big trucks. I ride in one of the trucks with a cousin. It is still snowing. During the twenty-minute ride to the village cemetery where Uncle is going to be buried, I stay quiet.

When we arrive, six pallbearers carry the casket on their shoulders to the plot. I get as close to the casket as possible. Several rows of people follow in solemn procession. We cross the bridge of a shallow creek to reach the grave. The casket is lowered to the ground next to the pit. Family members form a line along the sides of the excavation. Snow covers the bottom of the grave; I bow my head and stare into what seems like an abyss.

Some of the mourners can't stop crying. Others are quiet, observing closely with curious and even disbelieving looks. The imam begins saying the last prayers; dogs nearby howl as if they are mourning for Uncle Azem too. Mourners stand shoulder-to-shoulder to keep from fainting. As the casket is lowered into the grave, the dogs continue to bark. One of them barks louder than the others, exhaling cold vapor after each howl. I like to think he is protesting Uncle's death.

After the burial, Gëzime, Mami, and I linger at the grave. Finally, Mami grabs me by an arm and whispers, "Come on, it's time to go." Gëzime's fiancé gently takes her hand and leads her away. Uncle Azem is now alone.

When we go back to our grandparents' house, Grandmother tells us that if we go before sunrise to the room where Uncle Azem's casket was, we will see his face there. I am skeptical but curious. Younger cousins and I go, but we don't see the apparition. Besnik claims that we arrived too late. The sun had begun its ascent above the horizon. I'm certain that it's *rren e plakave* (an old wives' tale). We will never see Uncle again.

CHAPTER 28

VEDAT

For weeks, Mami cries frequently and never really gets back to normal. When she doesn't cry, we know not to bring up Uncle's name. Repeatedly she laments, "There was no other man like him. He always tried to help others. He didn't deserve this." When family members and friends come to visit, she can't compose herself. She always clasps a white handkerchief. She never seems to run out of tears. Her nose is red, dry, and sore. She worries aloud that without Uncle's support, our family and our aunts' families will struggle to make it. Throughout the night, she awakens and wails, "If anyone could bring a brother back to life with tears, I would be the one."

I stay quiet.

It is a tradition during these *ditë zije* (black days) not to have a TV on or music playing, but Babi is impatient and turns on the TV to watch the news. The news shows images of more massacres. Since Uncle Azem's death, we had almost forgotten about the war and the danger posed to our own lives. When cameras focus on bereaved family members, we understand how they feel. Now I know why they cry so much, why they lean against each other for support, and why they sometimes kneel on the ground and sob.

Distant gunfire is heard throughout each night. During the day, some of the grocery stores are closing and fewer buses are running. More and more Kosovar refugees, mostly women and children, wander aimlessly in the streets. Many husbands and fathers are probably casualties of the war. Families have been separated while trying to escape.

After the Serbians ousted them from their village, my nine-year-old cousin Vedat and his big sister became separated from their parents. Vedat's sister has brought him to our house, and she has gone to Aunt Hava's apartment. Shpetim, Fjolla, and I are closer to his age than Aunt Hava's children. We are happy to see them alive.

Vedat looks glum, shy, and vulnerable. With his floppy ears and sad eyes, he looks like a stray puppy. He is wearing a dirty blue coat, two sizes too small, with tattered sleeves that he uses to wipe his runny nose. He has thick black hair with natural brown highlights, evidently not combed or washed for weeks. We are willing to adopt him. Vedat lives in a remote village, so I am not as close to him as I am to Musa, Valdet, Fisnik, and Besnik. Since he is separated from his parents, I want to become his brother and share Mami and Babi with him.

Mami is sweet to him and treats him like her son. She washes and feeds him and politely encourages him to talk to us. Usually when Mami asks him questions, Vedat only says "yes" and "no" in a distinct voice. At the dining room table he keeps his head bowed while eating. Shpetim and I take him out to play *futboll*—something that he loves. After he gets used to playing with us, he becomes relaxed and talks to us.

Once enrolled in our school, he is like one of us; he becomes my little brother and *futboll* buddy. I am determined to protect him. We will get through the rest of the war together. While playing with Vedat and Burim, I wonder if Musa is still in his village. I refuse to dwell on the possibility that something has happened to him. If he were here, Musa would be playing *futboll* with us, two on two.

Meanwhile, Vedat has not said a word about his lost family. We avoid asking him anything about it: too sensitive.

"Vedat, do you miss your parents?" Mami suddenly asks.

Vedat doesn't answer. Instead, his face reddens; he bows his head and begins to cry. Mami should have known not to ask him that question. Of course he misses them. I hope they are still alive. When he isn't in school, I try to keep his mind occupied with *futboll* so he doesn't have as much time to contemplate the worst.

Just now I remember that yesterday—February 18—was my fourteenth birthday. I make a belated birthday wish for the killing and separations of families to end, and for Kosovo to be freed from Milosevic and the *t'zi*.

At night, the gunfire becomes louder. It sounds closer. What will we do if bullets shatter our windows? Such thoughts terrify me, especially when it is dark.

Once Vedat goes to sleep in Fjolla's room, Mami says she has something interesting to tell us. I suspect she is trying to keep us from thinking about the danger outside. "Last night, I heard Vedat sing himself to sleep in Fjolla's room," she says. "He has a lovely voice."

We go to his room, turn on the light, and start begging him to sing. "Vedat, if you sing, we can stay up late," I tell him.

"OK," he says, and he sings the Albanian song *"Sy me sy."* He begins softly, like a lullaby, and then his voice gets louder yet sweeter. Vedat can sing like no other child I have ever heard. His vocal range is wide and the top notes so high that he must be a tenor. Vedat's beautiful voice makes us appreciate his presence and life in general. He sings with his eyes closed. He seems tranquil and content. We feel the same way and momentarily forget the chaos around us.

We ask Vedat to sing for us every day. We want our lives to be a soaring, endless melody. Such a voice brightens our mood and fills our hearts with peace. Vedat sings as if he could go on forever. When he finishes, I desperately wish he hadn't.

Once again, our ears are assaulted by the ugly, piercing gunfire. Our respite from reality is over. We are at war.

It has been two weeks since Vedat moved in with us. Now most of the mini-markets are closed and most of the buses, including Uncle Fadil's, have stopped running. The streets are full of *t'zi* and Serbian soldiers, and Babi doesn't dare drive to the village to see what is happening there. Vedat and I want to play *futboll*, but Mami won't allow us outside. He and I decide to sneak out anyway and meet Burim to practice. We play in our fenced yard with the Serbian forces' presence all around us and the sound of gunfire in the near distance.

When Mami discovers that Vedat and I are outside, she confronts us.

"Get inside, now," she commands.

"Why?" I ask Mami.

"It is too dangerous out here, devil. Can't you see?" I realize now that war means no more *futboll*. War stops the game and the song; war stops everything but fear and death.

It is the end of February, and Vedat's big sister has come to take him with her. She wants to be with him before they get separated from one another too. We are sad Vedat is leaving us, and so is he. But we understand; they have only one another. They also have the stories of how they got separated from their parents—stories that just the two of them can relate to. We kiss them good-bye before they go to Aunt Hava's.

At school the next day, my classmate with the same last name as mine tells a scary true story. "I was chased by a man wearing black clothes as I returned home last night," he says.

Our classes begin later now, and when we leave for home, it is dark. I see a car burning. There are near-sounding shots. What if someone shoots me or tries to burn me alive? What will I do if a stranger tries to kidnap me? What if he can run faster than me? He may throw a grenade that blows me to bits; I can't imagine escaping.

"Are you serious?" someone asks.

"Yes, I ran away," says Adriatik Berisha. "I was so scared."

On my evening walk home from school, I hear loud explosions, the *rat-a-tat-tat* of artillery fire, and shrill sirens. I think about the stranger again. I picture him to be a masked man armed with a rifle, lurking around a corner. I run ahead to join other students who are walking hurriedly. With this group, I reach my apartment safely but shaken.

The next morning, Fjolla goes to school during the first shift but comes back after thirty minutes. "The Serbian police came to our school," she tells Mami, breathing hard from running home. "They kicked us out." My sister looks terrified.

I probably can't attend classes anymore.

CHAPTER 29

PRISONERS

My life stinks more than ever. All I do is stay home and watch horrible TV. During the day Mami won't let me play *fut-boll*, and during the evenings Babi does nothing but watch the news. Mami and her students have been evicted from school too, so she stays home and prevents us from going outside. We are stuck in the apartment like prisoners. From the TV news, I learn that there are riots near the city's center—protests against massacres and ethnic cleansing. The protesters are attacked by the *t'zi* and forced to disperse.

Today from Fjolla's window, I see a demonstration on the main highway. There are thousands and thousands of women walking in a line. There are no men. Each protester is holding a loaf of bread. The line is even longer than the ones during the funerals of Dr. Robaj and Uncle Azem.

"Mami, look outside the window."

She gazes at the scene for a minute.

"Mami, what are those women out there doing with the bread? Where are they going?" I ask.

"They are going to Drenice to take bread to the hungry there," she says. It is brave of these women to risk the danger of delivering food to those villagers.

However, fifteen minutes later, the line of women starts moving back toward Pristina. I wonder why. What happened? Why didn't they proceed to Drenice? Later, we learn that the *t'zi* had forced them back. This makes knots in my stomach. The people in Drenice will starve; the cruelty of the *t'zi* has no limits.

"We have no money," Babi says to Mami one day after he comes home from work. "What are we going to do in case we need to escape? Can we borrow some from Hava?"

"I can find out."

Mami decides to risk going to Aunt Hava's. Before leaving, she tells Babi, "Make sure Ilir doesn't go outside."

Isolated in the apartment, I worry about Mami. My anxiety escalates when she has been gone for over an hour. Fjolla is worried too. I hope the *t'zi* don't beat and rob Mami. Babi, however, doesn't seem too worried. He is preoccupied with the news on different channels, watching how the greatly outnumbered *t'zi* still managed to intimidate and thwart thousands of women protesters.

Finally, Mami returns and we quickly gather around her to learn why she was gone so long.

The first thing she says is, "Hysen, did the children go outside?"

"No," says Babi.

"Good. Hava gave me two thousand deutschmarks."

That is a relief; I am thankful that we have some money.

A week passes, and Mami still doesn't let me set foot outside the door. We hear that the vendor of a nearby mini-market has been killed by the *t'zi*. Babi doesn't go to work in the morning; he fears the same thing will happen to him.

I beg Mami yet again to let me go outside. This time I present a good argument. "The bullets being fired outside are aimed in a different direction from the parking lot where I play."

"I told you no already," she says. "There are tanks outside also."

"Mami, the tanks have traveled up and down the main highway all my life. How come Burim is allowed outside? His mom doesn't say anything to stop him," I say.

"Burim probably doesn't even ask his mom to go out. There are so many kids living in that small apartment that if one goes out you can't tell the difference," she says.

Now that I am stuck inside, our living room becomes my *futboll* field. I kick the ball and it bounces off the big armoire and TV stand. Mami yells at me from the kitchen, but I ignore the warning. She can't stop me from doing everything.

I hear my neighbors working in the lobby. I quickly exit and see that Babi and the other neighbors are putting new locks on the building's front doors. Mr. Vokshi is welding metal frames to reinforce the glass panes of the doors. Mr. Sejda and Mr. Krasniqi are lifting a long piece of metal. When it gets dark, the neighbors lock the main front door and place the long metal bar across it. We have never locked this door before, but now we fear that some *t'zi* will storm our building at night and massacre us.

The next day we prepare a bunker. Our apartment building has a room in the basement with a door and a low ceiling that is specifically designed for war situations. We have never used the bunker before, so it is messy. Inside it are spider webs, cockroaches, dead insects, dust mites, mosquitoes, and rats. It takes all day for several men to make the bunker habitable. If the Serbian police come, we now have a place to hide and possibly survive.

Even though Babi has gotten slapped by a *t'zi* for carrying an Albanian newspaper, he still keeps buying it. Since I have nothing to do, I grab it to read the sports section. I flip through pages with pictures of massacred bodies and homeless refugees. Above is a headline reading, "NATO, just do it."

Babi doesn't bring the paper home the next day. The Serbian police must have shut that place down because of its editorials pleading for NATO's help.

CHAPTER 30

NATO

Today is March 24, 1999. The daylight has turned to dark, and there is no electricity. Fjolla, Shpetim, and I are playing Ping-Pong on our dining room table by candlelight, and Mami and Babi and some neighbors are sitting in the living room. Suddenly we hear the roar of an airplane. The energy of it brightens the night. From its piercing sound—like whistling amplified a million times—I sense that it is getting closer to where we are. A big *booooom*, like an enormous clap of thunder, follows. NATO is bombing the military base where the Serbian tanks are located. The impact of the strike shakes the floor of our apartment. Those tanks are worthless now.

Fjolla, Shpetim, and I immediately run into the living room. Mami and Babi order us to sit on the floor. Fjolla goes to Mami, and Shpetim and I do as we are told. Keeping our heads down, we grab our knees with our arms so that our legs are close to our chests. Babi goes to a window and pulls back the edge of the curtain to peek outside. In the dim candlelight, I can see a grin on his face.

"Yes. I swear they are attacking them," he says to us. Our neighbors, Mrs. Kaqa and her husband, Mr. Sejda, smile.

"Congratulations," says Babi.

"Congratulations to you too," says Mr. Sejda.

"Ah, NATO, America and Bill Clinton, Tony Blair and Great Britain are saving us," says Babi.

"Ah, Bill Clinton, ah, Tony Blair," says Mr. Sejda as he rises from his seat. In Kosovo, it's customary to stand when you talk about somebody you are thankful for.

I am as happy as Babi. Since we don't hear more NATO jets approaching, I begin to clap and dance in celebration. After the pass of the bomber, there is a lot of Serbian antiaircraft fire, but that plane has probably returned to its base by now. Fjolla, Shpetim, and I jump up and down and give each other high fives. Even Mami seems happy for the first time since Uncle Azem was murdered. NATO has finally taken charge; we will be freed from the Serbians. Milosevic is going to pay a heavy price for kicking us out of schools and stadiums, for taking the lives of Kosovars.

Serbian guns continue their loud *paw paw* sounds. They have never seemed so near as they do tonight. It seems that ammunition is being fired toward our side yard. My father blows out the candles, leaving only one lit in the corner of the living room. I assume that he doesn't want anyone outside to know that we are here.

Mrs. Mejrem, whose daughter is in the Kosovo Liberation Army, comes with her husband and her two sons from their upstairs apartment to ours. They don't feel safe being so far above ground.

Babi and Mrs. Mejrem's husband, Mr. Latif, are congratulating each other that NATO has finally taken action. The intensity of the firing continues, so we huddle on the floor. The lone candle illuminates our faces. We exchange smiles. Other neighbors come to shake hands and express their hope and relief about the arrival of NATO.

Another NATO plane drops its payload. This hit isn't as close to us, but it still shakes our apartment building—but it's a good shake, a vibration that we love. On the other hand, I wonder how the pilots are able to see their targets at night. Still, I trust them. After all, these airplanes are from America, from President Clinton, and they will not fail in their mission.

The explosions of bombs and the street sounds of car alarms and sirens ring sweetly in our ears—like a fanfare of liberation.

Once the NATO bombings cease and the shooting subsides, I fall asleep on the carpet. The next morning is quieter, but I still hear some car sirens and the occasional *paw paw* sound. Carefully I draw the curtain of Fjolla's window to see what is happening outside. Smoke rises from the Serbian military base near my home. I notice the streets are empty.

"Looks like NATO has bombed the Serbian base nearby, Babi," I say.

"Yes, they sure have," he responds happily. "Don't look out the window anymore," he cautions me. We know there are a lot of Serbian snipers positioned on top of apartment buildings. Serbian forces, angry that NATO has come to our rescue, will retaliate by shooting some of us.

When I open the refrigerator door, the smell of rotting food sickens me. The meats and other perishables have gone bad. We eat some stale bread coated with sugar and melted margarine. I gag on every bite, but manage to flush it down my throat with lots of water.

When darkness falls and the gunfire intensifies, Babi and two neighbors hurry to the building's entrance, lock the doors, and place the metal bar across them again. What are the Serbian forces shooting at? I haven't heard a NATO jet tonight. I hope they are not shelling apartment buildings like ours.

In the darkness, Shpetim, Fjolla, and I sit on the carpet to form a triangle. We get a ball and roll it with our hands to one another's open legs. We played this game when we were very little, but it is babyish for a fourteen-year-old like me.

My siblings and I can barely see. We don't speak much. I have trouble keeping my mind on this boring game and avoiding thoughts of bullets flying in our direction. I hate not kicking the ball. A month has passed since I have been able to play *futboll* outside.

At about nine at night, a NATO jet roars overhead. This time it sounds as if it is flying right over our building. Its lights flash in our window. The noise is louder than any thunderstorm I have ever heard. A huge blast follows. The entire earth shakes. One window in our living room shatters. My internal organs shift violently. I gasp for air. My heart pounds wildly. Then I release a big sigh and fall to my knees. I flop onto the floor and cover my ears with my hands.

Silence hangs in the air, menacingly, for fifteen minutes. Then I hear voices and the sound of babies crying. Even though the NATO plane is gone I hear gunshots and Serbian artillery fire. I laugh. The Serbians are being defeated. It is time for them to go. Another bomber streaks overhead. The Serbians can only shoot at its echo.

Still, Babi doesn't look as happy as he did last night. He is covering the broken window with a blanket, and Mami is telling him to beware of the broken glass littering the floor. The smells of smoke and explosives permeate our apartment. Cold air penetrates the blanket and makes us shiver.

The young mothers in our building have difficulty putting their babies and little children to sleep. I can hear them crying.

The excitement brought by the NATO attacks doesn't last. The Serbian forces don't surrender. Since we support NATO, Bill Clinton, Tony Blair, and General Wesley Clark, the Serbian forces will annihilate Kosovar Albanians.

I can't sleep. Fear keeps me awake, and our apartment is freezing cold. Lying on the hard floor doesn't help. Fjolla is on our mother's warm lap, snuggling in Mami's arms. Mami is gently scratching Fjolla's back and rocking her as one would a baby. Despite all this comfort, Fjolla still doesn't fall asleep. As the shootings continue, she clings tightly to Mami.

The neighbors barely whisper to one another, as if talking will provoke a hail of bullets. The gunfire never stops, and it muffles our attempts to communicate. If Mami has to say something to Babi, she whispers. If our parents don't want us to understand what they're saying, they speak rapidly and in Serbian.

We pay great attention to the entrance of our apartment building for fear that someone will break down the double doors. We listen for a big bang, a kick, and the sound of the metal bar hitting the floor and making a clanging sound. When we hear footsteps in the hallway, we wonder if it is a person who lives in our building.

We listen closely to every sound inside our building. Each one is scary at first. Even when our armoire, TV set, and other furniture make tiny, random sounds, I get scared, and then I convince myself that the sound is coming from inanimate objects. The fear is in my imagination, I tell myself.

The scariest times are trips to the bathroom, because at those times I know I will be inside a small, dark room alone. Tonight I have avoided urinating for a long time. The bathroom is only a few steps away, but I am not brave enough to go in there. My stomach starts to hurt, and my bladder feels as if it's going to burst. I really have to pee, but I am too embarrassed to ask Mami or Babi to accompany me. Eventually the pressure in my bladder becomes unbearable.

I enter the bathroom and leave the door open. I pee as fast as I can. It is dark; I am peeing onto the toilet seat, making the urine splash back onto my thighs. I push so hard that peeing stings. Still, I can't purge my imagination of sounds that portend death. At any moment, someone will kick the door down and find me in the bathroom alone. Where could I hide if a stranger barged in? Maybe inside the washing machine, I think. No, I can't fit in it. I flee to the living room. I stumble as I pull my pants up while running.

The living room feels no safer because I worry that bullets, grenades, bombs, or missiles are going to crash through a window. I remember the shops in Ulpiana, where the bomb exploded. During the next few hours, I cover my ears, shut my eyes, and try to sleep.

Around two or three in the morning, I finally fall asleep. When I wake up, I learn of more people getting evicted from their homes, more houses being burned. The war is as widespread as ever.

CHAPTER 31

FORTY MEN

Due to frequent blackouts, Babi must listen to the news on his battery-powered radio. I wake up to the sound of the news in Albanian—the morning edition. Serbian forces have killed over forty men in Bellacerka. The victims were forced to undress in front of their wives and children, who were then ordered to leave. The women and children heard gunfire but didn't see the executions by firing squad. But no one survives an execution. The women wailed and wept uncontrollably, desperately clutching their bewildered and frightened children.

I wonder what the killers' mind-set was before firing their AK-47s. How did they justify their actions? How could they commit such crimes and then sleep peacefully each night? Apparently killing has become a habit—a routine that doesn't impose any guilt or remorse.

What must the victims have felt, knowing that their gruesome deaths were moments away? Why didn't they resist? I try to picture a scenario in which the forty of them could have rushed and knocked down the five Serbian paramilitary troops assigned to the firing squad. That was certainly a possibility. Yes, the prisoners could have become victors. Before making their escape on foot, they should have bound their foils to trees and beaten them, saying, "You motherfuckers, you were trying to kill us and we did nothing to you. You chose evil and sealed your fate. Did you think we were going to let you kill us without a fight—a fight not only for our lives but for our families?"

Then I think about reports of civilian Kosovar men who were marched before a firing squad and realized that the Serbians were only terrorizing them. Agron, Musa's cousin, was put on the firing line twice but didn't get killed. Guns were raised, an audible count-down began, and then the Serbians started laughing. Perhaps being killed is more merciful than this psychological torture, but Serbian executioners would never intend to be merciful. They are barbarous and proud of it.

Where is God in all this? It has been reported that some vic-tims pray aloud before they are shot. What is their final wish? An instantaneous death? That their wives and children may be spared? That justice may ultimately prevail? Or do they curse God for aban-doning them, their families, and Kosovo? The victims are innocent, devout—yet God permits their murders.

Did those men have time enough to recall their regrets? I often have regrets about things I have said or done. They may have regret-ted something that they did and believed death was their punish-ment. *Why did I not heed the warning before it was too late? I should have just gotten my family and myself out of harm's way as soon as I learned the Serbian forces were near.* Babi says he regrets having stayed in Pristina and not predicting that the war was coming to our city.

I imagine what the sons of those fathers must have felt like when they got separated from them. They must have feared the worst. Did they love their dads as much as I do? Did they know about the occa-sional mock executions and hope their fathers would be spared, like Agron? If Babi had been captured, I would have died by his side. I would have figured out what the Serbians were going to do with Babi, and I would have stayed with him no matter what they said. There would be no reason for me to survive Babi, because the rest of my life would have been intolerable without him.

CHAPTER 32

THE BUNKER

I get up from my sofa and go to the bathroom. At least emptying my bladder provides relief of a sort. When I try to flush and then wash my hands, I notice that the water pressure is lower than ever. Soon we may not have water either.

I go to the kitchen. Mami offers me some bread. The margarine and sugar toppings disgust me, so I tell her plain is fine. The windows of the apartment are covered with blinds and curtains, but the warm temperature inside suggests that the weather is sunny and pleasant. Unfortunately, I can't venture beyond our front door because gunfire can be heard day and night nearby.

I distract myself by thinking about Pruthi, my classmate who moved to America. Lucky kid—he doesn't have to endure this. He is living in a high-rise. I wish I were in America, living in an apartment in one of those elevator buildings. This is how I picture America, full of skyscrapers and big crowded neighborhoods with lots of friends who love to play *futboll* on lush fields in nice parks. Pruthi is able to go outside and be free. He could visit the White House and maybe meet President Bill Clinton. That is one of the first things I would do if I went to America.

Then my thoughts return to Kosovo; I wonder where Musa, Valdet, Fisnik, and Besnik might be. Are my dear cousins alive? I hope they have eluded Serbian forces. I could not live without them;

they have been my best friends my entire life. Labinot and Betim too. Have they dodged all the bullets, bombs, and grenades?

I hear my teenage neighbors talking in front of our building. They are Enis, our next door neighbor, Albert, from the fourth floor, and Besnik and Edanis, the two brothers from the sixth floor. They like me because I always make them laugh. I slip on a pair of blue sandals that we always keep near our apartment door and sneak outside without telling Mami.

It is a warm, gorgeous day, almost like a summer day. Albert and Edanis light their first cigarettes in a while. They never smoke in front of their parents. It feels good to just breathe some fresh air. While Albert and Edanis worry that their dads are going to appear and catch them puffing on cancerous cigarettes, I fear that my mom is going to catch me breathing fresh air.

We don't venture farther than the main front door because we hear guns firing not far from where we are. We are shielded somewhat by the walls of other tall apartment buildings and Mr. Sejda's garden. His roses climb high. Sadly, their heavenly fragrance is overwhelmed by the smell of gunpowder, smoke, and the residue of other explosives.

"What do you think of NATO?" Albert asks everybody.

I consider telling them how I nearly peed in my pants the night of the bombing raid to make them laugh, but I decide against it. I don't want to admit how scared I feel on such nights, but then I find out I am not the only one.

"Man, we should really start spending the nights in the basement, in the bunker," says Albert. "I talked to our old men, and they think it's a good idea too."

Enis looks down at Albert and teases him. "You are scared—is that what you are telling me?"

"Enis, don't be a fool, man," says Albert. "You don't understand the danger we are in. The *t'zi* could break down our doors during the night and massacre us all. Tonight will be our first night in the bunker."

The plan is for all of us to be in there, except the children and "old men," as Albert calls them, starting at eight tonight. Our secret meeting.

An old man walking our way greets us. "Happy Eid," he says.

Oh man—today is the end of Ramadan; I forgot that. We nod at him and shout back all at once, "Same to you." Then he goes into his house across from our apartments.

"How can you even have time to think that today is Eid?" says Albert.

We see Shpetim coming down the steps. "Did you ask Mami to go outside?" he asks.

"I'll go tell her in a minute," I say.

I don't even stay a minute because Mami is going to be livid if I don't go inside now. I leave the boys to explain to Shpetim the plan for tonight at eight.

"Why did you go outside?" Mami yells.

"Mami, it has been a month since I've been outside."

"You should have asked me before you went out. I didn't know where you were. You just disappeared."

"I'm sorry. I'll ask you next time before I go outside."

"Next time, you are going to stay inside," she says.

So I stay inside until eight, cursing the bullets, the people who manufacture bullets, the people who use bullets, the inventor of the bullet, and anyone else who has anything to do with a bullet. It's their fault that I'm trapped in the apartment and have missed a beautiful day outside.

Later, as planned, my friends and I meet at the entrance to the bunker. We enter through the small metal door, which is only about three feet squared. Albert, who proposed the idea that we get in there, holds a candle and tells us to be quiet. The flame flickers and looks as if it is about to die; it could be a symbol of our own fates. I pray the candle will stay lit. Enis's height poses a difficulty for him. He gets his head through the bunker's doorway and then screams when it hits the low ceiling.

"Be quiet, and squirm your way inside," says Albert. There are eight of us young men. Shpetim and I are the youngest. Denis, a Turkish neighbor from the second floor, stands behind me. I'm puzzled as to why he would feel threatened by the *t'zi*, since the Turks and Serbians get along fine. Berat, a college student from the third floor, is next.

When my turn comes, Albert tells me to quickly get inside. The bunker ceiling is so low that I must duck down and walk while bent at the waist. I can't see anyone in the dark, but I can hear voices and Enis's complaining that he can barely move. It smells damp; I stumble into spider webs headfirst. I think of all the cockroaches that we removed when we cleaned this pit. Since spiders are back, the cockroaches must have returned too. I think of the rats and mice; I'm glad it's dark so I don't see them.

We hear a big *boooom*—NATO's first bomb of the night. The Serbian guns, automatics, and antiaircraft missiles follow, and the bunker ceiling vibrates. If the ceiling collapses, we will be buried alive in here like miners trapped underground.

"They can shoot at the NATO plane all night long. It is already gone, fast as lightning," says Edanis. We laugh a little but stop when Albert tells us to shut up. Ironically, bombs are lifesavers, provided they kill people like Milosevic. I hope the NATO pilots know exactly where that genocidal maniac is.

The Serbians still fire at the long-gone NATO plane. Trying to down a NATO plane is like shooting at a running man's shadow. It's futile. They don't realize that.

Albert blows out his candle. "The *t'zi* might be outside and hear our voices," he says. "Keep quiet."

Albert's warning terrifies me. I do as he says. Edanis giggles. He seems tempted to say something funny, but Albert is serious. A gunshot sounds as if it's close by. Then I hear shuffling noises—footsteps, perhaps. I fear that armed *t'zi* are coming toward the bunker door.

Someone in the bunker moves. Another coughs.

"Don't move or make noises because that is freaking me out," says Albert.

"It must have been the rats—or the mice or the cockroaches," I say. Everyone but Albert laughs.

"That is not funny," Albert scolds me. We just slouch in the dark. After the noises from outside cease, we become calmer.

After an interminable silence, Denis the Turk says, "I am getting out of here. I'm going up."

"Go up," I tell him. "You are a Turk anyway. No one is going to touch you."

"Be quiet, Ilir," says Albert.

"If we stay here, they are going to kill our parents, and if they kill our parents, what's the use of us living?" Denis says as he exits.

Enis quickly follows him. "I am about to pass out from claustrophobia," he says.

We are weary of staying inside this cramped, dark hole. Albert is the last one to leave it.

I go up one flight of stairs to the lower level and hear babies crying in Ymer's apartment. The echoes of shootings and bombings are louder here and even more so on the first floor, where our apartment is.

I knock on our door, and Babi opens it, holding a lamp that illuminates his startled face. "What happened? What happened?"

"Nothing happened, we just left the bunker," I tell him and then explain the details. Babi sighs and Mami laughs at him for being scared.

Mami is the bravest. "We have nothing to worry about," she tells us. "We were born once, and we will die once. There should be no room reserved for fear." She makes me think about dying. Death is extinction. There will be no more Ilir forever. No consciousness. No thoughts. No feelings. Nothing. I won't be able to play *futboll* again; I won't even know that I'm dead or what I'm missing. That should comfort me, but it doesn't. An eternity of unawareness. I shudder.

I am just fourteen years old and Mami is forty-nine; she sounds unafraid to die, but I'm not ready. I want to live. The thought of dying is my greatest terror. I sink rapidly into a harrowing depression; it's like drowning in quicksand. Everyone will eventually forget me. I won't ever drink another Coke; I won't ever eat another chocolate or hamburger. I won't spend another summer with Musa ever again.

I approach Mami. She is holding Fjolla. "Mami, whenever I think of dying, I think that I won't exist anymore. Thoughts of not feeling or eating scare me so much that I might lose my mind."

"Dying is a natural part of life, *pllumb*. Everyone experiences it." I don't like her philosophy about something so frightening. Once I thought about dying bravely and honorably alongside my dad. Now I don't feel that dying is a privilege.

"Oh, don't be scared, *pllumb*. Everything is going to be all right."

Another NATO plane arrives and drops tons of explosives on the nearby Serbian military base. The earth shakes; my eardrums pop. The jet passes quickly, leaving a thin whistling sound in its wake. I've never felt my death as close as I do now.

If the bombings end soon, I'll be able to go outside. If I survive the war, things will get much better. There won't be any more *t'zi* on the roads beating us, no more Serbian bullies ruling our *futboll* and basketball fields. Milosevic will be dead; NATO will have killed him. When the war ends, life will bloom again, like Mr. Sejda's garden.

CHAPTER 33

THE BASEMENT

In the morning, I overhear Mami and Babi's conversation. "Why did they have to kill his two sons? They were young and they didn't do anything," says Mami.

"He didn't do anything to them either," says Babi.

I learn that the Serbian forces killed a famous Kosovar human rights lawyer, Bajram Kelmendi, and his two young sons. Mami is crying. "Oh God, oh God, poor sons," she says.

"Mami, why did you say, 'Oh God, oh God'? I thought you didn't believe in God."

"I never quite said that. There is something supernatural out there, whether you call it God or Nature."

I can't rely on God to help me survive the war because Mami taught me that "Nature" is God. I've never understood that concept. How can the air and water be the same as God?

I want to believe that there is a God; from heaven he looks at Earth with eyes so big he can see everybody. I want him to end the war, but I don't even know how to ask him that. How do I talk to God? If I just bow my head and pray aloud, will he hear me? If so, will he grant my requests?

Mami must be right. She is smart and knows better. Mami teaches science. She said, "Oh God, oh God," as an expression of anguish.

She starts to cry again. Her mood darkens. She must be thinking of Uncle Azem. "He used to ask you to massage his leg," she recalls. Her heart is fragile. She will never recover from his passing.

"I know, Mami." Then I try to distract her. "What's there to eat?"

"I haven't had the chance to cook anything because the electricity hasn't come back on," she says, stifling her weeping. "I'll fix you some bread. Do you want sugar or margarine on it?"

The bread is freckled with mold. I take it plain. I am really hungry and have no other choice, even though yesterday I ate bread twice. I eat around the "greenies," as I call them, but the entire slice smells of mold. It's disgusting. Kosovar parents teach their children that if they are given bread that is moldy or stale, they must kiss it three times before throwing it away. I do so and take a glass of water. As scarce as food is, I now understand why we have so much reverence and respect for bread.

I hear the teenage neighbors talking again as they descend the stairs. I want to see them and go outside for a bit. Mami is seated in a corner of the kitchen; she is still crying. When I ask her permission, she protests that it is too dangerous to go out. I promise that we won't step beyond the building's front doors. "Ask your father," she says. Babi is visiting a neighbor upstairs, so I join my friends.

Albert and Edanis are smoking and Enis is plucking leaves out of *muri i gjall* (the "living wall," or hedge) and stripping them vertically with his long fingers. Today is sunny and breezy—another beautiful day—but we still hear guns being fired.

"Hello, Mr. Ilir," they greet me.

"Hello."

They start to mock Albert for being so afraid last night in the bunker.

"Shut up," says Albert. "We should do it again tonight."

Everyone responds with snickering and laughter. No one, including me, wants to be in the dark bunker. Suddenly we hear the rumble of tanks traveling on the main highway.

Albert says, "Didn't you hear them earlier? They have been on the move all morning long. They are transporting some of their artillery to the bus station."

"To the bus station?" Why do that, I wonder.

I glimpse Albert's dad descending the stairs, and I warn the guys, "Mr. Krasniqi is coming." Albert and Edanis flick their cigarettes into the garden and shove their hands in their pockets.

"What are you boys doing out here?" Mr. Krasniqi asks us.

"Nothing. We are just getting some fresh air," says Albert.

"Do you know that snipers are stationed on the roofs of buildings around here?" He makes a circle in the air with his index finger. "Do you know what a sniper does?" We know, but Mr. Krasniqi tells us anyway. "He shoots you dead, right where you are. Get inside," he commands.

We obey and close the double doors after us.

Mami is still in the kitchen, crying. I don't think she realizes that I left the apartment.

Babi enters. With eyes cast downward, he sighs deeply as he sets his radio on the living room table.

At twilight, Babi stops listening to the news and helps Mr. Sejda lock and bar the double doors. Babi returns and locks our apartment door. He checks the door handle twice to make sure that it's secured. I hear no footsteps in the hallways or on the stairs. A tense silence prevails.

A NATO jet zooms directly overhead with a *ppppphhhhhhh-hhiiiiuuu* sound. I press the palms of my hands tightly against my ears but still hear a bomb explode. The impact shakes our apartment building so intensely that I fear the structure might collapse. The large pane of glass on our balcony door shatters. Babi runs to the sunroom, slightly parts the window's curtain, and peeks out.

"NATO has bombed the bus station," he says.

"The bus station?" NATO knew the Serbian tanks and artillery had been moved there earlier in the day. How can the pilots be so accurate at night?

Still, the bus station is nearby, and a miss could destroy our apartment building. I reassure myself that we are safe because these are American and British jets sent by President Bill Clinton and Prime Minister Tony Blair to liberate us. I know better than to doubt them.

I try to help Mami collect the pieces of broken glass that litter the floor, but she motions for me to stay away. It's dark. I'm not wearing slippers, so a shard of glass could cut my feet. Luckily the balcony door is reinforced with a second pane of thick glass, which didn't break.

After she finishes picking up the big pieces, Mami puts them in a large wastebasket and then embraces my crying sister. Suddenly we hear footsteps on the lower level.

Babi places one ear against our door. Have the t'zi come to kill us? They got through the door without our hearing them until now. Too late. What are we going to do? Someone knocks on our door. We are as good as dead now. Albert warned us to hide in the bunker again tonight. Ignoring his advice will cost us our lives. Serbian paramilitary troops—the same ones who probably killed Uncle Azem— have come to call. Arkan has somehow heard me curse him and now has come to kill me and my family. Just shoot us, I silently implore him. Don't inflict torture first. With a bullet to the forehead or heart, death will be instantaneous.

Babi still stands by the door, and we are behind him. He looks through the peephole, but I doubt he can see anything.

"Hysen, open the door. It's Ymer."

We nearly collapse with relief.

Babi opens the door. "You scared us," he says.

"I am sorry, but I have to ask you something. The children and babies of my sister are so hungry. They won't stop crying. Do you have any bread or milk?"

Neighbors crack open their doors and peer out. They sigh and complain, "Ymer, you scared us." We don't have any bread or milk, but Mr. Sejda donates some bread and says he hopes that will satisfy the crying children.

Babi sighs again and says, "All of us are going to spend tomorrow night in the basement."

The following night all of our neighbors, my family, and I are crowded into the basement. NATO targets are so close to us that a bomb might land on our apartment building.

My eyes are adjusting to the darkness, but I am shivering from the cold. Albert holds a gas lamp for illumination. In the basement there are ten small storage rooms—one for every family—but they are filled with old furniture, bicycles, old clothes, and other junk, so we stay in the hallways. Older men and women huddle together with little children and babies. Albert's older brother, Floren, holds his little boy and girl while the mother sits on the dusty floor. The two refugee mothers from Drenice, Ymer's sisters, don't have husbands to hold their children because those men went to Slovenia long ago. Between the two they have eight children, five of whom know how to walk.

The artillery fire intensifies steadily. It so frightens the children and babies that they can't stop crying and screaming. The refugee mothers attempt to calm them.

Mami and other women offer advice. "Give her your breast," one of them says.

"She is too big to breast-feed," replies the mother. "She needs solid food and a warm bed."

"Let me hold her," another lady says.

The hallway is like a nursery without electricity. The babies wail even louder. The men are edgy and order the young mothers, "Make those babies shut up." The young mothers try hard to implement some of the older women's advice to make their children quiet, but it is not working very well. Babies don't understand war.

I can barely move because of all the people. Serbian soldiers could drive a tank through the locked main doors, quickly followed by troops who would gun us down on the spot.

The older children who can walk are quiet but have wrapped their arms around their parents' legs and are asking them, "Why are we in the basement?…Why guns?…Why bombs? …Why is there no food?…Why can't we stay in our apartment?"

The ones who have fathers get answers along the lines of, "Shut up. Don't you understand that we are in a war?"

As I pass Albert, I trip on his foot, and he reminds me that he is holding a gas lamp and he doesn't want to drop it and set all of us on fire.

One of the storage rooms has a broken window through which the cold and smell of explosives seep. I am scared that our voices will be heard, the *t'zi* will throw a hand grenade, and we'll all be blown to bits seconds afterward.

I curse Milosevic. If it weren't for him, children wouldn't weep. We would have food and electricity. No one would be helpless, injured, or dead.

Body counts don't tell the whole story of this holocaust.

The next night we find ourselves in the cold, dark basement again.

I hear the young mothers and other women complain about the war.

"Oh, we have a tragic fate," one of them says. "We have no hope."

"Yes, yes," another one agrees.

"We have been cursed," says a third.

Babi mentions that he heard on the radio that NATO bombed the old post office where the Serbian forces had stored ammunition. He says that NATO is also targeting critical Serbian strategic structures such as gas reservoirs and bridges.

"NATO is tracking them down," Mr. Krasniqi proclaims.

Then Mr. Krasniqi asks, "Did we secure the door tonight?"

"Yes," Babi assures him.

As if a door could stop the *t'zi,* troops or tanks from invading our building. Still, doing something is better than doing nothing.

Five more days pass in our locked apartment building with very little food. Five more nights in the basement, fearful that the *t'zi* will break in and kill us. Five more nights full of dread. Five more nights of babies crying inconsolably. Five more sleepless nights.

CHAPTER 34

VDEKJA ËSHTË MË AFER SE KMISHA E TRUPIT (DEATH IS CLOSER THAN THE SHIRT ON YOUR BODY)

It is April 3. The electricity comes on for a minute, and Mami tells me that she is going to cook some eggs that she got from a neighbor. Babi uses this time to turn on the TV news, and I watch it with him while waiting for breakfast.

Babi flips through the different news channels and stops at an English-speaking one featuring coverage of the war in Kosovo. Kosovar refugees march in long rows. The *t'zi* patrol the perimeters to keep the hostages contained. The people are herded together on a highway beside a mosque, and I recognize it immediately as the street in Pristina where Uncle Hasan lives; that is only a fifteen-minute walk from where we are.

Mami comes to the living room from the kitchen to announce that the eggs are ready, but when she sees the TV she asks, "Are those people in Pris—?"

"Yes, yes," I interrupt her. "They are from the Kodra e Trimave neighborhood, where Uncle Hasan lives."

"*Qkaaa* (Whaaat?)?" she says. "Do you see Hasan and his family?"

"Xheva, let me listen to the news," Babi barks, even though he understands little English.

I sit closer to the TV and scrutinize the faces to see whether Uncle Hasan, his two children, and his wife are among the captives. I see babies, children, and old people, but not Uncle Hasan and his family. Some kids ride on their fathers' shoulders; others are held in their mothers' arms. People carry their belongings in paper or plastic bags. They obey the commands to walk briskly in the prescribed rotation. The *t'zi* hold AK-47s, index fingers against the triggers. I don't want to believe that this is happening. Uncle Hasan and his family must be in one of those rows, but I just can't see them. I think of Jeton and Jeta, the children of Uncle Hasan, being massacred like other children shown on TV. It's a terrible feeling to know that I am helpless to protect them. Jeton is a six-year-old boy who has never taunted the Serbians, and his sister, Jeta, is a pretty two-year-old who doesn't even speak yet, much less say anything insulting to provoke the *t'zi*. I then think of Musa and picture him dead. He would have fought back, but no one can match the lethal power of an AK-47.

The camera records the captured as they arrive at the train station. Babi sits on the edge of the sofa and turns up the volume. The Serbian policemen are pushing them onto trains. Where are they being sent? To a field in the countryside for a mass execution? None of those people will be alive in a couple of hours. My head and heart ache. More of my people are going to die.

The doomed passengers wave to loved ones as the death trains depart.

"Where are they being taken?" asks Mami.

Babi doesn't respond.

I know that the train station is only about a fifteen-minute walk from our apartment. *Oh Zoti im.* Our turn will come soon. We may even be rounded up later today.

I am grateful when the news switches to other stories and relieved when the electricity goes off again. If we're going to get killed, I'd rather not see a preview of it on TV.

I want to eat all of the eggs in the frying pan, but Mami tells me to leave half of them for Shpetim and Fjolla, who have just woken up. I have never enjoyed eggs so much in my life. I quickly eat more than half of them before Shpetim and Fjolla sit at the table.

"Ilir, you ate all the eggs," Shpetim complains. "Mami, Ilir ate all the eggs."

"No, I didn't," I say. "I ate less than half."

"You all be quiet," says Mami.

Even though Mami and Babi have bigger appetites than we do, they eat sparingly. They want us to consume all the available food, and they eat whatever we don't eat, including moldy bread with bland margarine.

In the hallways I hear the voices of Enis and others. I unlock the door and see that they are going outside. I am a little surprised because this is the first time they have gone out since Mr. Krasniqi demanded that we stay indoors.

Knowing that people in Pristina are being hauled out of town in trains, I am too afraid to go outside now. I don't want to be sent away, and my friends don't want to either. They probably haven't seen the news. Their dads don't watch as much TV as mine. I retreat into the living room and stay with Babi. He is scanning the radio channels for more news. Even though the radio and TV are the sources that keep us best informed about the war, I can't endure much of those horror stories. I want something pleasant in my life once in a while.

I hear footsteps approach the entrance downstairs.

"Babi, I think someone is coming."

He puts the radio aside, jumps up, and says, "Who is it?" I think of Enis, Albert, and Edanis being outside and remember that there are Serbian snipers on top of buildings. Perhaps my friends have been shot. They might have been chased by the *t'zi*. The footsteps stop at our apartment door; the doorknob is turned. This is the end. The *t'zi* are here. We will be taken to the train station and then shunted to our deaths. I never expected that my fourteenth year was going to be my last.

Instead of a Serbian policeman, Enis's somber face appears.

"Oh, Mr. Hysen! They are here and want us to leave!" says Enis.

Enis runs to tell others before we get the chance to ask who "they" are. Soon everyone in the apartment is informed. I follow Babi outside. People from the entire neighborhood have gathered on the street.

I notice two SUVs with tinted windows. I have never seen them until now. The vehicles are painted in camouflage, but the paint job isn't done right because you can see the manufacturer's red paint underneath. Babi stays in front of me. Neighbors stare at three men who exit the SUVs. They wear camouflage uniforms, but the sleeves and pants are cut short. Two of them wear black caps and their faces are painted. The third wears a ski mask. They hold AK-47s and point them at us. These must be paramilitary troops hired by the Serbian government to torture and kill civilians. Two Serbian policemen compound the threat. I am sure they want us to go to the train station.

A neighbor who lives in a nearby building whispers to my father. "Hysen, they want us to leave in five minutes."

A bald Serbian neighbor of ours named Boshko appears. He wears a black leather coat and jeans with a handgun tucked inside his waistband. The paramilitary troops and the *t'zi* refer to him as "boss."

Apparently Boshko is a leader of paramilitary troops. Babi and others beg him to let us stay.

"Hey, neighbor," says one man in the crowd.

"Hey, Boshko," says another.

Boshko looks toward us. "Yes?" he says.

"Would you persuade them not to evict us?"

"Please, Boshko," pleads Babi.

"Tell them we are your neighbors. Please save us, Boshko."

"You must leave," says Boshko.

"Oh, come on," says Babi. "We beg you."

"Please, please," says another neighbor.

"We won't ask you for another favor again."

"If you stay here, your safety will not be guaranteed," replies Boshko.

The two *t'zi* come to Boshko and say, "Hey, boss, is everything all right?"

Before Boshko replies, one of the *t'zi* shouts, "Get out of here. You have five minutes to get ready."

The crowd disperses immediately. People run back to their apartments to pack. Babi and I are running back too. Mr. Vehbi, my former music teacher who lives in our building, comes to our apartment and asks us what is going on.

I look back one more time and notice two men on top of the building across from ours. One is standing and smoking a cigarette, and the other is pointing a rifle in our direction. Mr. Krasniqi was right to order us to stay inside; Enis, Albert, and I could have been shot standing outside of our apartment building.

When we tell Mami, she screams, "*Qkaaaaa*? In five minutes?" I stand in the middle of the living room, not knowing what to do first. I watch Babi take a big framed family picture from an armoire drawer. It is the portrait of my brother and me when we were little, before Fjolla was born. He always loved that picture. He wants to save it as a record of our existence. We are going to be taken to Serbia and murdered.

"Get some clothes that you might need," says Babi. I choose a pair of black corduroy pants from the closet. Babi snatches them out of my hand and puts them in a duffel bag. I feel dizzy and let Mami pick out all the other clothing for me. It must have been over three minutes since we were ordered to leave. Why worry about pictures, clothing, or anything, given what will happen to us? We won't live long enough for it to matter.

From our open door I see Mr. Sejda and his family exit. I run to the hallway but don't want to go any farther by myself. Mami and Babi are not taking the deadline as seriously as I am. But why rush to accommodate my assassin? I don't know whether the three masked men or the *t'zi* are going to shoot me, but one of them will. I will see the bullet coming toward me. It is going to travel so fast that I won't have time to evade it.

I think of an Albanian proverb taught in school: *Vdekja eshtë më afer se kmisha e trupit* (Death is closer than the shirt on your body). Now I understand its full meaning. My death is imminent. To the Serbian troops and the *t'zi*, it's all in a day's work. I hope they kill me before severing my arms and legs and tossing them to their hungry dogs—kill me before gouging out my eyes, slicing off each ear, and mutilating my privates.

Neighbors from upstairs are hurrying down the stairs. What is taking my family so long? Mami carries a bag of clothes and is coming toward the door. Fjolla and Shpetim follow her, stark terror etched in their faces. Babi carries another bag. We leave behind all other possessions.

Mami bites her lower lip so hard it bleeds. We are all in the hallway and watch Babi close the door to our apartment.

All of our neighbors have gathered near the building, just outside the double doors. Some hold back their tears while others weep; Ymer's wife fears the worst because he hasn't returned from an errand. He had gone to collect his wages. Babi advises her to leave with the rest of us, assuring her that Ymer will join us later. But she doesn't want to leave.

"Let's hurry and get into the car," says Babi. I thought we were going by train.

I see other neighbors with their car keys in hand. The plan for those who have cars is to leave Kosovo and cross the border into Macedonia. Those without vehicles must go to the train station. Only half of the families own cars. Now we say good-bye to the ones who don't. "I hope that we will see each other again." It's like expressing condolences to friends before they die.

Mr. Vehbi, my music teacher, sobs. In school, he was the one who made students cry by slapping the palms of our hands with a wooden ruler, but now he is crying as much as we did then. Shpetim is breaking down too. I refuse to cry, for that will only make the situation worse and increase our chances of angering the masked men.

Finally, Ymer's wife decides to leave, although reluctantly. The families without cars separate from us and head to the train station. Everyone is leaving Kosovo except Mr. and Mrs. Krasniqi. Mr. Krasniqi has a sister who is protected by her Serbian neighbors, so he and his wife are going to her house. My sister, Fjolla, says good-bye to her best friend, a girl also named Fjolla, whose family doesn't have a car. They used to skip rope together after school. Now they hug each other and cry. The masked men and the *t'zi* order all pedestrians to stand in rows, and then their walk to the train station begins.

Three neighbors' cars are in front of us; one is behind us. Fjolla, Shpetim, and I sit in the back seat of Babi's Opel Ascona. Directly in front of us are Mr. Sejda and his family, and behind us is Mr. Vokshi with his wife. We feel sad about our neighbors who are now forced to travel by train. I have known them all my life. I especially feel bad for Mrs. Mejrem's family. Her sons, Besnik and Edanis, have always been pals of mine. Surely they are going to Serbia. I won't see them again. I wish we had enough room in our car for them. Babi offered Besnik a ride, but he wanted to stay with his family until the end.

Babi starts the car, and we begin our journey to the Macedonian border. I look back at our apartment. For two months I felt incarcerated there. Now I miss it already.

Traffic on the main highway is unusually light. It is a clear and beautiful day, free of rain or fog or snow, yet we encounter few cars. I'm surprised. This highway is always heavily traveled. I expected an exodus of cars traveling bumper-to-bumper.

We feel isolated, so we follow each other closely. The calm is scary. I sense a trap and expect the worst—a roadside bomb, sniper fire, grenades. Gunfire erupts in all directions, but we don't see the source. We don't say anything to one another, as though we are on the way to another funeral.

We slump in our seats but still peek out the windows. Babi drives slowly and shifts his eyes constantly. He checks the rearview and side mirrors often. Thus far, we have traveled several miles without getting stopped by the *t'zi* or Serbian troops, but they will appear soon. Refugees are a favorite target of theirs.

Smoke drifts across the road. There are houses burning on either side. Even in our car we feel the heat of the flames and smell the acrid smoke. The sides of houses still standing are riddled with bullet holes. I've seen the same images on TV. We pass a three-story house that resembles our summer home. Has our village been looted and burned too? We soon pass by another village that has been torched.

Two tanks and a military truck, each bearing the Serbian flag, are heading straight toward us. Babi and the rest of the cars in our convoy slow a little, but the tanks are roaring toward us at high speed. The gunners are in position. They are going to run us off the road and then murder us. Babi pulls the car over and slows down more. We have nowhere to hide. I glance at Fjolla and Shpetim, whose eyes are wide with despair. We are about to pay the ultimate price for freedom, even though we are civilians.

Mami looks at us and whispers, "They are just passing. It's all right." I question Mami's optimism. How could she know?

I look at Babi's face reflected in the rearview mirror. His face is ashen. If the troops are just passing and everything is all right, as Mami says, why does Babi look so pale and scared?

The first tank passes us with a deafening roar. The second tank and the military truck zip past us too, and we are still alive. I thought for sure that our car would be blown up. I gasp and feel lucky to still be breathing.

Babi and the neighbors get back on the highway and resume the same slow speed. I stare ahead and never look back. They might turn around and pursue us. It's a long while before I relax enough to believe that is not the case.

After traveling several more miles, we see a checkpoint ahead. Four *t'zi* are stationed there with their guns and batons at the ready. Serbian forces must be patrolling the route to the Macedonian border. We should never have attempted our escape by car. Initially I thought it was a good idea, but I didn't take into account the tanks and checkpoints on the way. I sense that something far worse than a fire or a beating awaits us.

The three neighbors' cars pass right through. I wait for the *t'zi* to stop us, but we are allowed to pass. They direct Babi and the others to take the longer route to Macedonia. That highway winds through more mountains, and the border crossing will lead to Tetova instead of the capital, Skopje.

Once the narrow road ascends the steep terrain, there are no guardrails along the edges of the cliffs. We spiral up more mountains. Tall trees cast dark shadows on the road. I break a sweat. Paramilitary troops may lurk at the edge of the forest and ambush us. If Serbian military vehicles run us off the road, we will plummet to our deaths. Our bodies will never be discovered. No one back home will ever know what has happened to us.

Ahead is a tunnel. I shut my eyes. Then we encounter a bridge. A stream flows beneath it. I am thirsty and yearn to drink cold, refreshing mountain water. The road continues to snake uphill. The altitude begins to bother me; I feel dizzy; my eardrums throb. Near here is Lubeten, one of the highest points in Kosovo, 7,500 feet above sea level. I don't know, of course, that as we ride there are Kosovar mothers with babies and little children climbing barefoot around the peak on a two-foot-wide snowy trail. They could easily slip and fall down the mountain before reaching the other side and the Macedonian border.

CHAPTER 35

MOUNTAINS

After an hour and a half of being alone on the road, we see other cars going in the same direction as we are. This is a relief. I am happy to share the fear with other people now. As time passes, we notice even more cars, so I am not scared at all. Now there are even cars behind us. There are so many cars that all traffic stops, and we exit for a moment to breathe the fresh mountain air.

After our short break, we rejoin the line of cars, which moves slowly now. We don't understand the cause for the delay until we see a slow tractor ahead, pulling a wagon. Crowded onto the wagon are women, children, and elderly people. They appear to be cold. Poor people. They make me feel grateful to be inside a warm car. Soon afterward, we pass another tractor with the same pitiful human cargo—Kosovar refugees.

I try to think positively. Soon we are going to cross the Macedonian border and will be free from the bombings and shootings. We are going to get out of Kosovo and leave the war behind. We are going to be safe. There will be plenty of food and water and nothing to worry about. Macedonia's population is approximately 30 percent Albanian. I will become friends with some of them, and we'll play *futboll* all day long. I can put behind me everything that has happened recently. I can forget about the Serbian forces, and I won't have to be so scared anymore.

Suddenly all vehicles stop. Perhaps there is an accident ahead, but news about the delay soon reaches us: Traffic can't proceed because there is a seven-mile queue between where we are and Macedonia. That means thousands of cars and hundreds of tractors are waiting their turn to cross the border before us.

Babi turns on the radio for the first time. During the whole trip he has been alert and observant, but now he sits back a little and turns the dial, trying to find some news. Since we are stuck here, I get out and stretch. The air up here is much colder. I see mountain after mountain. A tall mountain gives shade to a shorter one. All the mountains are blanketed with trees—trees of all kinds, many unfamiliar to me. They are quite varied in appearance: tall, short, wide, narrow, deciduous, and evergreen, with leaves of all shapes. I don't see fruit trees, which is a shame.

Albert and Enis are also standing by the road. Albert looks much happier and speaks much more casually, not just telling us to shut up and stay quiet.

Enis, Albert, and I inform the motorists behind our cars that they might as well get out and stretch because the line may not move for quite a while. There are children and babies in cars who cry and scream. Some refugees decide to move their vehicles into the left lane and pass the line so they can reach the border more quickly.

This continues until a Serbian military truck with six soldiers seated on two side benches in the back moves into the left lane. The soldiers make stern faces while holding their AK-47s, so drivers quickly make room for them. The military truck moves freely in the left lane and goes in the direction of Kosovo, where the soldiers might torture and kill people.

When it gets dark, NATO continues its usual air raids. We can also hear the Serbian gunshots and antiaircraft missiles. I hear multiple bomb explosions, one after another, with the last one being the loudest: *booom, boooooom.* The bombs and the gunshots sound as if they are very close to us.

It is really cold and no one seems to be sleeping. To save gas, instead of starting the engine every time the line moves a bit, we keep the car in neutral, get outside, and push it. We are all tired and want to sleep, but there is not enough room in the back seat for my siblings and me to get comfortable and rest.

"How long are we going to be here, Mami?" asks Fjolla.

Mami tells her she doesn't know. She tries to cover my sister and me with a jacket. Shpetim drapes his legs across the two of us and seems to be sleeping.

"Don't put your stinky feet in our noses," we yell.

Fjolla leans her head on my shoulder, and pretty soon Babi and I are the only ones awake. Babi tries to find a radio station that broadcasts news. He also pays close attention to any forward movement of the line.

At midnight, the line halts. As I close my eyes to doze, I feel Fjolla's head quickly rise from my shoulder. She starts screaming, "Look, look, look! Watch out! Get out of the way!" Then she screams even louder. "Watch out! Look, look! Get out of the way!"

Everyone wakes up.

"What? There's nothing. We are all right," I tell her.

"Get out of the way, get out of the way," she says. She doesn't believe that there is nothing outside. "Help me, help me," she says.

Mami shakes her a little and puts her hand on her cheek. Fjolla barely opens her eyes.

"You are all right, *pllumb*. You are all right. Everything is fine," says Mami.

Mami trades places with Shpetim so she can be closer to Fjolla. She embraces her and repeats that everything is all right. Fjolla begins to calm down. Babi offers a bottle of water to her. She takes a drink and finally realizes that we are no longer in our neighborhood; we are no longer in our apartment; we are in the mountains.

Most drivers are asleep now because the line of cars still hasn't moved. On the roadside, however, a lot of people chat with one another and smoke cigarettes. Their sad faces are made visible by the headlights of cars behind them. Judging from their expressions, they seem to be wondering how all this happened. *How did we end up here? What is going on? Why does everything seem to be happening so fast? Why do we deserve to be forced out of our homes? How does a minority displace the majority population from its homeland?*

I can't sleep in the back seat. I can't stretch out my body as I did on the floor or sofa in our apartment. How are five people supposed to sleep in one car? I am exhausted. My eyes and head hurt. I wish for nothing more than a warm bed. There isn't a worse feeling than being exhausted but unable to sleep. My stomach growls—another reason for my insomnia.

Mami is awake, and Babi is constantly shifting his body, trying to get comfortable. I am not surprised my mother isn't asleep. Since Uncle Azem died, every little sound startles her. At least she doesn't mutter to herself anymore.

I open the door slowly and go to pee; one must be careful where to use the bathroom. One risks falling off a cliff, especially at night. I only go where no one will see me, especially if it's daytime. The elderly who can't walk have no choice but to wet and soil their pants.

When I get into the back seat again, I fall asleep, but only for about six minutes. The seat is too hard, and my feet are numb. I doze again, waking up after a short while. It takes a few seconds to remember where I am and how I got here.

By morning, my back feels as if it is broken. I am shivering, and my fatigue is worse than last night. The newest worst feeling in the world is to wake up feeling cold with severe back pain.

"Good morning," says Mami.

"Good morning," I say. I notice that the line has moved a little. "Is there anything to eat, Mami?" I ask.

Mami opens a plastic bag and takes out a loaf of bread. She divides the loaf of bread into three equal parts for my siblings and me. After eating my portion, I feel even hungrier.

I get out to stretch and observe what is going on. Many people are outside. Our neighbors and Babi are chatting with one another. I see Enis, Shpetim, and Albert.

"Hey, Mr. Ilir," they greet me.

I yawn. "What you doing?"

"You want to come with us down to the border?" says Albert.

"Sure," I say.

We head toward the border, walking along the left lane and on the lookout for any Serbian military vehicles. Enis complains of not sleeping because he can't get his tall body comfortable in the car. At home he has an extra-long bed, and he can barely get comfortable on that.

We stride past a lot of cars and overhear conversations among people outside. They use gestures to emphasize to one another how the Serbians invaded their homes or how they heard the enemy coming and quickly fled by car, tractor, or bus. Some things they describe are terrifying, so I try not to pay attention. Still, I can't help but overhear some horror stories.

A dark-skinned man whose eyes are red from crying tells how his father refused to leave the house despite the family's attempts to remove him by force. "He told me, 'I was born here, and I am going to die here,'" says the son. "So I left him. He wouldn't leave. He wouldn't. I left his fate to the mercy of the Serbian forces. He's probably dead."

Many people stare at us—most likely because they have never seen anyone as tall as Enis. He says hello to them, and we keep walking.

After about twenty minutes, we see a village, its houses burned, on the left side of the road. Black ashes cover the caved-in walls and collapsed rooms. In the yards, refugees are filling containers with water, and some women are hand-washing clothes.

My eyes shift to a girl in front of me. I recognize her from my little cousin's birthday party. Her name is Pranvera, and I used to have a crush on her. Now I don't even consider speaking to her. She doesn't acknowledge me either.

A white Russian-manufactured NIVA sport utility vehicle full of *t'zi* comes toward us. I forget about Pranvera. We jump over the guardrail and crouch as low as possible. The *t'zi* driver keeps his hand on the horn and zooms by us, not bothering to take precautions for the children and other people who are in his way.

We resume walking but don't see the border. We stop and talk to a group of people.

"How long have you all been waiting here?" asks Albert.

"Three days," they tell us.

We walk a little more and then see a boy my age whose blond hair sticks straight up. He is carrying a loaf of bread and a brown lunch box.

"Hey, kid, where did you get that?" we all ask. "Hey, kid, could you share that?"

"No," he says. "You can get your own food at the border. They are giving out a bunch of bread and lunch boxes." Shpetim, Albert, Enis, and I start running toward the border. Others follow us.

When we reach the border we notice three teenagers who wear white vests with red crosses on the front. They carry cartons filled with lunch boxes. Approximately one hundred people are crowded around each of the three teenagers. They push, shove, and reach frantically for food.

We don't get a box. None are left.

I learn that there are over 2,000 people trying to cross the border on foot. The Serbian border patrolmen rarely allow anyone to get through. People wave their passports in the patrolmen's faces, but most pleas are ignored.

When the humanitarian workers return from the other side of the border, we start running toward them, surrounding them like a pack of wolves circling their prey. Then I and other kids my age scream because we are being pushed aside by adults. I almost fall because they shove me off balance. A humanitarian worker gets frustrated with the rowdiness and says, "We are going to bring food for everyone. Calm down. Quit pushing, quit pushing!"

He hands out more lunch boxes, but I don't get one. It's useless competing with grown men, but Enis and Shpetim succeed. The box itself, inscribed with pretty foreign lettering, looks inviting. I can't wait to see what kinds of foods are inside.

As we walk to our cars, people ask us where we got our lunch boxes. A short man starts begging Enis, "Could you give me one of your boxes?"

"No, I really can't," says Enis, "but they have plenty of them at the border." That's a lie. The poor man will probably get pushed around as I did and not get anything.

"Look, I have four kids, and they have not eaten in two days. Not one thing," he says. We look toward the back of his car and see the sad faces of two little girls and two boys. "*Të lutna, të lutna,*" the father begs. "I can't leave them by themselves. I have to stay with them. My wife went to get some water."

Enis hands one of his boxes to him, and the man thanks and hugs Enis.

When we reach our car, I see that the line has moved forward a short distance. The burned village is in sight.

Mami is very happy we have brought food, since that is her biggest concern.

It is almost two o'clock; my family is hungry. We wait impatiently to see what is in the box that Shpetim got. There is not much inside. Each of us could eat everything in at least two of them. We must share the contents of this one box. Shpetim pulls out a pouch of rice soup, peanut butter and crackers, and a fruit bar. Mami and Babi want us to eat all these things, saying they are not hungry. But they must be.

Shpetim, Fjolla, and I sit on the back seat of our car and prepare the meal. We argue about who gets the seemingly bigger portion.

On the left side of the road are two civilian cars passing slowly. We find out that the people in the second car are mourning the death of an elderly woman whose corpse is on the back seat of the first car. They bury her on the side of the road. At least she is resting in peace and doesn't have to worry about making it through another miserable day.

Ever since we returned from the border, the caravan of vehicles has slowed down drastically. I doubt there is enough room for all us refugees in Macedonia.

Babi thinks differently. "There is plenty of room," he says, "but Macedonians fear that we are going to enter their country and never return to Kosovo. They think Milosevic will never let us return, and they are probably right."

The night turns bitterly cold, and we are still far from the border. It is below freezing. People are trying to start campfires. Three cars behind us, a man with glassy blue eyes can't gather enough fuel to keep his fire going longer than five minutes. With help from the people around, we gather more paper and tree branches to keep it going for another thirty minutes.

"How long are we going to be here?" Fjolla asks again.

No one answers. The Serbian and Macedonian border patrol admitted fewer cars today than yesterday, and we are still several miles from the border. It may take us two or three weeks, but I refuse to tell Fjolla that.

I hear there are wolves, snakes, and bears that inhabit these vast mountains. When I have to pee, I don't venture far.

Finally, dawn breaks. I thought it would never come. However, the morning did not come for another old lady who died during the night. She is buried on the side of the road near the grave of the other lady.

This is our third day waiting to cross the border, but it feels as if we have been stuck here for weeks. The weather is rainy, but I have to trek to the border to get more food. I go by myself and decide to be aggressive and push this time, just like the adults. If someone pushes me like the last time, I am going to raise my voice and protest, "You jerk, stop pushing me. I need to get food as much as you do."

Along the way, I think that on a rainy day like this there won't be a lot of people waiting, but when I get there I see that I was wrong. Crowds gather around every humanitarian worker handing out food. I notice that the Serbian and Macedonian border patrolmen are slowly admitting people on foot. In addition to the UNHCR and UNICEF lunch boxes, the aid workers are distributing loaves of bread. Thanks to my determination, I end up with a loaf of bread and a lunch box in my hands. I start back with a grin on my face.

Walking back to our car, I see hardship that I'll never forget—women and children sitting on uncovered wagons, most of them crying because they are drenched by the cold, steady rain. Strangers try to shelter them by raising and securing a plastic cover over the wagon, but the wind and the rain knock it down. They must be hungry too. I pass them, my head bowed. I conceal my food, feeling guilty. They don't have their husbands and fathers to get food for them.

I put the food in the car and then fill a two-liter bottle with water at the spigot of a destroyed house in the village. I have to wait in line for water just as I did for food. There are greedy men who push me back, but after an hour of struggling, I succeed. By the time I fill my bottle, our car has advanced to a spot across from the water source. Babi is so thirsty he grabs the bottle out of my hand and starts drinking from it.

I get in the car and stay inside because it is cold. The rest of the day, I nap.

The Serbian troops force us from our house and take us to an open field. A man wearing civilian clothes and a mask places a pistol in my hand and orders me to shoot my father in his right temple.

"If you don't pull the trigger, I will kill the rest of your family," he says. I close my eyes and turn my head to one side, but I can't pull the trigger to kill my father.

The man slaps me and says, "I'll do it myself."

To avoid seeing my father get shot, I start running. My legs move, yet I remain stationary. I try harder to sprint forward but remain in the same place. I try again and finally move forward before I hear the gunshot.

I wake trembling and sweating. I find Mami holding my hand.

"Are you all right, Ilir?" she asks. "What happened?"

"I had a scary dream," I say.

"You're safe, *pllumb*. Don't worry. Go back to sleep." I refuse to go back to sleep without drinking some water first. The nightmare makes me feel lucky that Babi is still alive and we are all together.

The next morning we receive good and bad news. The good is that the line has moved some more, and the bad is that Enis and Albert have crossed the border on foot. They had their passports and went ahead. I hope we'll be reunited one day.

When I go to the border for food, I see men who are renting their private cell phones to others. I desperately wish for a conversation with my cousins, hoping to learn they are still alive, but I don't have any money. And how could I contact my cousins, since I don't know where they are? If I could talk to them, though, all I would want to hear is the first word that you say when you answer the phone, "Hello." Just one simple word. That would convince me they are all right. Their voices are locked in my heart.

I feel like screaming their names. Maybe the mountains would echo my voice to wherever they are. I want to cry out, "Musaaaaa," and wait for the sound to travel to his ears, then hear him call my name in response. I would be so happy to hear that my cousins are alive. If they have been murdered, I will be as good as dead. As close as I am to them, life will not be the same.

I join a conversation between Mr. Sejda and Babi. They're discussing the latest news heard on the radio.

"The NATO bombing," says Mr. Sejda, "will continue until Milosevic has signed a peace agreement with the NATO commanders."

"I know," says Babi.

"I don't think he will ever sign it," says Mr. Sejda.

"Probably not."

"Hey, Sejdo," continues Babi. "Did you hear that one of my friends got killed the day we left our houses?"

This is the first I've heard about it.

"No," says Mr. Sejda. "Are you serious? Which one?"

"His name was Afrim Loxha. The police shot him near the post office. Left three kids. He was a good man," says Babi.

"Are you sure, Hysen? Who told you?"

"Yes, Sejdo'. *Të lutna*. I talked to some people in line here who knew him. Who would lie about such a thing?"

"Poor children. They will live without their father now," says Mr. Sejda.

"I was devastated when I heard it," continues Babi. "I've known him since 'sixty-two. Went to high school together. His wife was a doctor. After they kicked him out of work, he opened up a bar in Kurriz."

Wait a second. Kurriz is the name of the underground strip mall where I used to sell cigarettes. I think I know this person.

"Babi, wasn't he tall and blond? I may have sold cigarettes in his bar."

"That's him."

What a small, sad world. He was a nice man. He always let me sell cigarettes in his bar. Now people won't ever be able to go to his place again. People used to go there to relax, probably trying to ease their anger toward Milosevic.

I sit near a campfire in the lot where a coffee shop once stood. Now the shop is completely abandoned. People are gathered around the flames, cooking potatoes. They tell us that they found the potatoes in vacant village houses. Shpetim and I immediately run there. We are overjoyed when we find some. We cook them in the fire and gobble them down. They are the only hearty food we've had in a couple of months.

As the night progresses, Serbian military troops in trucks pass our cars. By now I am a little more adjusted to their appearances, but they still make me angry. They know that they have reached their goal of evicting us from our homes and still they aren't satisfied. It's not enough that we lack food, water, and bathrooms. They want to inflict more misery. I know they could easily execute all of us just for being in their path.

Through all our years of hardship, I never thought that one day it would be difficult to leave our own country.

CHAPTER 36

HOSTAGES

Two mornings later, I wake up to terrifying information: Serbian forces are going to move their tanks and other heavy artillery from military bases to the left lane of the road, beside our cars.

We are going to be used as human shields now. We are going to be killed by the precise NATO bombs, which follow the Serbian tanks and artillery. Our own heroes, the NATO pilots, are going to kill us.

Both the Serbian and the Macedonian borders are closed. No pedestrians or vehicles are allowed to cross. This only compounds the problem and kills our hopes of at least getting over the border to escape the bombs. Worse, more military troops are patrolling the line of cars. Babi and the neighbors meet, but they do not decide anything. We have two options, neither of which will take us to safety. One option is to go back to our apartment, which is to say, go back to the *t'zi* and paramilitary troops who ordered us not to return. The other option is to stay here and wait for NATO to bomb us. Mr. Sejda suggests that we return to our apartments, but I think the Serbian forces in Pristina will be eager to have us back. That would give them a reason to kill us. Thankfully, Babi agrees with me. By going back home, he says, we will simply hand ourselves over to them.

Time passes slowly. We are hyperalert. We watch every little move the military trucks make. The troops say nothing. They let their presence be menacing.

In the end, we decide to stay put. If we go back, we are dead for sure, but if we stay, there is a chance that the NATO pilots will see us and not bomb. Some people climb the hills to escape into the forest. I consider doing the same, but I don't want the resident wolves and bears to eat me.

It is almost five o'clock in the afternoon, and we expect the flow of tanks and other military vehicles to appear any minute now. The news has spread. Some people have decided to risk returning to Kosovo. The heads of the households face a horrible dilemma. They don't know how to save their families. Their unshaven faces convey feelings of despair and helplessness.

Now it is dark. They could be here at any minute. We wait for their chains to thunder down the left side of the road. Presently we hear gunfire and NATO bombs.

No one even suggests lighting a fire outside to get warm; we all want to hide inside our cars, as if somehow that will save us. As Babi turns the dial on the radio, he finds a station playing soothing Italian music. After the song, the host of the show gives a commentary. Since the Italian and Albanian languages have some words in common, I can understand some of what he says. Whenever a listener calls, the host says, "*Bravooo.*" They often laugh and tell jokes.

It occurs to me that Italians—and most other people in the world—don't have the worries we do. They might be out partying and having a good time or sleeping comfortably in their beds, but they don't have to worry about tanks coming next to their houses or bombs being dropped on their cars. They don't have to worry about starvation, the cold, wolves, thirst, snakes, claustrophobia, or bears. I wonder whether they know what is happening to us. Would they even care? I desperately wish I were in Italy so I could laugh and celebrate life.

Our anxiety is so high that we almost pee on ourselves, yet the tanks still haven't come. I get little sleep during the night. The next morning the sun is brighter than on preceding days, but the wind is blowing and chilling the air. Even though the view to the left of our car is of the sorrowful torched village, we feel relief that it is not of the Serbian tanks. We are safe for another day.

Later, Shpetim and I go to the border and see the patrolmen maintaining tight security. The humanitarian workers are still handing out loaves of bread and lunch boxes. Fewer people are clamoring for food. Maybe fear has kept them away despite their hunger. After waiting less than fifteen minutes, Shpetim and I get two lunch boxes each.

When we get back, Babi tells us that Milosevic has made an agreement with NATO commanders. People have heard on the radio that now it is safe to go back to our homes. This is almost too good to be true. Mr. Sejda is happy, but Mami seems skeptical. There are about one hundred cars and some buses and tractors in front of us. Mami suggests that it might be wiser to wait and see whether the border might reopen. I doubt the Serbian forces will be willing to withdraw from Kosovo.

The news spreads up and down the line, and men whom we have never seen before come and ask us what we think about the news. We see some cars going back, so there are obviously people who really believe it is safe to return. A man comes running toward us and says, "Milosevic is defeated and has surrendered to NATO."

"We should not have to wait here any longer," says Mr. Sejda.

Babi agrees. We will see for ourselves just how safe it is to be home.

CHAPTER 37

THREE MASKED MEN

It is slightly past noon and the day is beautiful, sunny and windy. Babi looks to the left side of the road to see whether there are any Serbian trucks or military vehicles coming, and turns our car around to follow Mr. Sejda home.

In a way, I am glad we are going home because I am tired of waiting in this never-ending line. I am tired of scrunching my body into the back seat to sleep. I am tired of being cold all night, and I am tired of having to use the bathroom in places where everyone can see me. I am tired of the nasty smell of my hands and my whole body. In our apartment, at least we won't be scared of having tanks park right beside us.

There is still a long convoy of cars, tractors, and coach buses on the other side of the road waiting to cross the border. Those people must not have heard that it is safe to return home. Maybe it will take a while for the news to work its way from the beginning of the line to the end of it.

Our cars are back on the snaky mountain roads. Only a few vehicles are ahead and behind us. Babi drives slowly and we stay quiet. We reach a mountain village but don't see anyone in it. Shpetim, Fjolla, and I are in the back seat. Our car turns sharply to the left and our bodies are thrown hard to the right. My head hits the window.

I stay wide awake, even though I have not had a good night's sleep in a couple of months now. Because the roads curve sharply uphill and downhill, we can't see what is coming ahead of us. A tank. A Serbian truck. A roadblock. Now that we have been on the road for a little, there are no cars behind us.

Mr. Sejda drives slowly, even when the mountain roads end. I'd rather not go this slowly. I want to tell Babi to pass Mr. Sejda and start going one hundred miles per hour so if someone is about to shoot us or stop us we will whiz right past him like a NATO jet. I have wanted Babi to drive faster than he does all my life, never mind now that we are probably still at war.

Once off the mountain roads, we pass the burned villages. Some houses are still burning. I turn and look through the back window. The flames are being fanned by the wind. The roofs are releasing smoke and fire into the blue sky. If the war has ended, why are these houses still burning?

In one yard, a dead cow lies on its side. I say, "Oh, look at that cow," and everyone turns to look. The poor animal still has its eyes open. Blood is dripping out of its mouth. The war can't be over.

After the dead cow, we see a broken tank, just lying on the side of the street. We don't see anyone around it, but I am afraid that a middleman is going to pop up and shoot us.

"Why is Mr. Sejda driving so slowly?" I finally summon the courage to ask.

Babi doesn't answer me.

I hate Mr. Sejda for driving so slowly. I hate Babi for not passing him and not answering my question. I hate the Serbian forces for trying to kill us. I hate Slobo for starting this war in the first place. Burning houses, a broken tank, dead animals—what is next?

We are almost home, but soon hear the sound of automatic weapons in the distance: *trr, trr, trr, trr*. I am beside myself. I want something to happen now. I want one of those bullets to hit and kill me. I can't stand being terrified anymore. I want all of this to end. I thought the war was over. Why the *trr, trrs*? We should have known better. We should have known Milosevic would never surrender.

I can hear the city siren, screaming like the sirens of the Serbian police cars, only slower. If it is safe to be back here, why is the city siren blaring? Why are there no cars on the street? Why are we the only ones to have returned?

Babi parks beside our apartment, and we exit the car quickly. No one else is in sight. None of our neighbors are here. They might not even be alive. I expected to see at least Mr. Krasniqi, since he stayed in the city after we left.

Hearing the distant shots and the city siren, I feel unsafe. The silence in our neighborhood is unnerving. We start to run into our apartment building. The last thing we want is to be shot by one of the snipers.

As we are about to enter our apartment, I turn my head to check the place where the two Serbian SUVs and the paramilitary troops were stationed when they kicked us out, but the only thing I see is a Serbian lady walking back to her apartment across from ours. I raise my head and look at the top of the building where I had seen the two snipers. They are not there. I sigh with relief.

Once we enter our building, Babi and Mr. Sejda lock the main double door and place the big metal bar across it.

Mami turns the knob of our apartment door to discover that it is still locked. Babi comes with the key and opens the door. Mr. Sejda and Mrs. Kaqa enter their apartments. There is no electricity. The water level is low, but sufficient for me to wash my hands with soap. Thank God for the soap. Above the sink I see my reflection in the bathroom mirror. I look ugly. My face is bony, and my black hair has gotten thick and coarse, with cowlicks pointing in various directions. I feel like putting my whole head under the faucet.

When I finish using the towel, Shpetim washes his hands and says, "Get out of my way, and give me this towel." He snatches the towel out of my hands, and I go back to the living room. Amid the rush of leaving, some of the drawers of the armoire were left open. Even though it is daylight outside, it's dark inside the apartment because all the blinds and curtains are closed tightly.

I sit in the living room and start to eat from one of the lunch boxes until everyone is finished using the bathroom. I take some clean clothes and go to the bathroom again to wash my hair and take a bath with cold water. Shivering, I finish washing my hair and body.

I see the ball on top of the washing machine. Even though it has mud on it, it still makes me happy. I know I won't be able to play outside, but the sight of the mud-covered ball makes me hope that one day I will. I want to think that the day will come soon.

I grab the ball and return to the living room. I try to get Shpetim to kick it around with me, but Mami tells me to put the dirty ball back in the bathroom. What am I supposed to do, just sit in the living room and do nothing? Ignoring Mami, I sit on the couch and throw the ball in the air and let it drop back into my hands.

"Put the ball back," Babi screams as he threatens to hit me with his hand.

"Hysen, don't scream," says Mami.

It is not my fault that he trusted Slobo to have negotiated with the diplomats and believed that the war was over.

It is dark inside and outside now. The shots and bombs start all over again. I lie on the carpet, trying to sleep. But this time the bombing feels different; it is much scarier because all of our neighbors except Mr. Sejda and Mrs. Kaqa are gone. I feel alone and frightened. I want Mr. Sejda and Mrs. Kaqa to come stay with us. That will make me feel more secure.

I wonder why Babi doesn't want us to hide in the basement, but I don't complain, for I know that if a bomb hits our building, we are going to be crushed even if we are four stories underground.

I hear a faint sound as if someone is trying to push open our main double door. I don't know if it is just my imagination. I think about it carefully. I figure that if there is someone out there he would follow the faint sound with a big, noisy one. I am not nearly as afraid of the big explosions from the NATO bombs and the artillery fire that follows as I am of any sounds that might signify someone approaching our apartment.

I close my eyes. Now I hear a squeak. What is that? Oh no, someone is at the door. Babi jumps and says, "Who is it?"

Mami says, "It's nothing, it's just the armoire," and laughs softly at Babi for being so scared.

I open my eyes. I hate the sounds this big piece of furniture makes.

I am weary, and my back hurts. I want to go to sleep, but I don't want someone to kill me in my sleep. I might be able to hide in one of the drawers of our armoire and not be discovered. I wish that I could get in there right now and hibernate like a bear until the war is over.

I wonder whether the masked men who kicked us out know we are back. I picture them easily entering our apartment and conducting a search for anyone who might have stayed. Boshko's words come to mind: "If you stay here, your safety will not be guaranteed." I think of the words of the *t'zi*: "Get out of here. You have five minutes to get ready." These scary memories play in my head over and over. My whole body trembles. They must know we are back. They must. It is only a matter of minutes before they come.

I remember my karate trainer teaching us how to put our hands together and relax, saying, "Free yourself of all thoughts. Close your minds. Relax. Don't think of anything." I put my hands together, and I tell my mind to rest. I may be able to calm my mind, but I can't close my ears, which hear sounds that must be processed by my brain. I should be glad that I can finally stretch and be able to sleep in a warm apartment instead of a cold car, but I am not.

I am awakened several times during the night by the sounds and vibrations of NATO bombs, but in the morning it is calm. The night has taken all of the war sounds with it. I think of last night, and I don't understand why I was so afraid. Tonight I am going to pretend that daylight lasts twenty-four hours, and I won't be scared anymore.

Mr. Sejda and Mrs. Kaqa are visiting us, and they are talking about going to tell Mr. and Mrs. Krasniqi that we have come back.

Babi tells Mr. Sejda that he is concerned about going on the streets in this kind of situation. "This is how they killed my friend Afrim near the post office," he tells Mr. Sejda. I can tell that he doesn't want to go, but Mr. Krasniqi could tell us what is going on in town and perhaps find us a safer place to stay. Babi comes up with the idea of taking Fjolla with him and pretending that he is a Serb walking with his little daughter.

"Fjolla, can you come with Babi to see Mr. Krasniqi?" he asks her.

"I guess," she says and slips on her shoes. Mami kisses her and tells her that she will be all right walking with Babi. Outside I hear *paw paws* and *trr trrs*.

Babi returns holding Fjolla in his arms. She is crying.

Mami is distressed. "What happened? What happened?"

"What happened?" I scream. Did she get shot by a sniper? Is she wounded? I don't see any blood on her. They should have never gone out during this time.

We surround Fjolla and examine her. I look for blood again but don't see any.

"Hysen, what happened to the girl? Tell me now," orders Mami.

"When we got to the building of Mr. Krasniqi's sister's apartment," Babi says, "there were police at the entrance and I could not get in. I asked Fjolla to go to the ninth floor to tell Mr. Krasniqi that we have returned. On her way back down, apparently, a policeman yelled at her in Serbian. She then ran down the stairs as quickly as she could."

Fjolla's leg muscles are now paralyzed from sprinting down nine flights of stairs, and Babi says that he had to carry her home because her legs wouldn't work. Mami says to Babi, "Why did you let her go by herself when you knew there were Serbian policemen in the apartment building? You should have come right back when you saw them. Look at her now."

Fjolla is still crying. "Oh, I can't move my legs," she says.

She has to go to the bathroom. Mami grabs her and carries her there. I feel sorry for Fjolla. My legs would be spastic too if the *t'zi* had yelled at me and I had to sprint down nine flights of stairs. Mami returns from the bathroom with Fjolla in her arms and starts to massage and rub her legs. "Lift your leg up," she tells Fjolla, but she can't do it.

Fjolla still can't move her legs despite the fact that Mami has massaged them all day. Mr. and Mrs. Krasniqi have joined us and are now in their apartment on the fourth floor. I hear a NATO jet come and leave with a roar. It leaves behind a boom and an earthquake that shatters another one of our living room windows.

Babi gets up fast and peers from the edge of the window to see where the bomb has landed.

"Don't step on glass," Mami says to Babi as she begins to pick up the pieces of the windowpane. I have hit these windows with the ball numerous times—sometimes pretty hard—and they never broke. Now nothing touches them, but they break.

"Just leave it for tomorrow when it's daylight," says Babi. Mami ignores him and picks up the pieces anyway, using candlelight. Despite the broken windows, I am still grateful for Bill Clinton and Tony Blair. I dream of meeting Bill Clinton and talking as if we are close friends. I picture myself shaking his hand, thanking him so much for helping to liberate us, while looking closely at his gray hair and blue eyes.

"You are my hero," I say in my imaginary meeting with him.

I wake up to Fjolla's whining that she still can't move her legs. Mami is still massaging and exercising her muscles.

190

"Ohh, ahh, ohh," whines Fjolla.

When it's afternoon, Mr. Sejda goes outside to see whether someone else has come back to the other apartment buildings.

As Fjolla starts to move her legs a little by herself, we hear Mr. Sejda's steps. Babi and I go outside to see whether he has seen someone who has returned. We are surprised to see him with a swollen face. He is holding the rail while wobbling; he is barely able to stay on his feet. He has seen somebody, all right.

Babi and I run and each grab one of his arms. "What happened? What happened?" asks Babi.

"Ohh," moans Mr. Sejda as we knock on his door.

Mrs. Kaqa opens the door, puts her hand over her mouth, and says, "Sejdo! Sejdo! What happened? What happened?"

"Ohh," whines Mr. Sejda as we enter his apartment.

When Mr. Krasniqi arrives and sees Mr. Sejda, he says, "What happened? What happened?"

He refuses to say anything but, "Ohh."

Later, Mr. Sejda tells us that as he entered a nearby apartment building, he was seen by two *t'zi* who were looting.

"What are you doing here?" they asked. They knew Mr. Sejda and where he lived.

"Nothing—just looking for my neighbors in this building," Mr. Sejda replied.

"How many families are living in your apartment building?"

"Just me and my wife," Mr. Sejda lied.

"Just you and your wife, huh? Why are you lying to us?" Then they began slapping and punching Mr. Sejda until he fell to the floor. The *t'zi* kicked him in his ribs and face with their hard black boots. Once he was able to stand, they told him, "If the night catches you and your neighbors here, the dawn of the next morning will not!"

That night, three masked men break into our apartment. They take all of our money, Babi's documents, and his car keys. One of them wants to take my father too, but the other two respond, "We can't. We've got to get out of here quickly."

They turn toward us and say, "You *Šiptari* better leave town or we'll come back and kill you!"

CHAPTER 38

"DO NOT LEAVE THE HOUSE"

Mr. Sejda and Mrs. Kaqa come into our apartment, and I feel great relief. Mr. and Mrs. Krasniqi come down also. "What happened? What happened?" they say.

"I swear to God," says Babi. "They told us to leave or they'll kill us."

"What?" says Mr. Krasniqi.

"What are we going to do now?" asks Mr. Krasniqi.

Silence stills the room. We don't know what to do. Where can we go at night during bombings and shootings?

"Can we go to Kamenice?" asks Mr. Krasniqi, referring to the village where Mr. Sejda grew up.

"They took our car keys," responds Mr. Sejda, "and all of our money and documentation."

"Really?" Mr. Krasniqi says frantically.

"Yes, really," responds Mr. Sejda.

I am afraid that they are going to come back and find us here. "Babi, have you locked the door?"

There is more silence.

"Can we go to Drenovc?" says Mr. Krasniqi about our village.

"They took our car keys," repeats Mr. Sejda.

"I have my own car, and Morina's car keys too," says Mr. Krasniqi. Mr. Morina is a neighbor from another apartment building who owns a red Yugo. We are saved.

"It's more dangerous in Drenovc than it is here," says Babi. "Besides, listen to all these gunshots outside."

"You're right," agrees Mr. Krasniqi. "There are snipers on top of the buildings too."

We don't know where to go.

Babi goes down to close the door to the building, as if that is going to protect us. I study the armoire and consider which long drawer I could best hide in if they come back. What about Mami and Babi? There are no drawers large enough to accommodate them. I just hope the thieves won't come back, but they probably will.

Babi comes back, and we stay in our living room. All of the adults appear to be thinking hard about what to do next.

Two *t'zi* come to our apartment and Babi opens the door for them. They shoot Babi twice in his head. I immediately wake up in a cold sweat. Is this a dream or reality?

My breathing is rapid and shallow. I shake my head vigorously and then realize it was a dream. I am lying on the carpet. I am terrified yet relieved. Babi is alive, looking outside the edge of the window. His radio is on and sits on the carpet across from me. Our neighbors are back in their apartments. I really don't want to go back to sleep and risk another nightmare.

Now it is six o'clock in the morning, and I don't know how I managed to overcome the terror and then sleep for a few hours. We are leaving. We are going to go to Mr. Krasniqi's parents' house. Mr. Krasniqi has his own house next to theirs.

"Hurry up," my father tells me.

I get ready to leave this place and never come back while the war is on. We have wasted all of our life chances here, and we can't risk staying here any longer.

Outside it is still dark, with only glimpses of dawn. The bombing has stopped.

My family and I get into Mr. Morina's red Yugo, and our neighbors ride with Mr. Krasniqi. After a short while, we pass a big Serbian café with a camouflage cover. There are a lot of people in it, and the music is loud. It sounds as if the music is live, but I don't see a singer. There are some military men and young women seated at round tables, drinking and lip-syncing the lyrics. Wow. They are singing and having a good time while we are struggling to stay alive. We drive by fast, and I don't think anyone has taken notice of us. I imagine that is where all the Serbian paramilitary troops and policemen and soldiers go when they finish their job with us *Šiptari*.

The streets are deadly calm as usual. We pass tall apartment buildings, the sports complex where I used to practice karate, and the *futboll* stadium. Glass from shattered apartment windows litters the ground. A lone dog wanders across the road. The orphaned dog reminds me of my little cousin's plight. I wonder if Vedat is alive. If he were here he could sing to make us forget the war.

I am nervous that a Serbian police car is going to stop us. There are few Kosovars living in Pristina now. The city belongs to the Serbians and they don't want us in it.

We finally arrive at Mr. Krasniqi's parents' house, a three-story home big enough for several families. We call Mr. Krasniqi's dad Haxhi because he has taken a pilgrimage to Mecca, and that is how one honors people after they have completed that trip. It is written in the Koran that all Muslims are supposed to visit Mecca before they die, but it's unlikely that I will get out of Kosovo alive, much less make a pilgrimage.

Haxhi wears a white cap that he got in Mecca as a symbol to let the rest of the world know that he is a Haxhi, a good man. We are in his living room. Its walls are painted white and the furniture is attractive and comfortable. The silk draperies are white and hand-knitted. The wool carpet is beautiful and has wire heaters under it. But Haxhi does not look as if he is thrilled to have us in his house. He often stares at the carpet and avoids eye contact and conversation. I wonder what is wrong. Traditionally, a Kosovar host shakes each of his guests' hands with his right hand while holding his left hand over his heart. After the guests sit, he shakes their hands again while still holding his left hand over his heart, starting with the eldest guest and working his way to the youngest. A true Kosovar host will ask you, "How are you? How is your family? How is school going?"

But not Haxhi. He shook our hands only once when we came in, and he didn't place his hand over his heart. I am sure Haxhi is a nice man. What is wrong with him? We are in his house, and he doesn't even pretend that he is happy about it. Haxhi even looks at his son, Mr. Krasniqi, with the same disdain with which he seems to view us. Haxhi's wife stays quiet too. She stares at the draperies. As a Kosovar hostess, she is supposed to be more enthusiastic. She is supposed to be generous and have plenty of food and drinks on the table. Customarily, hot tea is served, and guests are encouraged to eat heartily. Haxhi's spouse is not gracious. I feel unwanted, the way a guest should never feel in a Kosovar's home. What is going on? Is the war also killing traditions? Haxhi's wife serves us only warm counterfeit Fanta soda pop in small cups. If Haxhi and his wife have enough money to go to Mecca, build this house, and furnish it lavishly, they must have ample food, tea, and other beverages in their pantry. How have we offended them?

I drink the Fanta in one gulp. It tastes flat and flavorless.

We want to stay in this big, warm house tonight, but Haxhi says, "When you finish your drinks, I will take you to the house where you and your family are going to stay."

We get up immediately. We would rather leave than stay in a place where we are not wanted. There are numerous rooms in Haxhi's house that he could let us use, but he does not want to have anything to do with us. Shpetim gets one of our bags, I get the other, and we leave.

Haxhi leads and urges us to walk quickly because there are Serbian forces nearby who would not hesitate to kill us. We move quickly on the sidewalk of Haxhi's house, which winds through his beautiful rose garden. On the other side of a waist-high red fence is Mr. Krasniqi's house, where we will stay. Unlike Haxhi's mansion, Mr. Krasniqi's house is not fully built, and it is only one story high. Its garden is small and unimpressive. If it were comfortable, Mr. Krasniqi himself would be staying in it.

The house has three unfurnished rooms, a small kitchen, and a dirty bathroom, which Mami begins to clean. Haxhi says that there were other refugees living here before us. In the kitchen there is a bag of flour, two bottles of cooking oil, and a little bag of dried beans.

As he walks out the door he says, "Do not leave the house and risk being seen, or else we will all be in big trouble. I will be in trouble for letting you stay here, and you will be in trouble for being here." He closes the door behind him.

I look through the door's yellow glass pane. There are three tall apartment buildings, and I see their Serbian residents walking in and out of them. Now I realize why Haxhi was acting the way he was. He is afraid that the Serbian forces are going to come and punish him for letting us stay here.

I walk into the room where we have dropped our bags and notice that the window doesn't have a curtain. From it I can see more apartment buildings and Serbian residents. If we can see them, they can probably see us. They can report us to the Serbian forces who in turn will arrest us. I go to Babi. He is turning the dial on the radio, probably trying to find BBC News or Voice of America broadcast in Albanian.

"These windows don't have any curtains," I say.

He puts down the radio to pick up a musty gray blanket to cover the window. "We need some pins or something," he says.

We find two nails and a screw in one of the kitchen drawers and use them as hangers to secure the blanket over the window. There are more blankets and some long foam mattresses that are commonly slept on by villagers. I assume that they were used by the refugees who lived here. I lie down on one of them and try to take a nap. The usual thoughts occupy my mind before I fall asleep. We cannot live here for long without being discovered by Serbian forces. I look around the room for places to hide. Unlike our apartment, there is no armoire with big drawers.

Shpetim and Fjolla explore the house. I get up and join them to look for a hiding place in one of the other rooms. We enter a small room across from the one that I was just in. There are some clothes spread on the floor. The refugees who were living here before must have had to leave in a hurry. Shpetim is trying on a black denim jacket, and Fjolla is considering how it looks on him.

"That's a good jacket," Fjolla says.

I am not interested in the clothes, so I ignore Fjolla and Shpetim and continue my search for a hiding place. There are no curtains in this room either, but luckily the window faces the side of Haxhi's house and not the apartment buildings inhabited by Serbians. The room has no furniture or closets. The same is true for the third room in the back of the house. From the bare window I see that the backyard has a tall tree, a tennis court, and a small, grassy area perfect for playing *futboll*. The room has two more foam mattresses, which I drag into the living room. I think we should all sleep in there.

I go to the kitchen and flip on the light switch. At least there is electricity and a stove. I open a kitchen drawer hoping to find a snack—a Swiss chocolate or chips or pretzels or popcorn—but the drawer is empty. In another drawer is a jar of Nescafé. I am so hungry that I take a spoon and eat some of the instant coffee, but it tastes so bitter.

Once back in the hallway, I look up and think I have found a hiding place: the attic. I don't see any steps, though, and I don't know how I would get up there.

"Shpetim, Shpetim," I holler.

He appears wearing his new denim jacket. "What? What do you want?"

I point to the ceiling. "How do you get up there?"

"There it is." He points to a rectangular shape above us. "Those are the stairs to the attic," he says. "We just have to bring them down."

He comes up with the idea of hoisting me to the ceiling. I plant my feet on my brother's thighs while he wraps his arms around my legs. Using all my strength, I pull down the wooden stairs. Now we are on to something, I think.

Mami comes out of the bathroom. "What are you two doing?"

"Nothing, Mami, we are just going to the attic," I tell her.

"Put those stairs up before Haxhi comes and catches you."

"Just for a minute, Mami," says Shpetim.

"No," she says.

"*Të lutna*," I say, "just for one minute," and we climb the stairs without giving her time to respond.

It is dark in the attic. The Serbian forces would never think to look for us in here. The air has an awful smell, though, and the space is cramped. You have to walk very carefully on top of long wooden joists to avoid falling. There is no way that we could safely hide up here. I see a chess board and a big plastic bag filled with clothes.

We grab the board and the bag and hurry down the wooden stairs to find Mami annoyed. Shpetim and I dust off the game board and align the chessmen for a match. This activity will keep us from going insane with boredom and fear.

After playing three games, we get tired of it. You can play chess for only so long, and then your head starts to hurt because you have to concentrate so intensely. I collapse onto a foam mattress and try to nap.

The sounds of NATO bombs and gunfire wake me up. We have moved so much I have trouble remembering where I am. After a few seconds pass, I get my bearings. For some reason, the echo of the *trr, trrs* is louder here. This makes me fear that some bullets might come in our direction. I wish I could sleep until the noises stop. Being with just my family makes me feel vulnerable.

As usual, we sit still. The bombs and gunfire make us mutter to ourselves instead of talking to one another. Mami is with Fjolla, Babi is listening to the radio, and Shpetim is with his denim jacket. Somehow, he says, he finds it very relaxing, as though it is sucking all the fear out of his stomach. Unlike the double door that was locked and reinforced in our apartment building, this front door is flimsy. The three masked men could have followed us here. Surely they are not finished with us.

I hear a big roar. I put my hands over my ears. I still hear the loud sound, feel the earth vibrate, and see the flashing lights of the jet. It's odd that the window didn't break. I hope the glass stays intact. Having no protection from the night chill would add to our misery.

The next morning is nice and warm, and I am awakened by the sun's rays that pierce the thin gray blanket covering the window. I am sweating. This time I am not going to even ask Mami's permission to go outdoors. It is too dangerous. I must be patient and cope with my predicament. Maybe Shpetim and I will play chess again.

The electricity is on; Mami could use that flour stored in the kitchen to make bread. "Mami, why don't you make something for breakfast? I am hungry."

"I am sorry, *pllumb*; I don't have enough ingredients."

"What about the flour and the oil in the kitchen?"

"To make bread, I need baking soda," she says.

"What about *krofne* (fried pieces of bread)?"

"I still have to have baking soda, plus milk and eggs."

I go to the kitchen, boil water, and put some Nescafé in a cup. I find sugar cubes in a small bowl and make my drink really sweet.

Shpetim and Fjolla want coffee too, so they start making their own. Behind the house I hear a group of people talking and occasionally shouting. Who could they be? With the cup still in one hand, I go to the room that has the view of the backyard. I carefully raise my head just above the windowsill.

A group of young people are playing *futboll* in the small grassy area beside the tennis court. I hear two of them argue in Serbian about a goal, and I immediately lower my head. I hear the sound of their feet kicking the ball and feel excitement in my heart. I love that sound. It gives me hope that someday I will be able to play again. As I sip my Nescafé, I listen to them kick the ball.

The sounds of the *futboll* game finally stop. The players' voices are fading. I wait a little longer and slightly raise my head. I see that they are gone. The grassy field is vacant and seems as if it is begging to be used again. I like to think it is calling my name to go outside and be with it. Since the Serbian boys are gone, why not go outside to the field? But then I remember where I am and the dangerous situation we are in.

Instead of playing *futboll*, I play chess with Babi, who listens to the radio at the same time—the droning radio that I am so tired of hearing. There is nothing but news about exiles or torched villages. I am distracted, and Babi's clever chess moves are beating me as usual. He is winning without even using his queen. Shpetim is waiting his turn, and Fjolla is watching us.

"Babi, how long are we going to stay here?" asks Fjolla. She has asked that three times now.

"Fjolla, I have told you that already. I don't know. We'll get out of here as soon as we can."

CHAPTER 39

HOPELESS

The next day we still don't have anything to eat. The day after that I wake up because my stomach hurts from hunger pangs. I want to be a tough kid and not complain, but when your stomach aches, complaining about it eases the pain. Since I didn't die from one of the bullets or bombs last night, I am surely going to die of starvation today. Mami is up, and I groan about my hunger and how much my stomach hurts.

I gripe until someone knocks on our door, and we all jump. Though I am terrified, I am glad this isn't happening during nighttime. Babi goes to the door and opens it, and Mr. Krasniqi and Haxhi, son and father, come in.

Mr. Krasniqi tells Babi that he is leaving for Macedonia with his wife, Mr. Sejda, and Mrs. Kaqa. He shakes our hands and says goodbye. What about us? Why can't we go with them? Then I remember that we don't have our passports. Plus, our neighbors might be scared that they would get in trouble for trying to save us.

We are stuck here in the house without options and burdened with boredom. I am so frustrated that I want to throw the chess set against the wall and scream.

The beautiful day has turned into a rainy night, and we are all sitting on the foam mattresses. We can hear the drops of rain hit the roof. Inclement weather won't keep troops, *t'zi*, or burglars away. We are at war. I cannot dismiss the possibility that masked men will knock down our door. I hate to tell Shpetim, Mami, Babi, or even Fjolla that I am scared because I am fourteen now—a big boy. My whining days are over. I can only whine to myself. Besides, I don't want Shpetim to think that I am frightened, even though he is scared too. He is quiet, like me and everybody else.

The rain won't stop the NATO pilots from bombing Serbian forces. On Babi's radio, I hear that NATO has accidentally hit a Serbian hospital. While NATO bombs are precise, mistakes occur that cause civilian casualties among the Serbians, including women and children. I take no pleasure in that.

Given the rainy weather and poor visibility, I am afraid that our house will be hit. The *phhhiiuus* and the booms sound so close.

I yawn. The rainy weather is making me sleepy, but I am too scared to go to bed. Serbian forces aren't deterred by the rain either.

If it's meant for a bomb to land on the house, I would much rather it was a NATO bomb. If I am killed by NATO, at least I will have been killed for a good cause. "Friendly casualty," I've heard them call such occurrences on the radio. It doesn't even sound as if you got killed. As lethal as those bombs are, it would only be a split second before we would be dead and buried beneath the rubble. The vibrations would violently shake the earth, causing Haxhi's windows to break.

I hear light footsteps, as if someone is tiptoeing toward me. Did a stranger enter the house? There must be assassins here to execute us. I am going to die, not from a NATO bomb but from a bullet. I swear, if we can live beyond this one moment—just one more night without being killed—we will never be war casualties. I wait anxiously, but luckily no intruder walks in. Now I attribute the noise to wind rattling the windows.

The rain stops. It must be one o'clock in the morning, and I am still awake.

The next day is another beautiful April day, but we are still confined to the house. No one says much, day or night. Babi finally breaks the silence by looking at me and saying, "Do you want to play chess?"

"No."

"This time, I'll take out my queen and the two rooks."

"I am tired of playing chess, Babi. I don't want to play. Besides, you don't have a chance at beating me without your queen and your two rooks."

"Let's set it up and see."

"No. Play with Shpetim."

Shpetim says, "I don't want to play either. Don't pass stuff to me. We play chess all the time. That's all we do."

I get up and wander from room to room, checking to see if they are empty, as I left them the last time, which they always are. It's as if I expect to find a dramatic change in them. This time when I enter the room at the back of the house, I hope to hear the sounds of a *futboll* game, but the Serbian boys are not outside.

The room that faces a side of Haxhi's house is empty. I leave the room too and decide to look through the yellow glass of the main door. My face presses against the tinted pane. The circles etched in the glass make impressions on my forehead. I see a Serbian woman carrying two loaves of bread in a transparent plastic bag. It reminds me of the time when I went to the bakery, and the bomb exploded. Despite that incident, I still want to go to the bakery. The bread is always soft and warm, and I imagine spreading some delicious feta cheese on it.

Looking through this window is like looking through the thick prescription glasses of my friend Labinot. It makes my head hurt. I see more Serbians walking freely outside. I move away from the window, thinking that they might see my silhouette darken the yellow glass.

I go to the kitchen for some instant coffee. The flour and oil remain untouched. I wish Mami had some baking soda. Sprinkle sugar on a warm slice of bread, and I would be one happy kid. Such a treat is only possible by imagining it.

I make another security check, inspecting each room, and then go back to the main living area where everyone is. I want to ask Babi, "How long are we going to be here?" but Fjolla has asked that question plenty of times. He doesn't know. We don't have a plan at all, and that is the worst part. This eliminates our hopes of getting out and leaves us with the singular goal of being able to make it to the next day without starving or getting killed.

"Babi, instead of playing chess, why don't we come up with a plan for leaving this place? Can't we just leave, like Mr. Krasniqi and Mr. Sejda?"

"No, we can't. We don't even have passports to cross the Macedonian border."

"Why do we need passports?"

"We fear the Macedonians won't allow Kosovar refugees to pass without passports any more. They have now brought more restrictions to cross the border."

I have two options here. One option is to go crazy because we can't get out of here, and the other is to be patient and see what happens. I consider these two choices and then say to Babi, "I can beat you at chess without your queen and the two rooks."

After Shpetim and I beat Babi, he says, "OK, this time I am going to play with all my pieces. You guys are getting good."

Chess gets boring again, because Babi beats both Shpetim and me twice with his queen and rooks. He wins with only a few moves. Chess is fun only when you can beat your opponent. I don't want to play anymore.

The next day, Babi can't persuade us to play chess. Shpetim and I repeatedly turn him down. We tell him that having food is our main interest. I don't understand how Babi does not get hungry like we do—or how he cannot complain about hunger.

"Are there no more lunch boxes?" he says.

"No, we ate the leftovers in them long ago," I say.

"Like two or three days ago," says Shpetim.

There is no way to get food, since we can't go out. NATO planes won't drop sacks of food from the sky onto the lawn.

"How about I teach you all how to play a new game?" says Babi. "A game that we used to play when I was your age."

That sounds good. I am curious and forget about my hunger. Babi goes to the kitchen and gets three cups and a bean. He aligns the three cups next to each other, leaving little spaces between them, and holds the bean between two fingertips.

"I am going to place this bean under one of these three cups. When I call your name, you have to guess where the bean is."

Babi lifts each cup just enough to allow room for his fingers, but his fingers are fat and I clearly see where he hid the bean.

"Ilir," he calls my name. "Which cup?"

I touch the middle cup and tell him, "This one, Babi. We all saw you place it in under there. That was easy. This game is boring."

"I'll let you guys try it. My hand is big and you can see me, but if you do it with your little fingers, and do it fast, we'll never know under which cup you put the bean."

With my legs crossed, the three cups close to me, and the bean in the tips of my fingers, I start. I tilt the cup just high enough to slip my fingers in. I move my hand fast from one cup to another and discreetly leave the bean in one of them.

So we go on like this until we all become masters of the game and the others can barely tell under which cup we leave the little bean. Even though the game is fun, it is no substitute for the satisfaction of eating a good meal or even a slice of bread. My stomach still hurts. It has been a day and a half since the last time I ate, but I feel as if I haven't eaten in a week.

We play the cup game until it is dark. In the end, I hold the bean in one hand. I stare at it until a thought comes to me. I have eaten raw spaghetti before; this can't be too bad. I put the bean in my mouth and start chewing it. It is hard and tastes nasty, but I swallow every little piece of it. I hope that eating a raw bean will make my stomach feel better rather than worse. I rarely ate beans when they were cooked, and now look at me.

The aftertaste is not bad, though. I could go to the kitchen and get a handful of raw beans and eat them, but it is nighttime and I am scared. The masked men could break down our door and find me alone in the kitchen.

I risk it anyway.

I light a candle and whisper to the others, "I am going to the bathroom." I don't want them to know my secret. I tiptoe to the kitchen. My stomach hurts from fear as well as hunger. Oh no. Oh no. Somebody is going to grab me and put a knife to my neck or a gun to my ribs. I quickly open the bag, get a handful of beans, and go back to my foam mattress. I am glad to still be alive. I start to munch the beans like sunflower seeds.

Shpetim is next to me. "What are you eating?" he says. He must have heard my chewing.

"Some beans. Shut up."

"Mami, Ilir is eating raw beans," he says.

"Oh, *pllumb*, I thought you went to the bathroom." She lifts her head, sees the beans in my palm, and laughs.

"Who gave you permission to eat beans, Ilir?" sneers Shpetim.

"I did. They are pretty good. They have a pretty good after-taste too."

"Eating them raw is going to hurt your stomach," Mami says.

"Well, it sure isn't going to hurt any more than it does already," I say.

Now everybody is laughing at me. I don't understand how their stomachs don't hurt after not eating for so long.

I sleep for five minutes and stay up for an hour, sleep for five and stay awake another hour. I hope that a bomb will drop on our house. At least that would eliminate the pain.

When morning comes, I see Mami with her curly black hair combed nicely. She has on the floral silk dress she wore when teaching. Babi is looking very sharp too in his white shirt and khaki pants. Seeing them dressed up and looking nice makes me wonder whether the war is over, but I can still hear the occasional gunfire.

"Where are you going?" I say.

"Back to our apartment to get some food," says Mami.

Their "disguises" are a good idea. They definitely look like Serbians. The *t'zi* will never guess they are Kosovars because a Kosovar would look like a scrub and avoid the *t'zi*. I am comforted they have decided to get some food.

Mami and Babi carefully open the door and quickly walk to the red Yugo.

Even though I frequently hear gunshots, with Babi and Mami gone they now make me more nervous. It feels like nighttime. Before they left, I didn't think I was going to be this scared. I thought that I could play the cup game with Shpetim and Fjolla to distract myself, but now I realize that if somebody saw Mami and Babi leave, he will burst in and slaughter us.

I worry that Mami and Babi will be captured and killed by Serbian soldiers. I don't know how Mami can be brave enough to go into our apartment building; the masked men and the *t'zi* made it clear that we shouldn't be there. Mami knew a lady who was killed by the *t'zi* in her apartment.

Shpetim, Fjolla, and I start to play the cup game, but my mind dwells on the front door and my parents, who left about thirty minutes ago. It feels as if they have disappeared from our lives forever. This time, when we successfully hide the bean under a cup, we don't get excited.

After another thirty minutes, we see someone coming to the door. It's Babi, and he is holding two plastic bags filled with food. In it there are some old biscuits, stale bread, and frozen cranberries. I grab one of the biscuits immediately. It's hard but not raw like the beans. After eating another biscuit, my stomach starts to feel much better.

"Mami, did you see any Serbian policemen or paramilitary troops? Did somebody stop you?" asks Shpetim excitedly.

She says there were no problems. Babi dropped her off half a mile from the apartment and waited while she walked to our building, looking like a Serbian woman without any worries. Mami got the breads from Denis's apartment and the cranberries from our fridge.

With my stomach filled with old biscuits and water, I walk around the three rooms three times happily. I wish I could use my energy to walk and run outside instead.

It has been two days since Shpetim and I begged Mami and Babi to allow us outside. We argue that they went out without getting into trouble and ask why we can't do the same. They grant our request, but our stay in the yard will be limited.

"Five minutes only," says Mami.

There is someone walking near the apartment buildings, but I don't think he is looking for us. Shpetim, Fjolla, and I quickly run to the back of the house. The weather is sunny, and I am glad to finally enjoy a beautiful spring day. It has been almost a week and a half since we have set foot outside. Now I know how it feels to be released from prison. There are no walls to confine me. I feel free.

We walk on the little grassy *futboll* field. I fear we might somehow be seen by Serbian forces. I remember Haxhi telling us to stay hidden. We might have already been seen by Serbian residents living across the street in apartments as we stepped out of the house. There may be snipers on those rooftops. I don't want to act fearful and be targeted as a Kosovar.

I kick the ground with one foot and watch grass and soil scatter. I would do anything for a ball right now. I wouldn't even care if a sniper shot me because at least I would be shot while playing a sport I love.

Five minutes later, Shpetim says, "We have to get back."

"Wait. Let's stay a little longer," I say.

"No. Right now," he says, heading back to our domestic prison. He must be scared of snipers, Mami, Serbian forces, Serbian residents, Haxhi—indeed, the whole world.

The next morning, Mami and Babi are dressed in the same clothes they wore three days ago when they went to get food from our apartment building. I wonder where they are going this time. We still have some bread and biscuits left.

"Babi, where are you going?"

"To get my birth certificate," he says. I remember that the three masked men had taken all of his documentation.

"Why do you need it?"

"In order to get a passport, you have to show a birth certificate. Without that, we can't go anywhere," he says.

As they walk out the door, Mami says, "Listen to Shpetim, and do not go outside. You understand?"

"OK," I say.

Now that she mentioned going outside, I want to do just that. If they expect nothing bad will happen to them, why shouldn't I expect the same?

Instead of going out, though, I decide to stay in and open the window with a view of the *futboll* field. A light breeze cools my face. This is just like being outside. I am enjoying this. I surrender all worries. I am meditating, as I learned in karate class. I am not scared of anybody coming into our house. If that happens, Fjolla and I will escape through the open window. Shpetim can follow us. We will run as fast as professional *futboll* players and the Serbian forces won't realize that we once occupied that house.

When Mami and Babi return, they look weary. I don't even let them sit before telling them, "I am going out for just a little."

Mami blocks my way. "No," she says. "It is dangerous out there. Let me tell you what happened to us."

"Oh, Mami. Come on."

She looks me in the eye.

"OK, what happened?" I say.

She goes in the other room and changes into sweatpants and a sweater and motions for me to sit down beside her.

She explains they went to the registrar's office via a coach line that had transported Babi's Serbian co-workers to a town called Milosheve. When they arrived, Babi went into the office, and Mami sat in the waiting room. After a while, two Serbian soldiers approached her and said they were going to kill Babi and that she was never going to see him alive again. She didn't believe it and moved away from them to another area in the building. Soon afterward, Babi appeared. "For all we know," she says, "those Serbian soldiers could have followed us, and that is a good reason to stay inside."

How could I forget that we are in great danger?

Mami continues her story. "This is funny," she says. "When it was time to go back to Pristina from Milosheve, we needed a ride, so we hitchhiked. A Serbian driver stopped and picked us up, thinking we were Serbians. Along the way he found out that we were Kosovars and ordered us out of his car."

I don't think that is funny. "How did you get back here?"

"We waited for another coach bus. Ilir, it is dangerous out there. Mami wouldn't lie to you. On the ride back we saw Serbian civilians on their balconies with rifles. On the streets there were gypsies and Serbian civilians looting stores, vandalizing property, and waving the Serbian flag. You don't want to go outside, *pllumb*."

"I believe you, Mami, but when are we going to get out of here?"

"Now that Babi has his birth certificate, we can apply for passports. Then we are leaving here."

When night falls, I become petrified that the two Serbian soldiers are on their way to murder us. There are rounds of ammunition being fired and bombs exploding. I sit here and wait for them to pound the front door at any moment. My eyes are staring at it with anticipation and dread.

I hear a sound. I always first imagine that it is made by some-one at the door. No other sound follows, so I relax. The noise must have come from the kitchen. At night we can clearly hear the kitchen drawers creak without anyone setting a hand on them; the hardwood floors squeak without anyone setting a foot on them. During the day, I never hear such things. At night the house becomes alive with unex-plained noises. It could be haunted by ghosts who want us to leave.

I am used to the sounds of NATO jets and the Serbians' antiair-craft fire and can easily identify those. However, any unfamiliar noises could signal trouble. I know they could lead to louder sounds—made by masked men knocking down the door, or Serbian soldiers setting the house on fire and threatening to shoot us if we try to escape. I wish that Mami had never told me about the soldiers. I don't fall asleep until dawn.

I sleep through late morning and early afternoon. When I wake up at two o'clock, I go into the kitchen and open drawers, hoping that I will find something to eat, even though I know that there is nothing. If only I could find something sweet like a Swiss chocolate. Wishing for food doesn't make it magically appear. I slam each drawer shut. I feel stupid for checking when I knew there was nothing in them.

I pace among the three rooms once, and then another time, and then yet another one.

I return to the kitchen again as if by now food has magically appeared in the drawers. I open them again. Empty. Now I hate myself for being so silly. Have I gone insane? I slam the last drawer so hard that its handle breaks.

I inspect the rooms again and again. Babi is listening to his radio in the living room. I sit opposite him and force a smile. The radio broadcaster is interviewing some Kosovar women who have been gang raped in their own homes by Serbian soldiers. One of the vic-tims says, "They threatened to kill our children if we didn't cooperate."

I think of Fjolla and Mami but can't imagine that Serbian sol-diers would molest them. Mami is old and Fjolla is a child. The sol-diers had better leave my mother and sister alone.

I am in the kitchen again, looking for a treat that I know isn't there. How nice it would be if I had a piece of chocolate melting in my mouth. I would savor its sweetness and smooth texture. I would enjoy its aftertaste. No chocolate in this kitchen. Why am I acting so stupid? We rarely had chocolate in our house during peacetime, never mind now that there is a war going on and we are exiles.

I stand on the countertops and check the cabinets. Nothing but dust. I feel desperate, almost crazy.

I jump down to the kitchen floor from the counters and look at the bags of flour and beans. I consider eating some raw beans, but I would rather eat grass. I open the bag of flour and take a pinch of it with my thumb and index finger. It tastes bitterer than the beans, but I eat more with the hope that the taste will improve. It doesn't. It gets worse. It reminds me of the times when I was nauseated, and Mami made me swallow baking soda without water so I could throw up and feel better.

I make some Nescafé. There is no electricity, so I can't boil the water. The coffee granules float, refusing to dissolve. I dump the disgusting concoction down the drain. I leave the kitchen, deciding that it is the worst room in the house. There is nothing worse than a kitchen without food or sweets.

After an hour I am back in the kitchen for a snack of moldy bread and rock-hard biscuits.

CHAPTER 40

KO TO KAŽE, KO TO LAŽE, SRBIJA JE MALA? (WHO SAID, WHO LIED THAT SERBIA IS SMALL?)

nother day and a half passes without food. Around noon, I am awakened by the buzz of flies. They land on my exposed skin and bite me. They have no idea that last night I could not sleep because I was hungry and scared. I wish I had a flyswatter like my grandfather had so I could squash the ooze out of these pests. In a rage, I roll up an old newspaper that Babi found in the house and kill two of them with it.

Mami and Babi leave to get more food. Just the thought of eating something gives me hope for another day.

My parents return with two bags of groceries. The air is hot and humid today, and Babi's forehead is covered with sweat that streaks down his face. Babi and Mami seem winded and tired.

"We didn't go back to the apartment this time," Babi says. "There were policemen, paramilitary, and soldiers patrolling the streets. I was not brave enough to go there." He plops the bags of groceries on a kitchen counter, runs his big hand across his sweaty forehead, and sighs.

"So where did you go?" I ask.

"We went to Shemsa. She gave us all this food," Mami says.

I immediately begin removing the contents of the bags. How nice of Shemsa, Mami's elderly Bosnian friend who used to sew her school clothes, to give us food. In it I see thawed cranberries, fresh bread, a can of Argeta like the ones we used to sell, and a bowl of bean soup (a welcome change from raw beans). I immediately grab a piece of bread, spread chicken paste on top, and gulp it down. I don't want to eat too much at one time. If I stuff myself then I'll be back to a diet of raw flour and raw beans.

Babi grabs a bottle of cooking oil and goes outside the door.

"Where's Babi going, Mami?" I ask.

"Oh, *pllumb*, we talked to a man on the street, and he told us that his family and other families were isolated in their apartment building without food. He begged and cried. He told us that there were a lot of university students hidden in basements and afraid to go outside. Babi will be right back."

I think about the university students and try to imagine what they must be feeling. They are in a worse situation than we are here, since students have always been prime targets of Serbian forces. I remember seeing the *t'zi* club young people on the street and then pile them into vans for a trip to the police station. I remember how they beat Agron, Musa's cousin. The students must feel that each day is their last.

"We got some good news, though, *pllumb*," says Mami.

"What's that, Mami?"

"The same man told us that a bus will go to Macedonia in two days, and we might be able to get on."

I want to know every detail. "That means that we won't ever have to come back to this house," I say.

"Possibly. Tomorrow we are going to try to get our passports. The man told us that they are issuing them in the Grand Hotel."

"Grand Hotel?" repeats Shpetim in a high voice.

"That is where they moved the passport office to," says Mami.

"What time does the bus leave?" I ask.

"Around two o'clock, he said," says Mami.

I can't even imagine leaving this place. If we can get out of here, I will not wish for another thing in this world.

When morning comes, we are all ready to go to the Grand Hotel to get our passports. Shpetim, Fjolla, and I are ecstatic. It feels just like the times when we would leave our boring apartment and go to the village for a fun-filled season.

We go out of the door and walk to the red Yugo. As we get into our car, I notice a Serbian man across the street carrying a bag of groceries. He turns his head and looks at us before entering his apartment building.

Babi grips the steering wheel and starts the engine; I see his face reflected in the rearview mirror. He looks determined not to run into any Serbian patrols. If we get stopped at any checkpoints, that will be the end of all hope for us.

There are few cars on the highway. That makes me nervous.

There are no people outside. When we approach a small strip mall, we see two paramilitary soldiers standing on a balcony holding Kalashnikovs. We are in trouble in this lawless country. They stare at our car. I try to compose myself, attempting to look like a carefree Serbian kid.

Babi looks straight ahead and drives slowly; I glance at Mami, and she looks calm. She plays that role best. Shpetim and Fjolla look in the opposite direction of the threat, pretending they don't see what is happening. Although I'm terrified, I can't help but look at the menacing faces of the two troops.

They are going to shoot us. They are not stupid. Who else but a Kosovar would travel with his wife and three kids at this time? I turn my head as we pass, waiting for a barrage of bullets to riddle our car. After Babi makes a right turn onto a narrow street, the paramilitary troops are no longer in sight. I sigh deeply, noticing that some of the sidewalks and roads are stained with blood.

Yet another danger presents itself immediately. Two Serbian police cars are parked on the side of the road. Both are occupied by officers. I nearly cease breathing. They will surely stop us.

Luckily they only stare.

Babi makes a left turn onto Korze, the main street where Mami and Babi met. This was once a bustling, cheerful place lined with trees and stores of all kinds, and full of shoppers. Now the people are gone and the businesses looted. Once, the trees complemented the beauty of the street. Now they seem ugly and misaligned, with a few of them tilting as though they have been run over and blown up by tanks. Korze is dead—killed for no reason, like Uncle Azem.

Shortly after, on the opposite side of the street, I see two military trucks coming. I jump from my seat. Each truck displays the Serbian flag. The vehicles speed toward us, and I worry that they might run us off the road. I see Babi's face in the rearview mirror. His face is bright red, as if he is about to choke. I think he is holding his breath. Miraculously, the trucks whiz by us. Babi sighs in relief. Soon we arrive at the Grand Hotel.

At a tiny ground-floor office, there is a short line of Kosovars waiting to get their passports. I never would have thought that during a war, passports would be issued. The Serbians must have decided that voluntary exile is the easier and cheaper way to remove us from the country.

Our pictures are taken. We hand over our birth certificates and in half an hour we have our passports. In my picture, I look shocked, and my eyeballs and nose look disproportionately large on my face.

Babi drives back by an indirect route, hoping not to encounter any Serbian military or *t'zi*.

When we reach Mr. Krasniqi's house, I think we are extremely lucky to be alive. "Since we haven't been shot by now, we are never going to get shot," I say aloud. Everyone laughs in relief, and we talk for the first time on the trip.

Now we have our passports, but will we make it to Macedonia tomorrow? The streets will pose as many risks tomorrow as they have today.

It is noon, and we are eager to leave this house, hopefully forever. We are all dressed and groomed nicely. I am happy that we are finally taking this chance, however risky. Mami has packed our clothing, and we are ready to go. Haxhi is waiting to follow us out of his neighborhood, and he is obviously as glad about our departure as we are.

When we exit the door, Babi hands Haxhi the house key and asks him, "If we aren't allowed to cross the border, can we come back to stay here?"

"Hysen, I am sorry, but no. I'm in great danger with you being here," says Haxhi. It is hard to blame him.

Babi says, "We are going to take the car back to our apartment and then walk to the place where the bus is going to pick us up."

Without incident, we arrive at our apartment and leave the car. Before we start our walk, Babi suggests that we form two groups to avoid looking like the Kosovar family we are. Fjolla, Mami, and I walk one route while Babi and Shpetim take another.

Fjolla and I grab Mami's hands. In the past, Mami insisted that we hold her hand whenever we walked with her in town and crossed busy streets, but today my sister and I don't need persuading. The streets are quiet, occupied by only the devil. We know there are snipers on rooftops, Serbian policemen and military on the streets, and Serbian paramilitary troops on the balconies, all of them ready for their target—Kosovars like us.

Neither Mami, Fjolla, nor I speak. The calm in the city should be comforting, but instead it is eerie. At any moment, violence could erupt, seemingly out of nowhere. We pass empty apartment buildings. There was a time when these buildings were filled with happy people and the activities of everyday life, when the entrance doors were unlocked all the time. Now they stand like memorials to the residents who used to live in them.

As we walk on a side street that leads to the sidewalk of a major highway, a gust of wind startles us. The air is getting cold.

At the sound of a car behind us, we look around. It is not a car but a military truck. *Oh Zoti im.* This is clearly the end. I quickly face forward. I squeeze Mami's hand, but I don't feel secure. The sound of the truck's engine is becoming louder.

"Calm down. It will be OK," whispers Mami.

We shift farther to the right of the sidewalk, away from the curb. We wait for the soldiers to stop right beside us and take us away to Serbia, execute us, throw us in some big hole, and cover us with dirt and mud. The truck slows down and pulls even with us. There are four soldiers, all holding big black guns, seated on benches anchored to the flatbed. They all stare at us. Fjolla and I stop walking, but Mami keeps going until we pull her back.

"It's OK, let's keep going," she says. The Serbian soldiers know that we are Kosovars. A Serbian family would never be scared of its own military.

The truck moves past us a little. Sensing our fear, a Serbian soldier stands and aims his gun at us. I release Mami's hand, crouch, and shield my face with crossed arms. I lie face down like Mami and Fjolla. Now I anticipate gunshots. I knew this was going to happen sooner or later. If only my heroes, the UÇK soldiers, were here to save us.

I want to awaken from a terrible nightmare, but this is not one of them. In my dreams something weird, awkward, and unrealistic happens. In one dream I was able to fly away from Serbian forces, like Superman. There is no escape now. This is a simple and realistic scenario, lying face down on the sidewalk. Nothing weird, nothing awkward, nothing unrealistic.

Instead of a gunshot, I hear laughter. I raise my head to see the soldiers laughing as their comrade points his rifle at us. They shift their bodies back and forth with their mouths open. Is he going to shoot us? What is so funny? I feel confused and dizzy, and I nearly faint.

A few seconds pass, and we are still alive. We look in all directions. The truck and soldiers have disappeared.

"I knew they weren't going to shoot us," says Mami. "They just wanted to scare us." We resume our walk. I should feel grateful that we have survived yet again, but sometimes I wish a soldier would shoot me. I am tired of the constant threat and terror. It's not a life worth living.

We turn right at the next intersection, where a café is blasting Serbian music. As the three of us continue walking, our faces down, we hear the song "*Ko to kaže, ko to laže, Srbija je mala* ('Who said, who lied that Serbia is small')!" This song is sung by Ceca, a famous Serbian singer who is married to Arkan, the leader of the paramilitary group responsible for massacres in Bosnia and now in Kosovo.

I glance at this café. It is crowded with Serbian civilians and soldiers. A soldier and a civilian are dancing to Ceca's song, arms swaying and bodies turning. They are having fun. I hope that this little café of criminals is on the list of NATO's targets.

We walk faster to get away from the café. After a short while, we see the bus stop, where a large crowd has gathered to await transport to Macedonia. We are happy to see Babi and Shpetim there.

The crowd is made up of mostly children, older men and women, and some young people. Most of them speak Albanian, but some are members of Pristina's Turkish community. I wonder whether more than one bus is coming, because not even three buses can hold this many people.

"Babi, Babi," I holler. "Is there more than one bus coming?"

"No," he answers.

There is a man near the group with money in his hand. The heads of families gather around him. They offer him cash, but he won't take it. They try to stuff it into his coat pockets, but he waves them off. He takes money from only those people who have reserved seats on the bus—Turks. The Kosovar people scream and yell at him and at each other. Babi uses his big body to push them aside until he reaches the fare collector, but the man refuses Babi's money.

We are stuck here. Without permission to board the bus for Macedonia, our passports are worthless. We are going to be in Pristina until we are killed. That is our destiny. Now there are even more people in this group. The bus won't hold even a fourth of us.

"What did he say? What did he say, Hysen?" asks Mami.

Babi doesn't answer.

"What did the man say?" asks Shpetim.

Babi still doesn't answer.

Finally he says, "He said there is no place for us, but that bus is not going anywhere without us." Babi raises his voice and says forcefully, "That bus is not going anywhere without us." Despite Babi's confidence, I don't think we are going anywhere.

The group gets more agitated and desperate as more men gather around the fare collector, each of them trying to pay and bribe him for passage out of Kosovo. The group of men is like boiling water. Eventually some give up and step away from the crowd.

A man with a lit cigarette in one hand sits on his bag as his wife yells at him.

"Get us seats on that bus," she screams. "Get us out of here. Do something."

The husband stares ahead and doesn't reply. "You are not worth anything," his wife continues.

The man takes a long drag of his cigarette, turns to her, and says, "I don't own that *qim nane autobusi* (motherfucking bus)."

A Turkish man warns the crowd in Albanian, "Calm down. If the police come, nobody is going anywhere." The Turks are worried that we are going to get them into trouble. The Turkish community in Kosovo doesn't side with either Kosovars or Serbians. They are neutral, and Serbians don't bother them much.

Babi says, "That is probably why they don't want us on that bus. They're afraid that Serbian police will punish them for helping Kosovars."

What are we going to do? Haxhi said that we can't return to his house. The three masked Serbian men said that we can't go back to our apartment. We are going to be stranded on the streets until nighttime, and Serbian soldiers are going to shoot us instead of mocking us. We have no chance.

As the bus turns a corner, it comes into view. The group rushes toward it like a tsunami. Babi quickly picks up Fjolla and tells the rest of us, "Follow me." He manages to make some headway, but soon he is blocked by the density of the crowd. The bus opens its doors and the Turkish leaders who arranged this trip stand in front of them. They screen passengers and allow only those who purchased tickets in advance to board.

There are at least one hundred people behind me, and they surge forward. I am nearly crushed. We can barely make way for the Turkish people to get in, and when they pass by me, their bodies and bags bump and bruise me. I try to picture us on the bus but can't even imagine it, because the bus is already almost filled. Babi thinks differently. Even while holding Fjolla, he charges forward to make room for Shpetim, Mami, and me to follow him. When we get to the door the bus is already stuffed with people sitting and standing.

"Where are you going?" a young Turk asks Babi.

"This bus is not going anywhere without my family," Babi says. "I have children too, and we have nowhere to go."

"There is no more room," the Turkish man says.

"Oh yes, there is," says Babi. The Turk tries to push Babi, but Babi pushes him hard and away from the door.

"Get in," Babi directs us, and we squeeze ourselves into the bus.

I can't believe we made it. I feel as if Uncle Azem is alive, and I am in his big, luxurious bus. I love my dad. We are going to Macedonia. We are going to a more peaceful country. We are going to be free—free to do anything we want. I am going to make Albanian friends there, and we are going to play *futboll* all day long. I am going to make up for all the lost time. By being on this bus, I am sure we have survived the war. This is it, the end of our struggle.

All the seats are occupied, so we stand. Many passengers sit on the laps of others. There isn't room to move, but I don't care.

More Kosovars break through and enter the bus. I start to sweat. It's almost impossible to breathe. People inside and outside the bus panic and scream. The bus starts leaving.

One man has only half his body inside the door. "Push forward," he screams to passengers. "I am about to fall off. *Të lutna*, push!" The door begins to close but he somehow manages to plant both feet onto the last step. Many people are left behind. Some run alongside the bus, begging the driver to stop. Some stumble and fall. Women and children weep.

I can barely breathe, and my legs have begun to ache already. I was worried about surviving the war. Now I wonder if I can survive this trip to Macedonia.

CHAPTER 41

IN THE LINE

Sweat oozes from my every pore and trickles down. My clothes are soaked. The humidity and cramped conditions on the bus are a torment. There are fifty passengers seated and fifty more standing. I never knew that a bus could hold this many people. The bus is leaning to one side. Babies and children are crying and adults are complaining. Some talk about the hazards we may encounter.

"There is a big checkpoint in Graqanice," a Kosovar says.

"I think that is where they divide the men from the women," another one says.

"They're not going to let us pass easily," the first man says. Then we hear two people speak Turkish, and I don't understand a word of it.

I fear that all families will be separated and then killed. All females will be raped and forced to witness the executions of their male family members. I remember the atrocities in Bosnia. A news program showed footage of a bus full of Bosnian refugees being stopped by Serbian forces. The Serbians pulled the men off the bus. The mothers, daughters, and the sisters started screaming and grabbed hold of the Bosnian men's shirts and coats. Serbians severely beat the women and girls until they could no longer hang on to their loved ones. Then they killed all the men. The din of crying, screaming, and wailing still pierces my memory with horror.

I picture Mami and Fjolla crying and grabbing me by my shirt and not letting me go. They are beaten as the Bosnian women were. My arms are outstretched to my mother, and I scream for her to save me, but she can't. I am dragged off the bus and shot in each leg, arm, shoulder, and the groin. A final bullet to the forehead kills me.

I sweat another quart of perspiration by having these thoughts. The last thing I need is to hear worst-case scenarios discussed among passengers. What good can that do anyone?

The bus passes a burning village, where a mosque, houses, and shops are charred and have partially collapsed. Somehow the bus keeps going, and I see more burned houses. There is the familiar *rat-a-tat* of gunfire. I'm so used to hearing it that if thirty minutes passed without it, I would wonder what had happened.

But I hope that no one is trying to shoot the bus.

We stop. We have reached Graqanice, the big checkpoint, and I panic when a military policeman boards the bus and orders all the men to get out.

Babi is between Shpetim and me and tells us to stay put. "Stay here. Don't get out," he commands. The policeman has left without taking a head count of all the men and boys. Before Babi exits, he promises us that he will be allowed back on the bus.

Mami's face turns ashen with fear but she doesn't cry. The other women follow her example. Shpetim and I scoot to the side and make room for other males to walk by us. The men walk up the aisle to the door, single file, slowly and silently. It is like a funeral march. I am frightened that Babi has gone to his grave, as have the others.

A fat young military policeman walks in. As soon as he sees Shpetim and me, he yells in Serbian, "What are you two waiting for? We said for all men to get out."

Mami grabs our shoulders and responds in a low tone, "But they are young. They are children, not men. What do you need them for? Please, let them stay here."

"Fuck your mother. I said let them go."

Mami stands her ground. She tells us, "You stay here. Don't listen to him."

The military policeman says, "Shut up."

All of the women urge Mami to let us go and reassure her that we will come back.

I worry that this stupid jerk is going to hit Mami, so I walk forward and lift Mami's hand off my shoulder. Once outside, I see all of the men aligned with their backs to the bus. Two brutish uniformed men monitor the line. They wear bulletproof vests and are armed from head to toe. One carries a bayonet. My heart beats wildly. Military trucks and more policemen surround the bus. I quickly claim a spot beside Babi. Shpetim has followed me and joins us.

"Why did you get off?" asks Babi.

"Ilir was the first one to walk out," says Shpetim.

"Didn't you hear the *t'zi* yell at us to exit?" I say.

Suddenly everyone is quiet. There are mountains all around. Nearby is the edge of a steep cliff. Are they going to push us over it? Two policemen seize every ID. Babi hands over our passports. We quickly learn that our IDs are being compared to those displayed on a computer screen inside a camouflage tent. The Serbians want to determine if any of us are members of the UÇK.

Other military policemen pace up and down the line of hostages and just look at us. Each is armed with a Kalashnikov. Occasionally one of them takes aim and cocks his weapon. A short distance from us, two policemen drink clear liquid out of a glass bottle and smoke cigarettes.

We are the only ones at this checkpoint. There are no other buses, cars, horse carts, or tractors. The policemen are free to do anything they want, and no one will protect us. They could throw us off the cliff, or order everyone to board and force the driver to speed down the rocky slope, sending us to our doom.

A policeman barks, "Turn toward the bus, and keep your hands up." This is it. Fjolla and Mami are going to see us get shot. The bus seemed to be our passage to freedom, but now I believe we should have stayed at Haxhi's house until the war ended.

In a thin and whining voice, a man in the line says, "*Oh Zot,* forgive our sins."

A tall policeman's shadow moves across the bus. He's going to start from one end and work his way to the middle, where I am, shooting two or three bullets at each person. I squint and wait for the first gunshot. Should I jump off the cliff before they shoot me? If I tumble down the side, there may be a chance that I'll live, but I won't survive being riddled with bullets.

"You got any more money?" I hear one policeman say.

"Where's your money?" says another one. The tall policeman searches Babi, but not Shpetim or me. He doesn't find any money on Babi. "Where's your money?" he asks.

"I don't have any, *gospodin.* All the money I had was taken by other policemen." Surprisingly, the *t'zi* moves along without hitting Babi or saying another word.

After a few moments, we are ordered to turn. The policeman who collected our IDs returns them and tells us to get back on the bus. The stunned men are stopped at the door and fleeced of jewelry and other valuables before climbing aboard. The bus is as jam-packed as before. We were abused, humiliated, and robbed, yet to our amazement, we are alive. The mass execution was either canceled—or merely postponed.

CHAPTER 42

NJERIU ËSHTË MË I FORT SE GURI (A HUMAN IS STRONGER THAN A ROCK)

The bus makes another stop by the border, and we get out. To the right there is a huge parking lot packed with empty cars, left behind by Kosovar refugees who had to cross the border on foot.

By now, most displaced Kosovars have crossed the border, so there are only a few people waiting in line. We go to a cabin where a Serbian policeman is sitting.

"How many people are in your family?" he asks Babi.

"Five."

He draws four straight vertical lines and a diagonal one in his notebook and directs us to the neutral zone. To the Serbians we are at best statistics crudely recorded in a notebook. A different Serbian border policeman refuses to let a young Kosovar pass. I hear him protest, "I am not in UÇK. I have never been in UÇK." He is seized and thrown into a barrack. The young man looks terrified; his face turns pale. I wonder if there will be a tomorrow for him. If I were his age, I too might have been detained.

The neutral zone between Kosovo and Macedonia is like a holding pen for refugees. There are twenty or twenty-five 600-foot lines of people waiting to cross the border. Multiple buses and trains, hundreds of cars, tractors, and horse carts have been unloaded in this zone.

There must be 10,000 people in here.

Many family members have become separated. When we get in the line, a woman asks us, "Have you seen my son? He is only nine. He has brown eyes and black hair. *Të lutna*, tell me you have seen him." There are hundreds of children here, and most have brown eyes and black hair.

Mami expresses her sympathy and explains that we have just gotten here. The distraught woman asks the same question to each person in line.

"Don't stray from here because you will get lost," Mami tells us. The lines here are not orderly; people move from line to line, and some try to get ahead. Others mill about aimlessly, so it is easy for a child to get lost. With their cameras and tape recorders, foreign journalists take pictures and interview people, but only a few. It would be impossible for them to record 10,000 stories. The world could never imagine the scope of the horror that has occurred in Kosovo. To most of those who see the images and read the accounts recorded here, it's just another civil war.

A young woman stands behind us. Her baby never stops crying. The sound is loud and thin, different from those of other babies. The young mother is trying to breast-feed her child. She looks exhausted. Her long, tattered red dress is stained with mud. Her dark hair is long and loose. Some of her hair gets blown into her baby's face by the wind. Her face looks yellow, and she trembles. She stands out from all other refugees. A small bag is set on the ground next to her.

Mami sympathizes with her and says, "Your baby sounds like a newborn." She takes a few steps toward the young mother.

"She was born yesterday," the woman says. "Serbian police came and kicked us from the village, and I had to leave. For three hours I carried her during the walk here. She's been crying like this ever since she was born. I don't even know if her father is still alive," she finally sighs.

Despite being surrounded by so much misery, we are still able to keep going somehow. I remember an Albanian proverb, *Njeriu është më i fort se guri* (A human is stronger than a rock). We all should have broken down by now, yet we somehow stand like *guri*. The line moves slowly and infrequently. In the past two hours we have moved forward only two or three steps. I should be grateful to be alive, but that's a challenge due to the everlasting tedium, exhaustion, and hunger. Occasionally Albanian humanitarian workers from Macedonia distribute food, but with every appearance they are pushed and surrounded by hundreds of people. A few refugees hoard multiple loaves of bread while many others get nothing.

There are people hungrier than we are, though. One father has three starving children. He pulls a biscuit from his pocket, crumbles it, and then drops the bits into each of his children's mouths, like a bird feeding its babies.

Shpetim gets permission from Mami to try to get a loaf of bread. Mami tells him to be careful and not forget where we are.

When it gets dark, we hear the night's NATO air raid. The bombs' explosions and the jets' roars are as loud as ever, but this time I feel safe. Here we cannot be used as human shields, and our door won't be broken down in the middle of the night.

Hearing NATO do its job makes me as happy as the first time they began the bombing. I know that Bill Clinton and Tony Blair are going to free Kosovo. The question is when we can return home. I don't even know when we can leave this neutral zone. I am tired of standing in this line and getting nowhere, so I sit on one of the two bags we have brought and complain about the long wait and the massive crowd.

A man sitting on his own bag nearby speaks to me.

"Let me tell you something," he says. "Did you know that in this place there used to be over four hundred thousand people when the war first started? Imagine that. Four hundred thousand people in this tiny neutral zone. People didn't even have room to sit like you and I are sitting right now. The Macedonians had completely closed the border and would not let anyone cross it. And that was when the weather was bad. You should feel lucky that there are not as many people now and the weather is nicer."

Babi nods in agreement with the man's comments. I try to imagine 400 times as many people as there are now in this half-mile-long neutral zone. How could that many people fit here?

I am reluctant to complain anymore. If I do, the man beside me will tell about worse things that I don't want to know.

PART THREE

"I was determined not to allow Kosovo to become another Bosnia."

—President Bill Clinton

CHAPTER 43

THE REFUGEE CAMP

We wait for seven excruciating hours in the neutral zone and then finally cross the border into Macedonia. Macedonian border patrolmen tell us to board one of many buses. It is overcrowded, but we manage to get in the back of the bus.

In front of us is an older woman with curly, dirty blond hair who is crying. She is by herself.

I don't even care to know where we are going on this bus. All I know is that we are out of Kosovo. I close my eyes. We have triumphed. We are alive. Better days await us. Our suffering is over. Surely it is. I won't have to worry about being killed.

When the bus stops I wake up, and passengers stand and stretch. I look out a window and see huge gray tents. An English-speaking humanitarian worker boards the bus with his translator and says, "Welcome to the refugee camp, Stankovec II. I want all of you to know that here you will see people wearing camouflage uniforms, but do not worry. They are not here to harm you. They are here to help you." As we exit, some French soldiers who apparently manage the camp hand each of us a gray blanket. They are polite and they smile. These are the first soldiers I've seen who don't try to kill or torture you. They direct us into one of the big tents.

The tent is empty. It is about forty-five feet long and fifteen feet wide. It has an eclipsed top, and blue sheets of plastic cover the ground. There must be one hundred of us in here. I lie on the ground beside Babi and across from Mami, Fjolla, and Shpetim.

The ground feels hard on my back, but I still prefer it to being at Mr. Krasniqi's house. In the tent, the haze of cigarette smoke, crying children, loud conversations, stinking body odors, people moving about—none of that bothers me. Now that I know I am safe, I will be asleep in no time.

A Serbian paramilitary wants to use me for target practice. He aims the gun, and Mami stands in front of me and begs him not to shoot. He laughs and forcefully pushes her aside. He steps forward until the tip of the barrel presses against my forehead. I put my hands together and plead, "Please, don't shoot. Please, please! I don't know why you are angry at me, but please don't shoot me!" He pulls the trigger.

Suddenly I awaken and sit bolt upright. I gasp and try to remember where I am. Except for a man outside smoking a cigarette and the woman with the dirty blond hair, everyone is asleep. I am not in the war zone anymore, but I am still angry that I have this dream, angry that I cannot sleep peacefully, angry that I am still scared, angry that the paramilitary troops are still alive and want to take my life. Can I not be free and safe even during sleep? How can I live like this?

I stand and shake the lurid images from my mind. I step outside. The man smoking a cigarette is staring straight ahead. He seems to be thinking hard. The motion of bending his arm to get the cigarette in his mouth is fast and furious. He inhales deeply to get the smoke into his lungs, and then relaxes his arm beside his leg while exhaling out of his mouth and nose like a dragon. He repeats this again and again—quick but deep inhalations.

I walk by him and say hello.

He waits a few moments and looks at me. "Hey," he finally says, but nothing more.

I think he is as angry as I am. We have reasons to be angry. We were forced to leave our houses and apartments and live in a tent. Who among us wouldn't be angry? Being corralled into a tent isn't the life we want or deserve. At best, it's a living death.

In the morning, I am awakened by the movements of people. I go outside to see what the camp looks like during the day. Hundreds of refugees roam the grounds. Some listen to Walkmans, others read newspapers. Many elderly people just sit and stare.

The camp is massive, even larger than I first thought. It is situated on a mountain slope. Select areas have been leveled by machinery, but the flattened ground hasn't been cleared of debris like stumps and gravel. We are at the bottom tier of the camp, where there are only big tents. Smaller white tents are higher up the mountain.

Just outside of our tent, I watch a British journalist and her Albanian translator interview one of the men from our tent. Somberly he tells the story of how he and his family fled their village as the Serbian military arrived. When he heard tanks enter the village, he led his wife and two little children out their back door and hid in the forest nearby. The journalist scribbles into her notebook as the translator relays the story to her in broken English.

Then the journalist asks the man if he knows anybody who was killed. He thinks about this question for a minute as if he is preparing a long answer—as if the question requires a complex answer.

"Yes," the man finally says. He recites names. One name, two names, three names, four names. I count in my head and wait for him to stop. But he doesn't. Five, six, seven. I remind myself that these are human lives I am counting. The translator spells the names of the victims to the British journalist as the man keeps uttering names. Eight, nine, ten, eleven. I realize that in the villages people were killed a lot more easily than in the urban areas. Twelve, thirteen...

I give up counting. I leave. I would rather go out and explore the camp.

During my walk I see that the camp is enclosed by fences so people can't leave. There is a main gate that is patrolled by Macedonian policemen. New refugees enter by bus.

Now that the day has warmed, some men and boys walk without their shirts and shoes. They are underweight and their ribs are visible. Their ears are their most apparent body part. My ribs and ears also stand out. Mami and Babi are thinner than I have ever seen them. Babi's belly is not as big and Mami's thighs are not as full.

Women and girls have their hair cut short. I remember how Mami warned me each summer, "When it's hot and you can't take a shower, fleas and lice are best friends with long, dirty hair."

A shirtless man with a radio is listening to the news. He has it lifted up to his ear, as if he doesn't want to miss a word that is being said. Several other people listen to their radios also. They must be anxious to learn the fate of their villages or hometowns.

Two girls my age, accompanied by their mother, go from tent to tent. They ask everyone, including the man with the radio, "Have you seen our father?" They say his name. "He is tall and bald on top of his head, but not on the sides." The mother, who has dyed red hair, looks in all directions for her husband.

"What is his name again?" says the radio man. They tell him again, excited that he might know something about him.

"No, I'm sorry, girls, but I haven't seen him. Where are you from?"

"We are from Pristina," they say, and they proceed to the next person.

I walk five more minutes, and I discover the center of the camp, where there are many queues. There is one for water, one for lunch boxes, one for sleeping bags, one for blankets, and one for telephones. Hundreds of people stand in these queues. The longest line of all is for the telephone. In a tent are a couple of cellular phones arranged by a humanitarian organization. This line is half the length of a *futboll* field, and there is more than one row. Some people are impatient and jump the line. The others protest and shove them back. The prevailing noise is mostly complaints about people cutting in line, the long wait, and the hot weather.

People enter one side of the tent and exit the opposite side after they've completed their phone calls. Many leave in tears. An elderly lady exiting the tent weeps. I wonder why she is crying. Then I see a man coming out of there sobbing, with his head bowed. What is going on? I hear others crying. Why these reactions after speaking on the telephone?

People in the telephone queue converse while waiting. They guess that callers must have found out that their family members or friends have been killed. "Poor guy," someone says. "Who knows? Maybe his son was killed."

Perhaps his son, his father, his mother. It must be someone dear, because he isn't even trying to hide his tears. He is sobbing aloud and swearing, "Screw this world and screw this land. It is all hell, and I am not afraid to express that. I have reasons."

I consider waiting in the telephone queue but decide against it. If someone in my family has been killed, I really don't want to know. No, not yet.

I walk away from the telephone tent and explore some more. There is a big white tent, the same size as mine, with the insignia of the Red Cross on it. I want to go there and ask if they can give me something that can make me stop dreaming of dying, but if medicines to prevent wartime nightmares existed, the queue for the Red Cross would be longer than the one for the telephone.

Several humanitarian organizations have tents: UNHCR, OXFAM, and UNICEF. There are also two other large tents next to each other, but I don't know their purpose. Near these tents there is a crowd, and a coach bus has parked outside. I step closer and see an English-speaking man addressing those gathered. A translator stands beside him. A barrier of yellow tape establishes a boundary between the speaker and his audience. The English speaker says, "Family Kra-snee-chee" with an approximate pronunciation of the common Albanian last name Krasniqi. His translator immediately pronounces it correctly, and a family of two children and their parents are allowed to join the translator and the man.

I find out that this family and several others called are going to Sweden. They receive instructions from the translator and then board a bus that will take them to the airport. From there they will be flown to their new country.

"Is Sweden the only place we can go?" I ask a man standing in front of me.

"No, they send you to Switzerland, Canada, America—even Australia. You have to sign up, though, early in the morning, and if you're lucky, your name gets posted."

Oh, wow. I want to go to America. I want to fly on an airplane. That would be so cool. It amazes me that something so large and heavy as a plane can even leave the ground, much less cruise at high altitudes. America would be a great place to go, but once the war ends, I want to return to a freed Kosovo. Will I be allowed to return to my homeland? I would miss Kosovo, as Uncle Skender did when he went to Switzerland. I would miss Musa and all my other cousins.

I return to the tent. Mami says, "Hey, guy, where have you been?"

"Oh, Mami, I've got to tell you. There is a tent where you can make phone calls."

"Really? Where? We need to call Uncle Fatmir in Switzerland and ask him whether he has heard news about our family and friends."

I also tell her about the other queues, and then she suggests, "Why don't you get us some water? Your brother went to get lunch boxes." Mami hands me two empty jugs that she got from a French guard. Soon I am at the end of an extremely long water queue.

The line moves at a snail's pace. There are people who have several gallon jugs to fill from two spigots and women who are hand-washing their clothes. They cut into the water line to rinse their clothes. To make matters worse, there are forceful men who jump the queue and act as if they own the refugee camp. Even so, the wait becomes worthwhile when I spy a beautiful girl my age. She has a gallon jug and one empty Coke bottle in her hand. She is ahead of me by ten feet or so, and whenever she turns her head to one side, I am entranced by her perfect profile and flawless, tanned skin. I wish she were nearer so we could talk.

Eventually my turn comes, and I get my gallon jugs filled with tepid water. Back at the tent, Shpetim has returned with food. I eat some peanut butter and crackers, which I never liked until now.

At dusk, several Kosovar civilians, including me, are herded by soldiers into a weird, rectangular building with no ceiling in the middle of a field. The Serbian military orders us into it quickly. Then for some reason, I get behind and don't get inside. That is when they open fire on me. Bullets hit my neck. I think I am dying. I can't feel my neck. I manage to scream.

"Are you OK? Are you OK?" I vaguely hear Mami's voice. "What is happening to you?"

I wake up and feel so relieved to see her, but I am still scared from the dream. I breathe hard.

"You're OK. You're OK, *pllumb*." Mami gives me some water. Only after I drink it can I fully orient myself to the present.

"I keep seeing these Serbian soldiers in my dreams," I tell Mami.

Then I get up and walk around a little. I take a walk around the tent, and Mami trails behind me.

"Tell me exactly what happened," she asks.

"I'll be all right. No need for you to follow me," I say.

"Well, go back to sleep, Ilir."

I am not going back to sleep. Every time I do, Serbians torture and slay me. I'm going to walk in order to stay awake. I never want to sleep again. It's like being murdered every night.

I keep walking around the tent and Mami follows. I don't want her to do that. I want to be alone. After an hour or so, I agree to go to bed.

CHAPTER 44

NIGHTMARES

In the morning I am like a new person. The sun makes all the difference.

I am surprised to see Mami talking with the blond-haired woman who cries. Usually she just cries; she doesn't really talk to anyone.

Later that night, when I am with Mami outside of the tent, refusing to go to sleep, I ask about her. "Why does that lady always cry?"

"Oh, it is really sad." Mami whispers so the woman can't hear us. She is still awake. She never sleeps. Like me.

"Serbian police have taken her two young daughters," Mami continues. "One of them was twenty and the other twenty-two. She said they took them from her arms, and she could not do anything about it. Today she spoke to some of her relatives on the phone to ask whether they know anything about them, but they told her that they didn't. She is heartbroken."

"*Qkaa*?" I say.

"Oh, son," she sighs and raises her voice. "A lot of these people have gone through so much. They have all kinds of horrid stories to tell. We are lucky compared to them. At least we are united and not separated like some families here." She pauses for a moment and says, "Now let's go to sleep, *pllumb*. Did you have any more nightmares after you went back to sleep last night?"

"No," I lie.

"You see, it just happened one time. It won't happen again, *pllumb*. You were shocked and scared by the threats to our lives recently. Here we are safe."

I listen to Mami this time.

I see a car coming to our house full of Serbian paramilitary troops. They are holding some wine bottles filled with gasoline. They trap us inside until they pour and break the wine bottles on the floor. I realize that they are going to light a match in the house to burn us up, so I quickly go outside and start running. One of the paramilitary troops sees me and lets the others know that I escaped. I don't stop running until I cross the border and jump over its strange walls and metal fences. Then I feel guilty that I was selfish and saved only myself, with little concern about my family.

I wake up in terror. My head feels heavy. It is full of violent thoughts and memories. I look at Mami and see that she is sleeping. I mustn't have screamed this time. Surely others in the camp have nightmares similar to mine—scenes of torture, decapitations, firing lines, burning houses, checkpoints. I expect for someone to sit upright suddenly, confused, wondering whether it is a dream or reality.

I stay awake until dawn, and only then do I go to sleep, believing that the daylight will keep me safe.

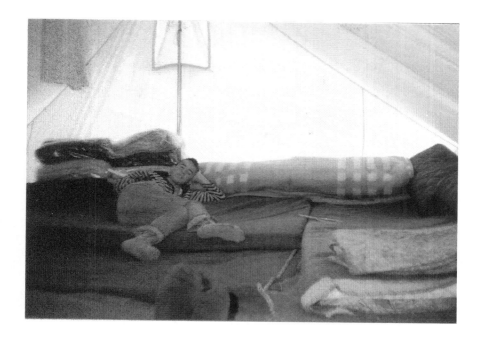

When I wake up, I hear Mami and Babi talking.

Mami says, "Oh, the poor guy should have stayed hidden somewhere and not tried to get out of Pristina."

"Yeah, he should have stayed in Kosovo," replies Babi.

"Who are you talking about?" I ask.

"Oh, did we wake you up, *pllumb*? I told you to be quiet, Hysen."

"I don't care, Mami," I say. "But who were you talking about? Who should have stayed in Pristina?"

Mami tells me that the Serbians have killed one of Kosovo's most admired men, Fehmi Agani, the vice president of Kosovo's leading political party and a sociology professor renowned throughout Europe. He had disguised himself as a woman and gotten onto the train to leave Kosovo. The *t'zi* recognized him, dragged him off the train, and murdered him.

Babi holds the Kosovar paper—which is now published here in Macedonia, since half of Kosovo's population has been forced out of the country—with the article about the murder on the front page. There are tears in Babi's eyes. He is crying for Fehmi Agani. I knew that Babi loved him very much. I knew that on election day, he had voted for Fehmi Agani instead of our beloved neighbor and friend, Mr. Vokshi, but I never imagined he would cry for him.

I am shocked. Never have I seen Babi cry. He didn't cry when the *t'zi* slapped him; he didn't cry when we didn't have any money; he didn't cry when Uncle Azem died; he didn't cry when he heard about his friend's death; he didn't cry when the three masked men stuck a gun in his ribs; he didn't cry when the fare collector told him there was no place for us on the bus. But he cries now. The Serbian forces have wounded him where it hurts the most. With the death of Agani, Kosovo has lost its best chance to prevail after the war.

I begin to understand Babi's reaction. Even as a fourteen-year-old, I know that Kosovo needs all of its smartest and bravest men and women. I realize that Babi probably also cried when the Serbians took away our autonomy, when they censored our television and newspaper, when they terminated his co-workers, when they kicked us out of school, when he heard about the death of the Kosovar human rights activist. He must have cried even then, but his tears must have run down his heart instead of his eyes. He must have hidden them in his heart all of this time, but he cannot hide them anymore. My heart and Babi's heart cry for our beloved Kosovo.

I remember seeing Fehmi Agani on TV. He always spoke softly, eloquently, clearly, and intelligently. I picture him dressed as a woman, with a little black head covering and a long dress, trying to mingle with a crowd and avoid being recognized, trying to save his life. I like the idea, but it did not work. I feel like crying myself.

When I walk around the camp today, some of the people look like Serbians to me. They look like spies. Their faces remind me of Serbian soldiers. Are they going to dress in black and come to our tent tonight? I don't trust them. The soldiers, paramilitary, and *t'zi* stalk us in our dreams or in camp. There is one person in particular who looks like a Serbian paramilitary I've seen. He is tall and menacing, and he walks stealthily, like a criminal. I follow him, but lose sight of him when he ducks behind a tent.

When it turns dark, thoughts about the spy escalate. Are there Serbians in the camp? Am I going to live through another night? My mind races. What is happening to me? I dwell on the faces of those men whom I saw during the day. They are spies. I know they are. I have this creepy feeling. How can I discuss it with Mami? She'll think I am crazy. I scoot toward Babi and pull my sleeping bag's zipper over my head so no one can see my face. Still, I'm scared.

I picture the shadow of a tall man with a knife coming toward me. He stops beside me. There is a long pause. I'd better poke my head out so I can see what is going on. With brutal force, a knife rips my sleeping bag and then my stomach. My torso is slashed vertically multiple times. My guts tumble out of the wounds.

Am I the only one who has these thoughts? Why is the rest of my family sleeping? Why don't they realize that we are in a great danger? Why is everyone else in the tent unaware of what I know to be true?

I pass the night with morbid thoughts and no sleep. I can only sleep during the day, when I feel safer. About three o'clock in the afternoon, Mami wakes me. I am lucky to have survived last night; no one stabbed me. All of the people in our tent are Kosovars. I must remember that. There are no Serbian paramilitary troops or spies here who are going to kill me.

"I have placed some gallons of water in the sun to warm so you can take a shower," Mami says. "The water should be ready by now."

Maybe the warm water will cleanse my mind.

I take the shower right in front of the tent and in view of the people. Mami pours water over my head, and I wash my hair. I scrub my scalp hard with the tips of my fingers as if trying to pry bad memories from my head. I lather my face and rub it vigorously. I want to wipe away all wartime images from my eyes. I want to have a new, fearless face.

I wash my chest, my armpits, my stomach, my legs, and my feet, and then I stop. It would be embarrassing to wash anything else. I dry myself off in the sun. My head feels so much lighter with all the dirt gone. I feel like a new person. Now that I am refreshed, I conclude that I was crazy to think that Serbian spies are in camp. I know better than that. In this camp, there are plenty of French soldiers who wouldn't let Serbians in here.

Later Shpetim goes to the phone queue to call Uncle Fatmir in Switzerland. When he returns, he says, "Uncle Fatmir hasn't heard from anyone. He said that we are the first ones to call him to let him know we are alive." Why has no one else in our family called Uncle Fatmir? Are we the only ones left? I would give anything to know that they are alive. As big as this camp is, they might be here.

I go to areas of the camp where I have never been, the highest elevation where the white tents are. I look from tent to tent for any familiar faces but don't recognize anyone. I try not to think of encountering a Serbian.

I see a man Uncle Skender's age. He looks as if he could be one of Uncle's friends.

"Do you know Skender Berisha?" I ask him. "He is from Drenovc and he has a son whose name is Musa."

"I am sorry, but I don't know him."

While looking for Uncle Skender, I discover a tent with a big TV inside of it. Several men have gathered to watch the news. I must tell Babi about this tent. Shpetim told me that they watch *futboll* games too, but I leave, because only depressing news is on.

I explore some more and discover a volleyball field, where young people are playing a game while others watch and cheer. The boys and girls who play look energetic and skilled. They are all older than me. Sometimes they argue about a ball landing out of bounds or touching the net when it was served, but no one mentions the war.

Eventually I become resigned that Uncle Skender and Musa are not in this camp. Watching the volleyball game keeps my negativity at bay, though. Instead of worrying about the Serbian military coming after me, I have erotic thoughts about the pretty girls who are playing the game. Their maturing bodies are alluring. Running and jumping make their breasts bounce. They wear shorts that reveal their lovely thighs. When the girls reach upward, I glimpse their smooth, tanned midriffs. Bending over brings attention to their firm, shapely hips. Except for the time I saw the pretty girl in the camp's water queue, I've not had such thoughts in a long while. The war made me forget about pleasures like this. I was only preoccupied with my body's discomfort. Dread displaced desire.

The teams switch sides and play until it turns dark and they cannot see the ball. I wish they played at night too. I find volleyball more interesting than anything else.

I come back and watch again the next day. After volleyball, I go to the camp's makeshift terminal, where people are boarding buses that will take them to the airport. I watch them enviously, wishing that I could go far away from Kosovo and leave the memories of war in the camp.

At the terminal, I am surprised to see Mr. Tahir, a neighbor from our village, leaving for the Czech Republic. He was the owner of the village's mini-market, where the men played chess and cards. He must know something about Musa, since his shop was directly across from Musa's house.

"No," he says after I ask him. "I talked to your father earlier and told him that I didn't see them. I don't know where they are."

"I was sure you would know something about them, Mr. Tahir," I say.

"Sorry, Ilir."

Mr. Tahir boards the coach bus and will be in the Czech Republic by tomorrow. We inherit his white tent.

So we move from the group tent on the lowest level to a single-family one higher on the slope. We grab our two bags of clothes, sleeping bags, and blankets, and complete the move in one trip.

If there is anything good about being a refugee, it is that you travel light. That makes relocating easy because there are only a few things to take. You miss your books, TV, bed, dining table, dishes, flatware, chairs, and your alarm clock.

This tent is much smaller than the one we had lived in, but we now have privacy. No other family or individual shares it with us. Nearby is a thick forest of fragrant evergreen trees. There are clusters of these small tents nestled on this side of the mountain.

We quickly become friends with the families who live in the tents around us—or, I should say, with separated and partial families grouped in one tent. To the left of our tent live three sisters-in-law. Their husbands and older male children were arrested and taken away by Serbian troops. Desperation and uncertainty rule their lives. Their last name is Preniq, and they come from a city near Pristina called Fushe Kosova.

One of them has red eyes, short blond hair, and a little son who always wears a blue cap sideways. Her son sometimes asks, "Where is my father?" She doesn't answer his question, but she hugs him tightly and cries behind his head.

The other one is really thin and has short black hair. She has an older daughter and a younger son about my age. She is missing her husband and her oldest son.

The other sister-in-law has long blond hair. She is the one who is most traumatized by what happened to her family. Each morning she wakes up and says out loud, "Oh my sons, where are you? I cannot see you. I don't know where you are. Where have they taken you?" The poor woman is delusional. She seems to believe that if her sons could hear her, they would respond. When she doesn't hear their voices, she asks again, "Oh my sons, where are you?" She reminds me of my mother when Uncle Azem died.

In the tent to our right, there are two older girls and their cousin. We meet and become friends with them. They are both originally from Drenice, but before the war, they were attending college in Pristina. One of them is a theater major and the other an economics major. Their older brothers and fathers have been taken from them by the *t'zi*, also, but they are optimistic that their loved ones are alive and will return. Mami and I find out from their cousin that the men have been killed, though.

One evening we invite the girls to our tent. The one who is studying to be an actress is funny and the one whose interest is economics has a sweet personality. The future actress is shorter and darker-skinned than the economics major. She tells us about the audition that got her accepted by the college of performing arts, and she makes us laugh. She had to mimic a gypsy woman—exactly how she talked. Her costume was a dirty, frayed dress, and she chose to dishevel her hair. The admissions panel loved her obvious imagination and humor.

Her story interests me because I want to be an actor too. I can use my talent for accents, mimicry, and comedy to favorably impress the judges who decide which students can study at the college of performing arts. I need to become a good actor and then I can go to America—to Hollywood.

One topic leads to another, and soon we are talking about my other passion—going abroad.

"Do you girls want to go anywhere, to a different country?" Mami asks the girls.

"No," says the future actress. "I have to get back home and stay with my brother and father. They will need me and I must help them around the house."

"Yeah," agrees the future economist. "Besides, we would miss them so much if we went to some other country. We would be so far away. Our house is going to be a mess, and they will definitely need our help."

These girls don't know the truth about their fathers and brothers. They are so cheerful and naïve. This makes me feel heartsick. Who will have the courage to break the sorrowful news to these girls? Who will have the courage to ruin their laughter and joy forever?

"I want to go somewhere. I want to travel in a plane," I say. "I think it would be so cool to fly."

"Oh yeah, that would be cool," the future actress says, "someday. That is in the distant future for us. The men in our families need us now. There will be lots to do when we get home."

I look away for several seconds to compose myself. Then I face the girls again and force a smile. "Show me that gypsy impression again."

Over the next few days, Shpetim and I become friends with some older boys in the nearby tents. Often we wait with them at the water and food queues. Sometimes we play volleyball in the forest nearby. At night we all walk to the water source together and brush our teeth with the brand new toothbrushes we received. We like going there after dark because there is no waiting in line.

I like hanging out with the boys because I feel safe with them. I hate when we come back because that means I will be in the tent without them. I get scared that someone is going to come to our tent. There is a rumor circulating that a man wearing all black lives deep in the forest. I picture someone like that coming to our tent and chopping us to pieces like firewood. I wonder whether the older boys think the same things I do at night. If I asked them they would probably laugh at me and call me a baby.

The nightmares still swirl in my head. I can't stop them. As I start to open the apartment building's front door on my way back from school, four snipers shoot at me from behind. One bullet hits my book bag. I run inside our apartment and see a gunman in the kitchen. I run to the sunroom and see Babi fighting another armed intruder. I get shot in my right leg.

I awaken and sit up sweating as if I have been running for my life. After shaking my head from side to side, I look down. Neither of my legs appears wounded. I haven't been shot.

I look around and see that we are in the white tent. Why do I so often awaken after being shot in my dreams? The boundary that separates life from death has become blurred.

I wonder what my life would have been like if I had been born in Italy to Italian parents. What would I be doing right now? I would not be a refugee. I would not live in perpetual fear of being shot. In my Italian apartment, I would have my dad serve a nice dinner: a Coke, a hamburger, and French fries. For dessert, I would slice fresh bananas over chocolate ice cream. I wish I were an Italian kid. Or a German. Or an American.

CHAPTER 45

LIBERATED

It is the beginning of June. We have spent a month in the Macedonian refugee camp. The weather is warmer. Exactly one year ago I was enjoying my summer at our village house. If I was there now, I would be playing *futboll* and basketball with Musa and Shpetim. We would fish in the river and collect blueberries and blackberries in the forest.

The camp is not too bad. We've adjusted to our refugee status and we are making the best of it. Some funny and interesting things happen here. For example, today a gust of wind uprooted a tent, making it sail upward like a kite. It was hilarious to see the tent up in the air while the things inside remained grounded. I laughed a lot. The resident of the airborne tent chased it for several minutes before the wind subsided and gravity brought it back to earth. His neighbors helped him to stake the corners deeper into the ground.

Yesterday a lizard crawled into Babi's shirt while he was sleeping. When Fjolla saw it, she screamed and ran out of the tent. Babi simply pulled his shirttail from his pants and wiggled vigorously until the lizard had enough and leapt to the ground. Babi continued to shake and shimmy until he and I began to crack up. It's been a long time since I last heard my father laugh.

The food has gotten much better now as well. We get Norwegian canned fish, tomatoes, peppers, cucumbers, and even oranges.

The French soldiers have built wooden stalls where we can take showers, so we no longer have to bathe in public.

One thing that hasn't changed in the camp is that people are still traumatized. I continue to have nightmares. The three sisters-in-law hope that their husbands and older sons will return to them. The two college girls from Drenice, however, are less optimistic now about the fates of the men in their family.

The number of dead reported is staggering. Fjolla met a friend who said her father had been killed. Fjolla didn't know what to say to her. "It was so sad," she said. "We hugged each other and cried."

Mami met a lady while waiting in the telephone line. "She broke my heart," Mami cried. "She said she left her youngest son wounded at the house, with one bullet in his shoulder and another in his stomach. Her older son promised to stay with his brother as long as the mother evacuated the house. When her turn in line came, she didn't hear a word from either of her sons. 'I don't know if my boys are alive,' said the lady. She was so distraught that she collapsed. She revived but was inconsolable."

At the terminal today, I notice a lot of refugee families who are bound for the United States and Canada, but I am stuck here. I am just one among thousands who wishes to live in one of those two places, especially the United States.

I meet an elderly man who lives in New York and is here to adopt a family in the camp and take them there.

"What is it like in America?" I ask him.

"Oh son!" he says. "It is wonderful. You can eat kilograms of bananas and drink liters of Coke for only a dollar or two."

Bananas and Coke were favorite foods that Mami and Babi could rarely afford. I rush back to the tent and tell my parents that they must find a way to get us assigned to America. Mami and Babi's dream has always been to send their children to a university in America.

"And then both Shpetim and I can get educated there," I tell them. "And Fjolla too." I am convinced that if I am that far away from

Kosovo, my night terrors will end. I will live beyond the Serbian forces' reach. I will drink Cokes and eat bananas every day. Good medical care will be available to my family and me.

One day our neighbor from Pristina, Mr. Vokshi, moves into our tent. After Mami tells him about my nightmares, he advises her to take me to the Red Cross tent and let the doctors examine me. They might recommend that our entire family go to America.

In the evening, Mami accompanies me to the Red Cross tent. While we wait in line, we hear the sound of a generator that supplies power for equipment. When my turn comes, Mami and I are called to see a doctor. I squeeze Mami's hand tightly and stay close to her.

The doctor directs Mami and me to sit on a bench. He studies me for a second. I look at him and then wrap my arms around Mami's legs.

"You're OK, boy," says the doctor. "Don't be afraid." Then he turns to Mami. "What's wrong with your son?" he asks her.

"He has nightmares every night. He dreams of being pursued and shot by Serbians. He is shell-shocked from all we've been through. I thought his distress would go away in the camp, but he continues to have nightmares."

The doctor tells Mami, "Well, we don't have anything to treat him with here, but I recommend we send your family abroad. I think that would be the best thing for him because staying here in the camp is not going to cure his stress disorder." He asks Mami where we would like to go.

Mami tells him that she would prefer Switzerland, Sweden, or America. She says Sweden because Babi thinks that they have a good medical system. She says Switzerland because Uncle Fatmir lives there. As for me, I want to fly to America.

The doctor writes our choices next to our names and lets us go back to our tent.

I check for our names on the bulletin boards around the camp several times a day. After three days, our names are posted. We are going to America! I am the first in my family to see this. I am so thrilled that I jump up and down with joy. I run to our tent, thinking only of our good luck and future happiness. I picture myself on the airplane destined for America. I imagine myself in the center of New York City, gazing at skyscrapers and being amazed by their height. I grin at the thought of eating and drinking whatever I want.

Shpetim and Fjolla are as excited as I am when I tell them, but Mami and Babi don't seem pleased. "Well, we might never return to Kosovo," they say. "How can you abandon your country and culture without regret?"

"We'll come back," I reassure Mami and Babi. "We won't forget Kosovo."

"Your children are going to be well-educated," says Mr. Vokshi. "Then they'll come back to their country and help to make it better. America is the best place for you now. You are going to love it. You are lucky to go there." Mr. Vokshi has been to America, so he knows. He had traveled to Texas and throughout the South on business before being fired from his job by the Serbians. He starts to drawl like Southerners do. "Hey, ha' y'all doin'? It's gotten purdy dam' hot roun' har' laytly." We laugh with Mr. Vokshi. His accent makes him sound like a cowboy. We ask him to translate what he said and then we ask him to speak more. I want to learn English so I can talk like a cowboy too.

During the next couple of nights, we are entertained by Mr. Vokshi's stories about America. NATO has finished its air mission, and now ground troops are preparing to enter, says Babi. But we are still not completely liberated. There are still Serbian forces inside Kosovo. We still can't leave the camp because the Macedonian policemen won't let anyone out the main gate.

A friend we have made in camp runs toward us. "The NATO ground troops are en route to Kosovo," he says, panting. "They are here. Their tanks are rolling by our camp. Let's go see them." He bends over and puts his hands on his knees, trying to regain his breath.

Shpetim and I are so excited that we race toward the fences that surround the camp. We are not the only ones. A crowd of little boys and girls is right behind us, running and screaming, "*Fitore, fitore!*" We raise our hands and point two fingers up in the air. Adults rush to see our liberators too. They run, shout, and cheer like us. Everyone applauds the international troops who are going to save our country, to save the people who are still alive in Kosovo. An elderly lady in a wheelchair smiles with gratitude and waves to the soldiers.

We press our faces against the fence and watch the massive tanks rumble past. We want to shake the hands of our heroes. The crowd manages to tear down portions of the fence. Some crawl underneath it, and some adults climb over it. In no time we are running alongside the tanks and troops here to free us. The soldiers smile at us, wave, and shake our hands. The crowd keeps chanting, "*Fitore, fitore!*" This is the celebration that we have been waiting for all our lives. Our lives can begin anew.

Waves of people surge forward to join us in celebrating this day. The Macedonian police can't stop us. Our numbers are too great. As American soldiers pass we cheer, "*Amerika, Amerika!*" Then we shout, "*Bill Klintoni, Bill Klintoni!*" The American soldiers flash the victory sign or wave at us. They are friendly. Their tanks, artillery, and weapons are far superior to those of the Serbians. Their guns shine, and they don't drink alcohol. They take their mission seriously, which is to defeat the Serbian military and free us forever. Milosevic's days are numbered. I jump up and down until I'm breathless. Shpetim is jumping up and down and smiling broadly. Everybody is.

More people stream from their tents. People take pictures, and others throw bouquets. I don't know where they found flowers.

Now we sing, "*Mirë se vini, mirë se vini* (Welcome, welcome)." The excitement continues to build. How else can we express our gratitude? We should stop and hug every soldier, but that might not be a good idea. These men have a critical mission to accomplish and shouldn't be delayed. Civilians in Kosovo are still being tortured and killed.

Once the convoy has passed and night falls, the celebration continues. Little boys and girls run in groups, shouting, "*Kosova, Kosova! UÇK, UÇK!*" They probably don't understand the significance of the event, but they can feel it.

The next day, I borrow Mr. Vokshi's camera to take pictures of our heroes who continue towards Kosovo. I stay for hours and forget to eat or drink. I am joined by the same throng as yesterday. Mami and Babi and Mr. Vokshi are here too, but I stay with the loud and enthusiastic youths. We are Kosovo's future, and our heroes will return our county to us. They bring us hope. They bring us the season I remember loving the most. They are the summer.

After being interviewed at the American consulate, we pass the required medical exams. We are scheduled to leave in two days.

I am excited, but my parents are far less enthused. They are afraid that we'll never come back. America is too far away, they say. I assure them that we'll be back as soon as I finish college and make some money.

The day of our scheduled departure, Mami and Babi say they are skeptical that it is such a golden opportunity. "It's better to wait until the war ends, when it is safe to go back. It won't be long," says Babi.

I get very upset and start crying. Fjolla wants to go too, and she starts crying. Shpetim stays neutral.

Mami is conflicted; one minute she says we are going, and the next she decides it is better to stay. I get frustrated and tell my parents, "I am never going to speak to you again. I will never forgive you for not taking us to America. Can we go, *të lutna? Të lutna, të lutna?* We will return, we will return."

We are to be at the terminal in twenty minutes. Our bags are not packed. My camp friends come over and ask me, "Are you going to America today?"

"No, because my parents are stupid," I say bitterly.

Mami hears me. She considers what I said and then tells Babi, "You know what? If we go, we may come back, but if we don't go we'll never have another chance. The kids will never forgive us."

Babi thinks about it. Mr. Vokshi talks to him some more, and then my dad starts to get ready.

My parents have finally decided that we are going. I am even happier than several days ago when we celebrated the passage of the ground troops. I tell my camp friends, and they are happy for us, but sad that we won't be here with them anymore.

"I hope your families are chosen to go to America too," I tell them. "Sign up today and ask to go to America."

We take time to comb our hair and look nice. You are supposed to look nice when you travel, especially when you travel to America.

At the terminal, two buses wait for refugees to board. We check in, but an American official tells us through her interpreter that there is a delay. "Bill Clinton," they say, "is visiting Stankovec I."

Wow. The camp is near ours, less than half a mile away. Is this a dream or what? Am I finally starting to have sweet dreams? I scramble up a hill and try to see Bill Clinton from it. I can see the motorcade, but I can't identify the people. I am a little frustrated that he is visiting Stankovec I but not Stankovec II. I want to shake his hand and thank him for saving our lives and our country.

Soon I relax, reminding myself that I will meet President Clinton in America. He made it possible for us to be alive and to go to his country. I am determined to meet him in America. I will do anything to make that happen.

The motorcade heads toward the horizon. I hurry down the hill to our bus.

Once the bus leaves the camp, I begin to feel hyper. In less than an hour I will be inside an airplane. My parents are quiet until Shpetim starts to cry. Mami and Babi tell him, "Shpetim, we don't have to go." He doesn't say anything but continues crying.

"Shut up. You are going to make Mami and Babi take us back," I tell him.

"You shut up," he snaps.

I remain nervous until I take my first step on the stairs leading to the airplane and realize there is no turning back. We are awed by the plane. Fjolla and I peek into the pilot's cabin, and he invites us to sit in his seat. I am amazed by the number of instruments pilots have to monitor. It is exciting to see an airplane's steering wheel.

We are on the way to America for sure. I can't believe it.

We take pictures of the pilot's cockpit and of ourselves with the friendly American flight attendants. Once the plane takes off and I realize that I am going to America, to the home of Bill Clinton, of bananas and Coca-Colas, of skyscrapers and cowboys, I think I am somewhere completely opposite from hell.

EPILOGUE
LUCKY MAN

It is the summer of 2008, nine years after the war, and I am on my way to Kosovo. The plane is descending to Pristina Airport. As I look back, I have been blessed beyond the dreams of a thousand men. I left Kosovo as a frightened, traumatized, scrawny fourteen-year-old, and I am returning as a healthy recent graduate of an American university. I left my beloved country in shambles and occupied by Serbian forces, and now I am going back to a new, independent Kosovo, free from Serbia. I fled the country without knowing whether my family members were alive, and I am returning knowing they have survived.

I found America to be everything that I had dreamed about. The American people welcomed us into their culture, granting us an entryway not only to their homes but also their hearts. They loved and respected us as though we were long lost family members. They helped us enroll in school, found jobs for my parents, found us an apartment, and paid the first few months' rent. They bought us clothes and food. They stood with us every step of the way while introducing us to the American dream. They told us that anything was possible in their country. One of them told me that I could write a book if I want. Who could have known that all this would be possible?

I have traveled alone. Shpetim is busy working as a computer and electrical engineer and Fjolla, who will soon be a senior in college, is studying abroad in Italy. Mami and Babi have made the visit before me. Even though Babi couldn't make the trip this time, his heart remains in Kosovo. With her political status as an independent state, he is the happiest he has ever been. On February 17—the day Kosovo declared its independence—he spent the whole day shedding tears of joy while watching the news in Albanian.

Musa has taken a day off from work to greet me at the airport. Besnik, Fisnik, and Besim have driven in a separate car to meet me. When I see their faces, I start to cry. I feel as if I am in another world. They snatch my suitcases and throw them in the trunk so I can be on my way to visit my other family members. On the road, my cousin is stopped by our very own Kosovar Albanian police force. We are fined for not wearing seat belts—but at least this was a ticket that we deserved.

I ask Besim how his *futboll* career is going, and he tells me that he is much happier and that his team no longer has to play on rocky, uneven, dusty fields. Our stadium has been returned to us now. New businesses have opened, and some of the restaurants and shopping malls are fancy, like the ones in America. Kosovar Albanian workers have returned to their former posts and are busy building our new country. I see Kosovar workers fixing the roads. The former dirt road leading to our village has already been paved with asphalt. Most of the houses have been repaired and renovated since the war. I no longer see bullet holes on their white facades. Musa's house looks stunning.

It feels wonderful to see my aunts and uncles, who smile constantly. It used to be that when a guest came to your house, you served him a small cup of soda, if you could afford it. Now my uncles and aunts bring the whole bottle to the table.

After I rest from my trip, Musa and I go fishing, just as we did in the good old days. It feels great to be here during this summer. My cousins and I organize a *futboll* match between us at a private turf field. I am thrilled that we are able to play together again.

Even though we have made great strides forward, Kosovo remains a developing country with one of the worst economies and highest unemployment rates in Europe. We are very thankful for the support of the United States and the European Union, and we count on them to continue to support us until we fully overcome the effects of the repression and hardship suffered in the years of the Milosevic regime.

While I am visiting, we celebrate the capture of Radovan Karadzic. After fifteen years of living as a free man, he has finally been brought to justice by the international tribunal. As a victim of one of the wars in the former Yugoslavia, I will never be fully satisfied until all the war criminals are brought to trial. If no one is held responsible for the atrocities that Kosovar Albanian and Bosnian people have endured—for the quarter of a million lives that have been taken here—then another war is waiting to happen. The international organizations must continually pressure those who are so thirsty for power that they will do anything, including committing massacres, just to maintain their status. It is in the interest of humanity.

My cousins and I and the rest of the younger generation in Kosovo have come to realize that while we must never forget the war and its victims, we must also move forward. We have learned to forgive and are optimistic about our future and our relationship with the Serbs. Those who run the institutions of Kosovo are now working hard to create a democratic and multiethnic country. Our leaders are lobbying for more nations to accept our independent status. The new Kosovo flag has six stars around the map of Kosovo, representing peace and stability among the six ethnic groups living there, among them the Serbians. No one star is bigger than the others. They are all equal.

We know that we can coexist. After all, we have done it before—during Tito's reign.

APPENDIX

GUIDE TO PRONUNCIATION
OF NAMES

Hysen [HOO-sen]
Xheva [JAY-va]
Shpetim [sh-PA-tim]
Azem [AH-zem]
Ilir [e-LEER]
Fjolla [fe-OL-la]
Sejda [SAY-dah]
Krasniqi [KRA-snee-chee]
Fatmir [FAHT-meer]
Fadil [FAH-dil]
Fisnik [FIHS-nik]
Valdet [vol-DET]
Besnik [BEHS-nik]
Besim [beh-SIM]
Drenice [dray-NEETS]
Gëzime [GZEEM-a]
Vedat [veh-DOT]

27838401R00153

Made in the USA
Lexington, KY
25 November 2013